Data-Driven Decisions and School Leadership

Best Practices for School Improvement

Theodore J. Kowalski
University of Dayton

Thomas J. Lasley II
University of Dayton

James W. Mahoney
Battelle for Kids

PEARSON

Boston New York San Francisco
Mexico City Montreal Toronto London Madrid Munich Paris
Hong Kong Singapore Tokyo Cape Town Sydney

Senior Series Editor: *Arnis Burvikovs*
Series Editorial Assistant: *Erin Reilly*
Marketing Manager: *Danae April*
Production Editor: *Paula Carroll*
Editorial Production Service: *Publishers' Design and Production Services, Inc.*
Composition Buyer: *Linda Cox*
Manufacturing Buyer: *Linda Morris*
Electronic Composition: *Publishers' Design and Production Services, Inc.*
Interior Design: *Publishers' Design and Production Services, Inc.*
Cover Administrator: *Kristina Mose-Libon*

For related titles and support materials, visit our online catalog at www.ablongman.com.

Between the time website information is gathered and then published, it is not unusual for some sites to have closed. Also, the transcription of URLs can result in typographical errors. The publisher would appreciate notification where these errors occur.

Library of Congress Cataloging-in-Publication Data

Kowalski, Theodore J.
    Data-driven decisions and school leadership : best practices for school improvement / Theodore J. Kowalski, Thomas J. Lasley II, James W. Mahoney.
        p. cm.
    Includes bibliographical references.
    ISBN-10: 0-205-49668-7 (alk. paper)
    ISBN-13: 978-0-205-49668-6 (alk. paper)
    1. School management and organization—United States—Decision making. 2. School improvement programs—United States. 3. Education—United States—Data processing. I. Lasley, Thomas J. II. Mahoney, James W. III. Title.
    LB2806.K69 2008
    371.2—dc22

                                                                                          2007016029

Printed in the United States of America

10 9 8 7 6 5 4 3 2 1   13 12 11 10 09 08 07

CONTENTS

PREFACE

Change occurs in schools in various ways. For example, some modifications are involuntary; typically they are initiated externally by policymakers responding to political interests or social concerns. Other alterations are voluntary; typically they are instigated by teachers and administrators. A fair reading of history during the last century, however, reveals that the most dramatic and enduring alterations to public schools have been external and involuntary. The landmark school desegregation case, *Brown v. Board of Education* (1954), and *P.L. 94–142*, commonly called the civil rights act for the disabled, enacted by Congress approximately twenty years later, are quintessential examples. Though such legal mandates effectively change structure and practices in schools, they do not necessarily reconstruct school cultures (i.e., the shared values and beliefs that influence the day-to-day behavior of educators).

Passage of the No Child Left Behind Act (NCLB) in 2001 is yet another externally initiated mandate requiring educators to change several normative practices. As was true with previous federal interventions, not all administrators and teachers have responded enthusiastically or even favorably. Some disagree with provisions in the law; some resent political-legal interventions; some simply resist change. Though this book is not a defense of NCLB, it is intended to improve practice in one of the law's foci—namely, the requirement that educators use data to make consequential decisions. We, the authors, believe that rational decision making is the standard in scientific professions, and therefore this process should have been normative in education even before NCLB. Without such rational (professional) decision making and without data as a basis for solving educational problems, education is reduced to a craft. There are certainly craftlike characteristics to the practice of education, but the goals of NCLB and the needs of young people in K–12 settings will only be met if professional decision making occurs.

We also believe that establishing data-based decision making as a normative practice in schools requires improvements in at least four areas.

1. Fundamental beliefs about decision making must be identified, analyzed, and, if necessary, changed. Though purely rational decisions are rare, scholars in scientific professions realize that evidence should not be disregarded simply because it conflicts with politics, bias, or emotion. In schools, for example, educators should not choose between values and facts, but rather they should understand how each can or should shape decisions that have critical consequences for students—and ultimately for society.
2. Immediately after the enactment of NCLB, a myriad of articles and monographs about data-based decision making were published. Many focused exclusively or primarily on research and statistics. Though these topics are undeniably relevant, such efforts to improve practice ignored the fact that the

vast majority of administrators and teachers had never studied decision making. Educators are far more likely to become proficient in making data-driven decisions if they possess this foundational knowledge. For this reason, the introductory portion of this book is devoted to examining theory and models, especially in the context of districts and schools.

3. Once educators have a fundamental understanding of decision making, they must develop the skills necessary to access, store, analyze, and apply data to their practice. Much of the content in this book is devoted to this objective—that is, substantial attention is given to accessing and managing data and then using those data to make consequential decisions.

4. In addition to practitioner knowledge and skills, districts and schools must have enabling technological infrastructures. That is, they must have a system for managing information, most notably databases, and they must provide employees with the necessary hardware and software to use the system as intended.

In summary, the primary purposes of this book are to integrate theory and practice in decision making and to guide the reader to develop essential skills for engaging in data-based decision making. In pursuing these objectives, this text differs substantially from others that have been published in the last few years. It is neither a primer on statistics, a guide to implementing NCLB, nor a simple "how-to" manual. Rather, it is a textbook providing foundational theory, process models, and practical knowledge that teachers and administrators can use to make data-based decisions.

Conceptual Framework

The book contains eleven chapters divided into three parts. Part I is intended to provide a foundation for understanding decision theory and models and their applications in districts and schools. The four chapters examine relationships between problem solving and decision making, decision-making behavior, various paradigms and action theories, and the benefits and potential pitfalls of group decisions.

Part II focuses directly on the use of data to make decisions. The four chapters define data-driven decision making; explain associations among research, statistics, and decision making; identify procedures for collecting, organizing, and distributing data; and describe ways that information technology can facilitate decision making in schools.

Part III is dedicated to applications of data-based decisions to problems commonly occurring in schools. First, this process is examined in relation to curriculum and instruction. Examples are provided in the context of various teaching paradigms and in relation to assessing student learning. The next chapter explains the nexus between data-based decisions and school improvement; specific topics include the need to challenge the status quo, meaningful ways to involve parents, and using assessment to make formative and summative decisions. The final chapter is devoted to implementation and monitoring issues; the content also bridges assessment with evaluation in relation to specific decisions and the collective effect of decisions on school improvement.

Intended Audiences

The book is designed as a text to be used in courses taken by both aspiring and practicing school administrators and teachers. It can be a primary or supplemental text in introductory courses on assessment, evaluation, decision making, and school administration. The book also is intended to be used as a reference book by experienced practitioners who have not formally studied data-based decision making or who wish to acquire a deeper understanding of the topic.

Acknowledgments

Many individuals contributed directly or indirectly to the completion of this book. We are especially thankful to Professor Scott Sweetland from Ohio State University for insights and recommendations regarding the scope and sequence of the content. Appreciation also is extended to three other groups of individuals. The colleagues offered constructive advice for improving and extending the content:

- Betsy Apolito, Montgomery County (OH) Educational Service Center
- Fred Dawson, Dayton Public Schools
- Karen Foster, University of Dayton
- Sandy Lowrey, Dayton Public Schools
- Mike Nicholson, Battelle for Kids
- Carolyn Ridenour, University of Dayton
- Diane Stultz, Battelle for Kids

The following colleagues completed reviews for the publisher and provided cogent recommendations:

Ronald M. Berrey, Lindenwood University; Kim T. Brown, University of North Carolina, Asheville; Leo P. Corriveau, Plymouth State University; Lance D. Fusarelli, North Carolina State University; Myrna Gartner, University of West Georgia; John L. Hamilton, Texas A&M University, Texarkana; Bob L. Johnson, Jr., University of Utah; Virginia G. Johnson, St. Joseph's University; Susan M. Kiernan, Eastern Tennessee State University; Mary K. McCullough, Loyola Marymount University; Kathy Peca, Eastern New Mexico University; Carol Shakeshaft, Hofstra University; and Luana J. Zellner, Texas A&M University.

Finally, the following individuals provided technical assistance in preparing the manuscript:

- Elizabeth Cameron, University of Dayton
- Mea Greenwood, University of Dayton
- Lucianne Lilienthal, University of Dayton
- Grace Murphy, Battelle for Kids
- Elizabeth Pearn, University of Dayton
- Colleen Wildenhaus, University of Dayton

PART ONE

Foundations of Decision Making in Schools

1

Problem Solving and Decision Making in the Context of School Reform

Chapter Focus

Historically, administrators and teachers have functioned as managers; that is, their role was to determine how to carry out policies and rules developed by others. The protracted period of school reform that arguably began in the early 1980s has broadened expectations for professional practice. Now educators also are expected to be effective leaders; that is, they must determine what should be done to improve schools. In this vein, they are expected to solve problems that prevent school effectiveness by relying on scientifically based research and other valid data.

This first chapter is designed to place data-driven decision making in the context of contemporary practice. The modern era of school reform is summarized and then the processes of problem solving, decision making, and data-driven decision making are defined. Last, the concept of reflective practice is described in relation to problem solving and decision making. After reading the chapter, you should be able to address the following questions:

1. How have the school reform targets and strategies changed since 1983?
2. What is the nexus between current reform strategies and the expectation that administrators and teachers function as effective leaders and managers?
3. What is the difference between problem solving and decision making?
4. What is the relationship between problem solving and decision making?
5. What is data-driven decision making?

CASE STUDY

Even before she became principal of Rogers Elementary School two years ago, Maureen Brown knew she would be assuming a difficult assignment. The school is located in the most economically depressed area of an economically depressed school district, the Bayville Community Schools. The city of Bayville's population has declined by more than 20 percent over the last twenty-five years, primarily because the steel mill that had been the community's largest employer closed. Many middle class families have left the community.

Despite the district's bleak demographic profile, Maureen accepted the position at Rogers Elementary School because of the superintendent, Dr. Mark Simon, an enthusiastic leader who has vowed to improve the school district. Strongly supported by the school board and Bayville's mayor, he has replaced about 75 percent of the district's principals during his five-year tenure. In addition, he has provided principals a great deal of flexibility and resources to pursue instructional improvement.

Immediately after beginning her assignment at Rogers, Maureen retained several consultants with whom she had worked previously to conduct workshops on reading and mathematics instruction. Her goal, communicated to both the faculty and the consultants, was to improve achievement test scores in the school by at least 5 percent a year. The year before she became principal, less than half of the Rogers students were scoring at or above grade level in both reading (49 percent) and mathematics (46 percent). After just one year of the consultants' workshops with teachers, the test scores increased; 60 percent scored at or above grade level in reading and 55 percent at or above grade level in mathematics. The principal and faculty were proud of the progress, and the contract with the consultants was extended for another year.

At the beginning of the second year of Principal Brown's tenure, the state board of education adopted new accountability standards. Included was a new benchmark for the percentage of students who were expected to score at or above grade level in basic subjects in elementary schools. The target had been raised from 78 percent to 90 percent, and schools not meeting the standard would be placed on probation and required to show incremental improvement. Failure to do so would result in further penalties such as reductions in state grants. The policy revision drew sharp criticism from educator groups because at least one-third of the state's schools had not yet met the old benchmark.

Principal Brown was deeply concerned by the new accountability standards, but her anxiety intensified several months later after Superintendent Simon informed her that the current year's test results for Rogers Elementary School were very disappointing. Only 56 percent of the Rogers students had scored at or above grade level in reading, and only 52 percent had done so in mathematics. Even worse, Rogers was the only school in the Bayville district that had experienced regression in its test scores from the previous year. Dr. Simon was not pleased, and he made that clear to Principal Brown. He told her that eight of the district's eleven schools were placed on probation, but none was as far away from the state benchmark as was Rogers. He told her she needed to devise a plan to improve achievement test scores within thirty days.

After the conversation, Principal Brown sat dejected in her office. She had been confident that the consultants had been effective and believed that the teachers had worked diligently to improve student test performance. But in light of this year's test results, she questioned whether either of her beliefs were accurate, and more importantly, she did not know what she could do next to improve the test scores. Given the social and economic difficulties experienced by most of her students, she concluded that the 90 percent benchmark was totally unrealistic.

Contemporary School Reform

The principal's ability to deal with the problem confronting Rogers Elementary School will depend largely on her knowledge of school reform strategies, problem solving, and decision making. Increasingly, administrators and teachers have to assume leadership responsibilities requiring them to make critical choices about school reform strategies and concepts. Moreover, federal and state policies are mandating that educators make rational decisions; that is, the choices they make should be guided by empirical evidence rather than emotion, personal bias, or political expediency.

Ever since the founding of a public education system in the United States circa 1840, educators and policymakers have attempted to resolve philosophical conflict endemic to this institution. Tensions have focused primarily on the purposes of schooling, a debate framed by several meta-values—such as liberty, equality, efficiency, and adequacy—that have guided public policy for more than 100 years (King, Swanson, & Sweetland, 2003). Though these meta-values have been and continue to be supported broadly in American society, political and social groups disagree over their relative importance (Kowalski, 2003).

As an example, conservatives see liberty as a dominant value, and consequently they usually support reform concepts intended to reduce government control and increase individual freedom (e.g., school choice and vouchers). On the other hand, liberals see equality as a dominant value, and consequently they usually support reform intended to increase government control as a means to ensure more equal educational opportunities (e.g., mandated desegregation, state equalized funding formulas). This divisive political context has existed for more than 125 years (Spring, 1994), and this partially explains why school reform movements wax and wane. Rather than resolving the causes of public dissatisfaction, previous reform eras have merely produced compromises that temporarily eradicate the symptoms but not the causes of philosophical disagreements (Cuban, 1988).

School Reform during the 1980s

Endurance and mutability have been two of the defining features of the current reform movement. Since the early 1980s, problem statements, change targets, and change strategies have been modified periodically, largely because of disappointing results. Many observers believe that the report *A Nation at Risk,* produced by the National Commission on Excellence in Education (1983) initiated the current reform period. Actually, this document legitimized a shift from equity to excellence that had been occurring for at least a decade (Finn, 1991). However, *A Nation at Risk* certainly spawned a flurry of other reports, all essentially repeating the conviction that a mediocre and declining system of public education already had endangered the nation's economic welfare (DuFour & Eaker, 1998). Even in the absence of compelling evidence to support this disapproving conclusion, many political elites, including most state governors, instinctively and quickly accepted it (Hawley, 1988).

School reform has commonly been described as having occurred in waves. The term *waves* can be confusing because historically it has been used to designate major reform periods. More recently, the term has been used to describe stages of contemporary reform. In this vein, some authors (e.g., Lusi, 1997) refer to two waves, one occurring from 1983 to 1989 and other occurring from 1990 to the present. Other authors (e.g., Smylie & Denny, 1990) refer to three waves. The latter description is followed in this book.

During the 1980s, reform initiatives focused almost exclusively on students and teachers, primarily because lazy students and incompetent educators were deemed to be the source of the problem (Kowalski, 2003). At the outset, state legislatures and other policymakers approved intensification mandates requiring students to do more of what they were already doing; examples included increasing graduation requirements and the minimum number of attendance days in a school calendar. Within two years, they started promulgating mandates for teacher preparation and licensing; examples included requirements for the broader study of the liberal arts, licensing examinations, and continuing education. Moreover, educators were relegated to an instrumental role; that is, their sole responsibility was to ensure that the mandates were implemented (St. John & Clements, 2004). Scholars who critiqued this reform strategy (e.g., Fullan, 2001; Sarason, 1996) concluded that it had failed and would continue to fail. They based their judgment on empirical evidence indicating that school cultures could derail political-coercive change paradigms. This was especially likely to occur if the underlying assumptions in a school culture were incompatible with the need for organizational change in general and the efficacy of the change initiatives specifically. Inside the sanctity of their classrooms, teachers ignored the mandates and continued to make pedagogical decisions based on the guiding beliefs in their minds and hearts—values they acquired through socialization to their profession and workplace (Fullan, 1996; Hall & Hord, 2001). Working in relative isolation, therefore, educators demonstrated that they were more likely to scuttle or at least attenuate reforms than to be changed by them (Cuban, 1988).

The power of school culture is exemplified by what are arguably the two most revolutionary changes in public education that occurred in the second half of the last century. The first, *Brown v. Board of Education* (1954), ruled that separate but equal public schools were unconstitutional. The second, *P.L. 94-142*, is a federal mandate and commonly referred to as the civil rights act for disabled students. These two federal interventions required school desegregation and individualized and integrated educational programming for special needs students. Many observers argue that these changes have been sustained largely by legal penalties.

School Reform after the 1980s

Circa 1990, policymakers began to pay attention to researchers (e.g., Hawley, 1988) who found that mandates had fallen short of expectations. In light of their marginal achievements, they began charting a new strategy and paid particular attention to four conclusions:

1. Focusing solely on students and teachers was insufficient (Parker, 1987); school governance (Frymier, 1987) and organizational culture (Elmore, 1987; Prince, 1989) were other variables that needed to be addressed.
2. Student needs, resources, and school environments were inconstant across districts and schools, and therefore generic state mandates proved to be ineffective for a significant portion of the public school population (Tyack & Cuban, 1995). School improvement efforts had to be refined locally (Allen, 1992; Passow, 1988) by granting school boards, administrators, and teachers the leeway to determine how they could best meet state goals (Saban, 1997).
3. The fact that teachers had little control over the services they rendered was a major barrier to school improvement (Sarason, 1990). If educators were to become authentic reformers, teacher professionalism and autonomy had to be enhanced (Kowalski, 1995; Noblit, 1986; Petrie, 1990).
4. Changing educator roles from implementers to leaders required at least three other actions: (a) efforts to make professional preparation and licensing more rigorous had to be continued (Timar, 1989); (b) new incentives were necessary to attract and retain more competent individuals to the profession (Hawley, 1988); and (c) educators had to assume greater responsibility for individual practice and overall school productivity (Timar, 1989).

Influenced by these conclusions, state policymakers embraced various iterations of a concept called *directed autonomy* (Kowalski, 2006). Applied to public policy, the strategy requires state officials (typically state legislatures and state boards of education) to (a) set broad educational objectives, (b) relax state policy and rules in order to give educators greater flexibility, and (c) hold local officials accountable for goal attainment (Weiler, 1990). The new strategy required administrators to function as leaders, especially in relation to building a local reform agenda through visioning and planning (Wimpelberg & Boyd, 1990). A comparison of reform initiatives pre- and post- 1990 is provided in Table 1.1.

TABLE 1.1   Evolution of Reform Initiatives

Factor	Pre-1990	Post-1990
Reform targets	Students and educators	Governance, culture, and organization of schools
Change strategy	Intensification mandates applied politically and externally	School restructuring applied through directed autonomy
Control	Centralized	Centralized and decentralized
Power and authority	Hierarchical, authoritative	Professional, democratic
Coupling of reform initiatives	Fragmented	Coordinated
Educator role	Management (implementers)	Leadership (designers) and management (implementers)

More recently, passage of the *No Child Left Behind Act of 2001* (NCLB) affirmed that the federal government is taking a conspicuous and direct role in school reform. As noted by Petersen and Young (2004), NCLB "readjusted the lens of accountability and focused it directly on school leaders" (p. 344). More precisely, this federal legislation requires administrators and teachers to (a) collect assessment data, (b) disaggregate those data by student groups, and (c) develop explicit plans for meeting the needs of students, especially those exhibiting low achievement (Protheroe, Shellard, & Turner, 2003). More than any other single policy or law, NCLB has visibly amalgamated directed autonomy, data-driven decision making, and school leadership.

School Reform and Leadership

The words *administration, management,* and *leadership* have been used carelessly in the professional literature, resulting in three recurring problems.

1. Many authors mistakenly treat these three words as synonyms (Yukl, 2006).
2. The words are rarely defined by authors who use them (Shields & Newton, 1994).
3. The indiscriminate use of these words leads many educators to view management and administration as pejorative terms, and as a result executive functions essential to organizational operations are devalued, primarily for political reasons (Kowalski, 2003).

As a result of these problems, graduate students in education express different and often erroneous perceptions of school leadership. For example, after asking education graduate students enrolled over a three-year period to define leadership, a California professor recorded approximately fifty different definitions (Glasman & Glasman, 1997).

Acknowledgment of dissimilarities between leadership and management can be traced back to Aristotle. He separated knowledge necessary to make things (a largely creative process) and knowledge necessary to make right decisions (largely a technical process) (Kowalski, 2006). Management involves decisions about *how* things should be done; that is, the role is directed toward controlling and using resources to achieve organizational goals (Hanson, 2003). The role focuses on sustaining organizational uniformity and efficiency (Orlosky, McCleary, Shapiro, & Webb, 1984). Leadership, on the other hand, involves decisions about *what* should be done to improve an organization. This includes functions such as visioning and planning. Distinguishing between managers and leaders, Zaleznik (1989) wrote:

> Career-oriented managers are more likely to exhibit the effects of narcissism than leaders. While busily adapting to their environment, managers are narrowly engaged in maintaining their identity and self-esteem through others, whereas leaders have self-confidence growing out of the awareness of who they are and the visions that drive them to achieve. (p. 6)

Administration actually is a broad term that encompasses both management and leadership (Yukl, 2006), and in the context of contemporary practice, school administrators must assume both roles (Kowalski, 2003). Summarizing this perspective, Guthrie and Reed (1991) observed the following about superintendents and principals:

> As managers they must ensure that fiscal and human resources are used effectively in accomplishing organizational goals. As leaders they must display the vision and skills necessary to create and maintain a suitable teaching and learning environment, to develop school goals, and to inspire others to achieve these goals. (pp. 231–232)

Teachers arguably are administrators too, but in the context of classrooms instead of districts or schools. From a managerial perspective, they ensure that the school's prescribed curriculum is being followed and that instructional materials are used effectively. From a leadership perspective, they develop goals for their students, individualize instruction, and inspire their students to do well academically (Willower, 1991).

Political-coercive change strategies deployed during much of the 1980s treated educators as instruments of change (St. John & Clements, 2004). Intensification mandates, for example, restricted their roles to implementing new standards that essentially made students do more of what they were already doing. This reform perspective reinforced two prevailing beliefs: that educators are essentially managers and that educators could not or would not make meaningful contributions with respect to deciding what should be done to improve schools.

After 1990, however, dispositions toward the role of educators in school reform started changing. Many states adopted new reform policies requiring educators to play an active leadership role—that is, administrators and teachers were expected to work with local school boards to decide *what* should be done to meet broad state goals. Using Aristotle's perspective, principals and teachers had to acquire and apply a different type of knowledge. Whereas the change initiatives they were ordered to implement during the 1980s were basically "simple, uniform, universal, and abrupt," the improvement efforts they were required to develop during the 1990s were supposed to be "handcrafted, school-specific changes" (Finn, 1991, p. 42). And because decentralized reform agendas were almost certain to be slow, gradual, and uneven, educators correctly recognized that leading would be difficult and risky. In the context of organizational administration, leadership is oriented toward success-seeking strategies—a problem-solving and risk-taking orientation (Bassett, 1970). Consequently, leadership decisions are almost always more abstract and difficult than are management decisions (Yukl, 2006).

Educator apprehensions about leadership responsibilities also are connected to institutional culture and professional knowledge. Administrators traditionally have been socialized to function as obedient school managers and teachers to function as subordinate classroom managers (Sarason, 1996). Unless prevailing cultures are altered, the effects of their socialization are not likely to disappear

(Schein, 1996). Moreover, many educators lack the requisite knowledge to function as leaders and change agents; most have no understanding of either school culture or organizational change (Sarason, 1996). Consequently, making leadership decisions necessitates (a) essential knowledge, (b) essential skills, (c) a conviction that leadership is essential to school improvement, and (d) a conviction that leadership is a professional responsibility. To appreciate the magnitude of these requirements, educators also must understand the process of decision making and its relationship to problem solving.

Problem Solving, Decision Making, and Data-Driven Decisions

Reflecting on the preparation of school administrators, Elmore (2006) concluded that traditional programs housed in universities and their cultures are ineffective. He bases this judgment on several observations including beliefs that administrative practice should be anchored in the instructional core of schooling and that systematic problems require systematic solutions. In the context of these convictions, protocols of practice should be the core of professional preparation and licensing.

When asked to describe ideal practitioners, both teachers and administrators offer an array of responses that typically describe personal and not professional characteristics of an administrator (Kowalski, 2003, 2008). For those who see practice as having a scientific foundation, the failure to discriminate between who a person is and what he or she does as a practitioner is indeed troubling for at least two reasons. First, this disposition circuitously perpetuates the assumption that effective practice is largely intuitive and artistic. Second, it deflects attention from the troubling fact that the preparation of school administrators is not guided by protocols that require specific knowledge and skills required to address systematic problems endemic in all public schools. This book is nested in the assumption that effective practice in education requires an intricate mix of scientific and craft knowledge. That is, superintendents, principals, and teachers must have sufficient knowledge to apply effective protocols to pervasive problems that cut across all schools, and they must have the ability to adjust these protocols to characteristics that make the problems dissimilar.

Clearly then, practice in the education profession should be centered on problem solving, and one essential protocol is the ability to frame a problem. Problem framing is diagnostic; that is, the task requires assessment, analysis, and evaluation. Moreover, diagnostic skills (application of the protocol) improve through reflection on practice (Loughran, 2002). Unfortunately, problem framing does not develop naturally even in very intelligent individuals. Medical students, for example, spend considerable time learning and applying scientific knowledge to diagnosing illness. Therefore, educators who have not learned to frame problems correctly are highly susceptible to making ineffective decisions because problem solving and decision making are inextricably linked.

Rather than applying proven protocols, teachers and administrators have relied primarily on intuition and routine to make complex decisions (Doyle, 2002). Those who find this condition acceptable or even favorable tend to believe that the attention being given to data-based decision making is unreasonable, if not unwarranted. In large measure, this is because most decisions made by educators involved *how* to implement predetermined curricula and instructional strategies; that is, the decisions basically required management skills. Consequently, the intent has been to manage and not resolve persisting problems, and even worse, little was done to improve learning for students who did not respond well to normative practices. After decades of pursuing reform, many scholars (e.g., Fullan, 2001; Hall & Hord, 2001) have concluded that school improvement requires a different perspective—one in which teachers and administrators lead as well as manage. This expectation requires practitioners to focus on *what* should be done to resolve problems (Kowalski, 2003).

In addition to acquiring knowledge and skills essential to problem solving and decision making, educators must engage in reflection. Reflective practice is professional introspection—a process through which teachers and administrators integrate theoretical knowledge and craft knowledge to make and evaluate decisions. When reflection is applied appropriately, problem solving and decision making become experiential learning platforms (Kowalski, 2008); that is, school leaders are able to grow professionally by virtue of their experiences in making important choices.

Problem Solving

Problem solving is often characterized as a five-stage process, as depicted in Figure 1.1. Each of these stages is essential to understanding the relationship between causes and solutions.

Stage 1: Understanding.   The first level of problem solving requires you to understand what you are trying do. There are two steps in this stage: *framing the problem* and *analyzing the problem.*

Administrators and teachers with similar levels of education and professional experience often frame (or define) a problem differently. Variance results because they usually perceive situations differently even when given identical information (e.g., contextual variables, description of an incident) (Kowalski, 1998; Kowalski, Petersen, & Fusarelli, 2005). Evidence interpretations result from a person's cognitive processing of personal knowledge, values, and experiences. These perceptual differences are extremely important. When educators deal with a problem, their preferred solution and constituent decisions are determined by their perception of the problem.

A problem's frame consists of a person's assumptions and attitudes with respect to dealing with a situation requiring attention. This process is limiting and enabling. As an example, our beliefs and values about standardized testing may limit creativity in deciding how to raise mathematics achievement scores. At the

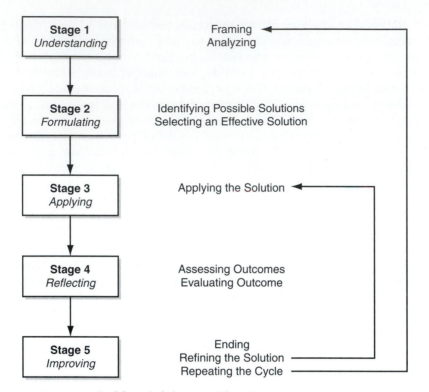

FIGURE 1.1   **Problem Solving as a Five-Stage Process**

same time, however, having a frame prevents the decision maker from losing focus or from considering improbable solutions (e.g., concern about mathematics achievement scores will simply disappear over time). Therefore, the challenge is to frame a problem accurately

According to Mayer (1983), cognitive psychologists commonly identify three features of a problem:

1. A current state (e.g., in the case study at the beginning of the chapter, 42 percent of the students in Rogers Elementary School were below grade level in mathematics achievement)
2. A desired state (e.g., the state's benchmark for acceptable performance is 90 percent of the students scoring at or above grade level on the achievement test)
3. The lack of a direct obvious way to eliminate the gap between the current state and the desired state (e.g., the principal and teachers do not know how they are going to be able to meet the benchmark)

The situation at Rogers Elementary School presented in the opening case study can be categorized by applying Reitman's (1965) typology based on four possible combinations of current and desired states of knowledge. Assuming that the desired state is reaching or surpassing the state benchmark (i.e., 90 percent of the students scoring at or above grade level) and assuming that the problem solver is the school principal, the following are the four possible combinations for identifying the nature of the problem (see also Figure 1.2):

- *A well-defined current state; a well-defined desired state.* If this category is applicable, the principal knows the percentage of students scoring at or above grade level and knows the state benchmark.
- *A well-defined current state; a poorly defined desired state.* If this category is applicable, the principal knows the percentage of students scoring at or above grade level but does not know the state benchmark.
- *A poorly defined current state; a well-defined goal.* If this category is applicable, the principal does not know the percentage of students scoring at or above grade level but knows the state benchmark. For example, his or her lack of knowledge concerning the test scores could be attributable to an inability to interpret test scores correctly.
- *A poorly defined current state; a poorly defined goal.* If this category is applicable, the principal does not know the percentage of students scoring at or above grade level and does not know the state benchmark.

Before the principal could frame the problem correctly, he or she would need to know both the percentage of students scoring at or above grade level and the state benchmark (the first category). If the principal does not possess either or both

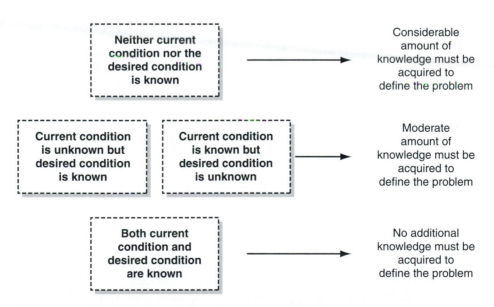

FIGURE 1.2   Possible Knowledge Categories for Problems

pieces of information, he or she must acquire additional knowledge in order to frame the problem correctly. If the problem is viewed as the gap between the current condition and the desired condition, the problem statement would read: *The percentage of students scoring at or above grade level at Rogers Elementary School needs to be increased from 52 percent to 90 percent; however, there is no clear path to achieving this goal.* In very simple terms, a problem exists when something is needed or wanted but the decision maker is unsure what to do in order to attain it (Reys, Lindquist, Lambdin, Smith, & Suydam, 2003).

Once a problem has been correctly identified, an administrator must analyze it. This entails asking and answering pertinent questions such as:

- *How serious is the problem?* The attention an administrator gives to a problem often depends on perceived consequences. Serious problems receive more and immediate attention.
- *What causes the problem?* Students often confuse causes and problems. Problems are products and causes are the variables responsible for the product. Not knowing how to eradicate the gap between current achievement scores and the state benchmark may be caused by factors such as a negative school culture, incompetent leadership, ineffective teaching, a lack of employee learning opportunities (staff development), or inappropriate instructional materials.
- *Can the problem be divided into manageable components?* By dividing a problem into parts, the search for a solution may be more efficient. For example, improving the percentage of students scoring at the proficiency level from 62 to 90 percent is a daunting task. If the problem is addressed over a five-year period, however, the principal can establish yearly benchmarks that incrementally move the school toward reaching the state benchmark.

Stage 2: Formulating.   This stage also has two elements: *identifying possible solutions* and *selecting a preferred solution.* Because information and time are common constraints, administrators and teachers usually identify only the most obvious solutions rather than all possible solutions, and they pursue a satisfactory solution rather than conducting a protracted search for the ideal solution. This behavior is known as satisficing, and is a defining characteristic of a concept called bounded rationality (Hanson, 2003). This topic is discussed in detail later in Chapter 3.

Consider an example of a superintendent faced with insufficient instructional space. He may opt to place an addition onto a school building, a solution that alleviates overcrowding temporarily but does not provide sufficient space to accommodate future growth. In this vein, the addition is an acceptable but not ideal solution.

Stage 3: Applying.   At this stage, the preferred solution is applied in effort to solve the problem. A solution's effectiveness is determined by a mix of its potentiality, the quality of application, and the context in which it is applied. Even the best solutions fail when they are applied incorrectly and inappropriately. As an example, placing an addition onto a school would alleviate the problem of insufficient instructional space only if it is large enough, designed properly, and acceptable to the public and school staff. In evaluating our choices, we must be careful to separate a solution's potential and application.

Stage 4: Reflecting.   The effects of the preferred solution should be assessed objectively and then evaluated. Assessment involves measuring (e.g., determining the percentage of students who meet the state proficiency). Evaluation entails judgment (e.g., determining if the amount measured is acceptable). Evaluation should be summative (i.e., determining the extent to which the solution actually resolved the problem) and formative (i.e., determining what could be done to improve the solution if the problem has not been resolved sufficiently). In some instances, both evaluations influence the administrator's decisions about moving forward. For example, the superintendent's assessment is that the addition provided 5 percent more instructional space. His or her summative evaluation indicates that this is insufficient because a 10 percent increase was needed. His or her formative evaluation indicates that continuing growth in the school district may require a solution other than facility additions (e.g., building a totally new school).

Stage 5: Improving.   At the improvement stage, one of three decisions is made: (a) the problem is deemed to be resolved so no further improvement is warranted; (b) the preferred solution is adjusted and the application stage is repeated; or (c) the solution is deemed to be ineffective and the problem cycle is repeated by returning to the understanding stage.

Decision Making

Educators make myriad decisions during the course of a school day, and in most instances they select a course of action either routinely or instinctively but almost always instantly. Fortunately, the bulk of these decisions are relatively inconsequential. As examples, a teacher decides to allow a student to show the class a gift he received from his grandparents or a principal decides to approve a request for a magazine subscription for the media center. Problems emerge, however, when educators fail to distinguish between important and unimportant decisions or when they do distinguish between them but fail to alter their decision-making behavior.

In relation to problem solving, decision making is less broad; problem solving actually entails series of decisions. Therefore, the value of a decision is often determined by its effect on solving a problem. Basically, a decision has three components: *a goal, options for attaining the goal,* and *the selection of the preferred option* (Welch, 2002).

School leaders face two primary decision-making challenges: *separating consequential from inconsequential decisions* and *engaging in decision analysis for consequential issues.* Arguably, these two challenges are not new; however, they have become ever more important for the following reasons:

- Society and schools have become increasingly complex social systems (Hoy & Miskel, 2005).
- The quantity and quality of information available to educators is much greater now than it was just 25 years ago (Popham, 2006).
- Society and schools have become increasingly political systems in which competition for scarce resources is manifested in a growing number of conflicting goals (Kowalski, 2006).
- School reform has heightened expectations that important decisions will be made democratically and accurately (Henkin & Dee, 2001).
- Both uncertainty and risk are higher now than in the past (Hanson, 2003).

Data-Driven Decisions

Whereas decision making involves choosing among alternatives, data-driven (or data-based) decision making involves using quantitative or qualitative information sources to inform choices (Picciano, 2006). Though the process has been promoted as a valuable management tool in education for more than fifty years, NCLB has been primarily responsible for making it a core topic in the profession. Summarizing the challenge, Doyle (2002) wrote:

> Today's education leader, whether the leader of the school district, the school building or the classroom, must change data into knowledge, transform knowledge into wisdom and use wisdom as a guide to action. But if data-driven decision making and scientifically based research are the necessary preconditions to wise decision making, they are not sufficient. True, without data and solid evidence the modern decision maker is helpless, but simply possessing data and evidence is no guarantee of success. (p. 30)

The hope is that superintendents and principals will come to "view data as the axis around which school improvement revolves" (Parsley, Dean, & Miller, 2006, p. 39).

Today, schools have access to more data than at any time in the past. Yet making data-driven decision making part of school culture is a difficult task as evidenced by the following conditions:

- Many educators have not been prepared adequately to engage in assessment, and therefore they have difficulty linking assessment data to their decisions (Popham, 2006).
- Educators who study research methodology and statistics often find the subject matter abstract and unrelated to practice (Kowalski, Petersen, & Fusarelli, 2005).
- Educators often see data as the enemy; they point out that information such as student test scores have been used historically to point the finger of blame at them (Doyle, 2003).
- The process is viewed as burdensome and time consuming (Doyle, 2003).

- Schools are social and political institutions, and therefore, values and bias have become common factors in decision making (Hoy & Miskel, 2005).
- Unlike practitioners in most other professions, educators have not typically engaged in collaborative assessment, analysis, and decision making (Popham, 2006).

Despite these problems, school leaders face the demand that they build, maintain, and use information systems for making important decisions, and especially those that directly affect student achievement. This task can be viewed in four dimensions:

1. Proficiency generating data—the degree to which principals, teachers, and support staff are prepared to conduct assessment and related research
2. Proficiency using data—the degree to which principals, teachers, and support staff are prepared to apply assessment outcomes to important decisions
3. Resource adequacy—the degree to which principals, teachers, and support staff have access to data, time, equipment, and technical assistance
4. Cultural acceptance—the degree to which principals, teachers, and support staff share values and beliefs supportive of data-driven decision making

Skeptics argue that data-driven decision making is nothing more than rational decision making—a normative management model that has long been criticized in the literature for being based on erroneous assumptions, such as the ability of the decision maker to identify all possible alternatives and to be completely objective (Hellreigel & Slocum, 1996). At the other end of the spectrum, however, one finds totally subjective decisions. These are choices made on the basis of intuition, personal bias, emotion, or politics. Clearly, such decisions are unacceptable in any profession because they ignore the need for scientific knowledge. Recognizing the limitations of rational decision making and the undesirability of totally subjective decisions, data-driven decision making is presented in this book as bounded rationality—a paradigm in which a scientific approach (i.e., data-based) is deployed but in the context of acknowledging the flawed assumptions inherent in traditional rational models. Decision models, including bounded rationality, are described more fully in Chapter 3.

Reflective Practice

Organizational behavior has commonly been described as the interface of role and personality (Getzels, 1958).[1] The former includes prescribed functions (e.g., roles and responsibilities) and goals (e.g., increased levels of efficiency and productiv-

---

[1]A more detailed explanation of organizational behavior as the interface of role and personality can be found in Getzels, J. W., & Guba, E. G. (1957). Social behavior and the administrative process. *School Review, 65,* 423–441.

ity) determined by the organization; the latter includes characteristics (e.g., personal needs, wants, and values) and goals (e.g., career advancement, praise) determined by the individual. For professionals practicing in a formal organization context, a third sphere of influence is germane. The professional sphere includes obligations (e.g., applying the profession's knowledge base and abiding by its ethical and moral codes) and goals (e.g., helping clients). In this vein, professional knowledge can be viewed as an intervening variable in decision behavior (Kowalski, 2003). Figure 1.3 provides an illustration of the three interacting spheres of influence.

A profession's knowledge base has two components: theoretical knowledge (derived primarily from research) and craft knowledge or artistry (derived primarily from experience) (Schön, 1987). The extent to which practitioners possess and use this knowledge base is thought to vary considerably in education. Dispositions toward the value of professional knowledge are critical as demonstrated in Sergiovanni's (2001) three categories of principals:

1. *Those who treat administration as a nonscience.* These principals reject the value of theory and research and rely on tacit knowledge, intuition, and more transcendental factors when making important decisions.
2. *Those who treat administration as an applied science.* These principals believe that theory and research are linearly linked to practice so they rely heavily, if not exclusively, on theoretical knowledge when making important decisions.
3. *Those who view administration as a craftlike science.* These principals believe that practice is characterized by interacting reflection and action episodes, and therefore they rely on a personal knowledge base that is continuously evolving when making important decisions.

Whereas Category 1 members reject the value of scientific knowledge, Category 2 members reject the value of experience. Category 3 members, however, meld scientific knowledge and experience and treat professional knowledge as a personal, dynamic resource.

The course of action of learning from our previous decisions is called reflective practice. The process is deemed essential because educators, like all other professionals, face complex, ambiguous, and political problems that may not be resolved by normative (prescriptive) theory. Schön (1983) argues that practitioners face three intermediate zones of practice:

1. Uncertainty: For example, the problems encountered by administrators and teachers do not always occur as well-informed structures.
2. Uniqueness: For example, problems encountered by administrators and teachers often are not discussed in textbooks, nor were they described precisely during professional preparation.
3. Value conflict: For example, possible solutions to problems often are not supported uniformly; individuals and groups holding conflicting values frequently promote opposing solutions.

FIGURE 1.3   **Spheres of Influence for Decision Behavior**

The challenge of decision making is deepened further by context. That is, uncertainty, uniqueness, and value conflict must be evaluated in relation to the conditions in which a problem exists (Erlandson, 1992; Kowalski, 2008).

Frequently, educators struggle to describe how they know what decision to make or why they made a certain decision. This is because their choices are guided by an embedded, tacit knowledge of their practice (Colton & Sparks-Langer, 1993). Occasionally, however, their routine behavior fails. As an example, teachers make on-the-spot adjustments in their lesson plans or their line of questioning, based on immediately prior student responses. When this occurs, the professional is engaging in reflection-in-action. Schön (1987) differentiates between "knowing-in-action" and "reflecting-in-action." The former is embedded in theoretical knowledge; the latter represents artistry that becomes critically important when problems and challenges are unique and less than rational.

Actually, the examination of an event can occur prior to, during, and after a decision (Kowalski, 2003). Consider a middle school principal who is contemplating how to deal with a first-year teacher who is several minutes late for his first-period class about 50 percent of the time. The principal could make a quick decision with little or no forethought, or he could engage in reflection about action. The latter alternative entails a conscious evaluation of choices and possibly a detailed plan. Reflection can also occur as the principal applies his decision (reflection-in-action). Assume the principal has decided to give the teacher a letter of reprimand based on the conviction that the letter will motivate the teacher to arrive in class on time. Without engaging in reflection at this stage, the principal misses an opportunity to assess his interaction with the teacher, especially in relation to determining if the teacher responded to the letter positively or negatively. Finally, the principal can reflect on the behavioral outcomes of his decision by studying the teacher's actions over the next few weeks. If the letter of reprimand proved to be effective, the principal's original conviction is reinforced; if the letter is not effective, the principal has reason to challenge his conviction. This third frame is called *reflection-on-action,* and it is critical to experiential learning.

The study of positive transfer between experience and future practice in relation to problem solving has been conducted for more than fifty years in both industrial and cognitive psychology (Mayer, 1983). Kolb (1984) describes experiential learning as a four-stage process:

1. Having an experience
2. Making observations of and reflecting on the experience
3. Abstractly reconceptualizing based on the experience
4. Engaging in experimentation

If the letter of reprimand cited in the previous example produces an outcome opposite to the one intended (i.e., the teacher is demoralized, rebels against the principal's authority, and comes to class late more frequently than in the past), does the principal learn from this experience? The correct answer depends on reflection-in-action and on-action. Without reflecting, the principal may simply conclude that the teacher is atypical and beyond remediation. Therefore, the principal is likely to use a reprimand again when confronted with a similar problem. On the other hand, reflection prompts the principal to think about what occurred when the teacher was given the reprimand and afterward. Since the reprimand failed to produce its intended effect, the principal may reconceptualize his disposition toward this option and subsequently try other options when confronted with a similar problem.

Unfortunately, many educators do not engage in reflective practice; some because they have rejected the value of professional knowledge; others because they have not learned to apply the process, and still others because they are unwilling to devote the necessary time. Regardless of the reason, not engaging in reflective practice diminishes a principal or teacher to the status of a technician; that is, he or she only makes decisions that he or she was been trained to make (Björk, Kowalski, & Browne-Ferrigno, 2006). As long as the problems they encounter are standard (i.e., problems on which their training was based), these individuals perform rather well. When they face challenges that defy textbook solutions, however, they struggle to make decisions, often relying on routines that have already failed. In every profession, the most effective practitioners are those who grow through experience. As a consequence of their reflective practice, their knowledge base is dynamic, and they are better prepared than their peers to address unique and highly complex problems (Schön, 1987).

SUMMARY

The importance of problem solving and decision making has been elevated markedly by school reform initiatives over the last three decades. Educators now are expected to be both reliable managers and creative leaders. Leadership is defined here as the process of determining what should be done to improve schools—and this responsibility obviously spans both administration and teaching. Historically, however, educators have been socialized to work in institutions of stability. Most were socialized to believe that risk taking was neither encouraged nor rewarded but now they are being pushed in an opposite direction.

Succeeding in an information-rich, reform-minded environment requires school leaders to alter their assumptions and beliefs about the necessity of change, risk taking, and their normative roles as decision makers. Moreover, they must acquire the knowledge and skills necessary to function as leaders, and that includes expertise essential to data-driven decision making. The purpose of this and the next several chapters is to provide a foundation for acquiring this knowledge base. Much of the book, however, is devoted directly to applications of decision making in curriculum, instruction, and school management.

QUESTIONS AND SUGGESTED ACTIVITIES

Case Study Questions

1. Immediately after being employed, Principal Brown retains the services of two consultants in an effort to raise reading and mathematics achievement test scores. What are the possible reasons why she made this choice?

2. After reading the chapter and reflecting on the case study, what other options could the principal have considered in relation to improving the test scores?

3. Individually or in a small group, frame the problem confronting Principal Brown.

4. Using the adaptation of Reitman's typology presented in the chapter, in which category does the problem presented in the case study fall?

Chapter Questions

5. What were the primary differences between the reform strategy pursued during the 1980s and reform strategy pursued subsequently?

6. How did the transition in reform strategies affect the normative roles of teachers and administrators?

7. How did the transition affect decision-making expectations for educators?

8. What is the difference between problem solving and decision making?

9. What is data-driven decision making?

10. Discuss the attitudes of educators toward data-driven decision making and identify factors that have influenced these attitudes.

11. What is experiential learning? Why is this subject germane to this chapter?

12. What is reflective practice? Why is this subject germane to this chapter?

REFERENCES

Allen, D. W. (1992). *Schools for a new century: A conservative approach to radical school reform.* New York: Praeger.

Bassett, G . (1970). Leadership style and strategy. In L. Netzer, G. Eye, R. Krey, & J. F. Overman (Eds.), *Interdisciplinary foundations of supervision* (pp. 221–231). Boston: Allyn and Bacon.

Björk, L. G., Kowalski, T. J., & Browne-Ferrigno, T. (2006). Learning theory and research: A framework for changing superintendent preparation and development. In L. G. Björk & T. J. Kowalski (Eds.), *The contemporary superintendent: Preparation, practice, and development* (pp. 71–106). Thousand Oaks, CA: Corwin Press.

Brown v. Board of Education of Topeka. 347 U.S. 483, 74 S. Ct. 686, 98 L.Ed. 873 (1954).

Colton, A. B., & Sparks-Langer, G. M. (1993). A conceptual framework to guide the development of teacher reflection and decision making. *Journal of Teacher Education, 44*(1), 45–54.

Cuban, L. (1988). How schools change reforms: Redefining reform success and failure. *Teachers College Record, 99*(3), 453–477.

Doyle, D. P. (2002). Knowledge-based decision making. *School Administrator, 59*(11), 30–34.

Doyle, D. P. (2003). Data-driven decision-making. *T.H.E. Journal, 30*(10), S19–21.

DuFour, R., & Eaker, R. (1998). *Professional learning communities at work: Enhancing best practices in student achievement.* Bloomington, IN: National Educational Service.

Elmore, R. F. (1987). Reform and the culture of authority in schools. *Educational Administration Quarterly, 23,* 60–78.

Elmore, R. F. (2006). Breaking the cartel. *Phi Delta Kappan, 87*(7), 517–518.

Erlandson, D. A. (1992). The power of context. *Journal of School Leadership, 2*(1), 66–74.

Finn, C. E. (1991). *We must take charge: Our schools and our future.* New York: Free Press.

Frymier, J. R. (1987). Bureaucracy and the neutering of teachers. *Phi Delta Kappan, 69,* 9–14.

Fullan, M. (1996). Professional culture and educational change. *The School Psychology Review, 25*(4), 496–500.

Fullan, M. (2001). *Leading in a culture of change.* San Francisco: Jossey-Bass.

Getzels, J. W. (1958). Administration as a social process. In A. W. Halpin (Ed.), *Administrative theory in education* (pp. 150–165). New York: Macmillan.

Glasman, N., & Glasman, L. (1997). Connecting the preparation of school leaders to the practice of school leadership. *Peabody Journal of Education, 72*(2), 3–20.

Guthrie, J. W., & Reed, R. J. (1991). *Educational administration and policy* (2nd ed.). Englewood Cliffs, NJ: Prentice Hall.

Hall, G. E., & Hord, S. M. (2001). *Implementing change: Patterns, principals, and potholes.* Boston: Allyn and Bacon.

Hanson, E. M. (2003). *Educational administration and organizational behavior* (5th ed.). Boston: Allyn and Bacon.

Hawley, W. D. (1988). Missing pieces in the educational reform agenda: Or, why the first and second waves may miss the boat. *Educational Administration Quarterly, 24*(4), 416–437.

Hellreigel, D., & Slocum, J. W. (1996). *Management* (7th ed.). Cincinnati: South-Western College Publishing.

Henkin, A. B., & Dee, J. R. (2001). The power of trust: Teams and collective action in self-managed schools. *Journal of School Leadership, 11*(1), 48–62.

Hoy, W. K., & Miskel, C. G. (2005). *Educational administration: Theory, research, and practice* (8th ed.). New York: McGraw-Hill.

King, R. A., Swanson, A. D., & Sweetland, R. G. (2003). *School finance: Achieving high standards with equity and efficiency* (3rd ed.). Boston: Allyn and Bacon.

Kolb, D. A. (1984). *Experiential learning: Experience as the source of learning and development.* Engle-wood Cliffs, NJ: Prentice Hall.

Kowalski, T. J. (1995). Preparing teachers to be leaders: Barriers in the workplace. In M. O'Hair & S. O'Dell (Eds.), *Educating teachers for leadership and change: Teacher education yearbook III* (pp. 243–256). Thousand Oaks, CA: Corwin Press.

Kowalski, T. J. (1998). Using case studies in school administration. In M. Sudzina (Ed.), *Case study applications for teacher education* (pp. 201–217). Boston: Allyn and Bacon.

Kowalski, T. J. (2003). Contemporary school administration: An introduction (2nd ed.). Boston: Allyn and Bacon.

Kowalski, T. J. (2006). *The school superintendent: Theory, practice, and cases* (2nd ed.). Thousand Oaks, CA: Sage.

Kowalski, T. J. (2008). *Case studies on educational administration* (5th ed.). Boston: Allyn and Bacon.

Kowalski, T. J., Petersen, G. J., & Fusarelli, L. (2005, November). *Facing an uncertain future: An investigation of the preparation and readiness of first-time superintendents to lead in a democratic society.* Paper presented at the annual meeting of the University Council for Educational Administration, Nashville, TN.

Loughran, J. J. (2002). Effective reflective practice: In search of meaning in learning and teaching. *Journal of Teacher Education, 53*(1), 33–43.

Lusi, S. F. (1997). *The role of state departments of education in complex school reform.* New York: Teachers College Press.

Mayer, R. E. (1983). *Thinking, problem solving, cognition.* New York: W. H. Freeman and Company.

National Commission on Excellence in Education. (1983, April). *A nation at risk: The imperative of school reform.* Washington, DC: United States Government Printing Office.

Noblit, G. W. (1986). What's missing from the national agenda for school reform? Teacher professionalism and local initiative. *Urban Review, 18*(1), 40–51.

Orlosky, D. E., McCleary, L. E., Shapiro, A., & Webb, L. D. (1984). *Educational administration today.* Columbus, OH: Merrill.

Parker, F. (1987). School reform: Recent influences. *National Forum: Phi Kappa Phi Journal, 67*(3), 32–33.

Parsley, D., Dean, C., & Miller, K. (2006). Selecting the right data. *Principal Leadership* (High School edition), *7*(2), 38–42.

Passow, A. H. (1988). Whither (or wither?) school reform? *Educational Administration Quarterly, 24*(3), 246–256.

Petersen, G. J., & Young, M. P. (2004). The No Child Left Behind Act and its influence on current and future district leaders. *Journal of Law & Education, 33*(3), 343–363.

Petrie, H. G. (1990). Reflections on the second wave of reform: Restructuring the teaching profession. In S. Jacobson & J. Conway (Eds.), *Educational leadership in an age of reform* (pp. 14–29). New York: Longman.

Picciano, A. G. (2006). *Data-driven decision making for effective school leaders.* Upper Saddle River, NJ: Pearson/Merrill, Prentice Hall.

Popham, W. J. (2006). *Assessment for educational leaders.* Boston: Allyn and Bacon.

Prince, J. D. (1989). *Invisible forces: School reform versus school culture.* Bloomington, IN: Phi Delta Kappa.

Protheroe, N., Shellard, E., & Turner, J. (2003). *A practical guide to school improvement: Meeting the challenges of NCLB.* Arlington, VA: Educational Research Service.

Reitman, W. R. (1965). *Cognition and thought: An information processing approach.* New York: Wiley.

Reys, R., Lindquist, M., Lambdin, D., Smith, N., & Suydam, M. (2003). *Helping children learn mathematics* (6th ed.). New York: John Wiley and Sons.

Saban, A. (1997). Emerging themes of national educational reform. *International Journal of Educational Reform, 6*(3), 349–356.

St. John, E. P., & Clements, M. M. (2004). Public opinions and political contexts. In T. J. Kowalski (Ed.), *Public relations in schools* (3rd ed., pp. 47–67). Upper Saddle River, NJ: Merrill, Prentice Hall.

Sarason, S. B. (1990). *The predictable failure of educational reform: Can we change course before it's too late?* San Francisco: Jossey-Bass.

Sarason, S. B. (1996). *Revisiting the culture of the school and the problem of change.* New York: Teachers College Press.

Schein, E. H. (1996). Culture: The missing concept in organization studies. *Administrative Science Quarterly, 41*(2), 229–240.

Schön, D. A. (1983). *The reflective practitioner.* New York: Basic Books.

Schön, D. A. (1987). *Educating the reflective practitioner: Toward a new design for teaching and learning in the profession.* San Francisco: Jossey-Bass.

Sergiovanni, T. J. (2001). *The principalship: A reflective practice perspective* (4th ed.). Boston: Allyn and Bacon.

Shields, C., & Newton, E. (1994). Empowered leadership: Realizing the good news. *Journal of School Leadership, 4*(2), 171–196.

Smylie, M. A., & Denny, J. W. (1990). Teacher leadership: Tensions and ambiguities in organizational perspective. *Educational Administration Quarterly, 26*(3), 235–259.

Spring, J. H. (1994). *The American school, 1642–1993* (3rd ed.). New York: McGraw-Hill.

Timar, T. (1989). The politics of school restructuring. *Phi Delta Kappan, 71*(4), 165–175.

Tyack, D. B., & Cuban, L. (1995). *Tinkering toward utopia: A century of public school reform.* Cambridge, MA: Harvard University Press.

Weiler, H. N. (1990). Comparative perspectives on educational decentralization: An exercise in contradiction? *Educational Evaluation and Policy Analysis, 12*(4), 433–448.

Welch, D. A. (2002). *Decisions, decisions: The art of effective decision making.* Amherst, NY: Prometheus Books.

Willower, D. J. (1991). School reform and schools as organizations. *Journal of School Leadership, 1*(4), 305–315.

Wimpelberg, R. K., & Boyd, W. L. (1990). Restructured leadership: Directed autonomy in an age of educational reform. *Planning & Changing, 21,* 239–253.

Yukl, G. A. (2006). *Leadership in organizations* (6th ed.). Englewood Cliffs, NJ: Prentice Hall.

Zaleznik, A. (1989). *The managerial mystique.* New York: Harper & Row.

2 Decision-Making Behavior

Chapter Focus

Behavior in organizations is complex, inconsistent, and often unpredictable. This fact is readily apparent in the decision-making actions of school administrators and teachers. The choices they make, even for important matters, are neither consistently rational nor unfailingly deferential to authority (i.e., policy and rules). Rather, their practice is affected by an intricate mix of personal, societal, and institutional variables. Consequently, simply ordering teachers and principals to engage in data-driven decision making and then sending them to workshops to acquire requisite skills does not ensure that they will abide.

In a rush to implement the No Child Left Behind Act (NCLB), far too many professors and administrators have focused entirely on training; that is, they have instructed educators to behave in a predetermined uniform manner. In scientific professions, this iteration of professional preparation is considered insufficient. In order to embrace a concept and to apply it effectively, practitioners must have a deep understanding of the nexus between problems (as defined by prevailing contextual variables) and decisions (responses shaped by diagnosis). Consequently, this chapter is devoted to describing social, organizational, and personal variables that influence decision-making behavior. After reading it, you should be able to respond correctly to the following queries:

1. What social forces influence decisions in schools?
2. How do district and school climate, and especially the element of culture, influence decisions?
3. What individual variables influence decision making?
4. How does your understanding of decision behavior affect your acceptance of data-based decision making?

CASE STUDY

Wendy Cooper decided to be a teacher when she was 13 years old. She was an excellent student in college and was employed last year in one of the state's most affluent school districts teaching first grade. In November, she had a conference with her principal as part of the school's required performance evaluation program.

The principal was very positive about her performance, and he had only a few minor suggestions regarding lesson planning. When given an opportunity to make comments or ask questions, Wendy sought advice about two students. In her opinion, both were having difficulty keeping up with their peers and both appeared to be less mature socially. The principal told Wendy that it was not uncommon for one or two students in each first-grade class to be retained.

"We emphasize academic excellence and we don't believe in social promotions," he told her. "If the students don't improve, we need to talk about it at our next conference in January. We may want to prepare the parents for the possibility that their children will be retained. Although parents occasionally object, the superintendent, school board, and community support our retention practices."

Wendy left the conference confused. Her former professors had given her a different perspective on retention. They claimed that the negative effects of retention far outweighed any positive effects. For example, any gain acquired by students was temporary—usually only one year or less. On the other hand, students who were retained were much more likely not to do well academically in later grades. Wendy contacted one of her former professors, who sent her a research article to read that supported the view that retention was basically ineffective in improving student performance beyond one or two years. She also went to the university library and read a doctoral dissertation that presented the same conclusion.

As Wendy prepared for her January conference with the principal, she contemplated what she should do with the students. They were not improving, but she was concerned that retaining them was not in their best interests. She kept asking herself, "What should I tell the principal?"

Understanding Educator Behavior

The situation Wendy faces in the case study reminds us that decision-based conflict is pervasive in schools. More importantly for this chapter, it demonstrates that the source of the conflict is dissonance among societal, organizational, and personal predilections. More precisely, Wendy is forced to choose between acting in accordance with her professional convictions and complying with the school and community's preference—an expectation that has been expressed to her by the principal.

Though individuals and groups do not behave uniformly in districts and schools, three categories of variables influencing decisions cut across all education institutions. These categories are social (societal factors), institutional (district and school factors), and individual (personal factors). These categories, shown in Figure 2.1, are discrete but not totally independent. As an example, community values often influence school values and school values often influence individual values.

Referring again to Wendy in the case study, four conditions are essential if she is to act on the basis of her professional conviction (a personal value).

1. Knowledge: She must understand the nature of the conviction and validation in the context of the profession.

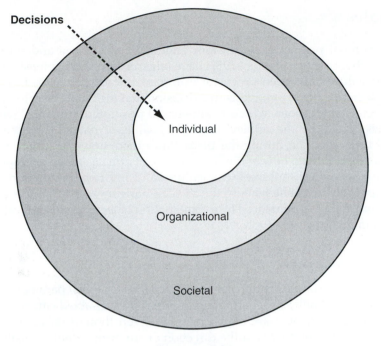

Influence variables

FIGURE 2.1 Levels of Influence Variables

2. Ability: She must have the skill necessary to act in accordance with the conviction.
3. Opportunity: She must have an occasion to act on the conviction.
4. Priority: She must view the conviction as being more important than other alternatives (e.g., competing values).

Rozycki (1994) noted that the issue of priority is especially difficult because it requires individuals to have a broad understanding of competing beliefs and their relative rank of importance.

Value-based conflict also can evolve into obligation-based conflict. A principal, for instance, has obligations to his or her profession, employer, students, and the public. As Wirt and Kirst (2001) astutely observed, school administrators must continuously reconcile two conflicting expectations: to provide professional leadership to employees and the community and to be sensitive to employee needs/interests and the public's will.

Understanding decision behavior is made more difficult by variability. That is, no two communities, no two schools, and no two educators are exactly alike. Nevertheless, we can develop a fundamental understanding of the factors that commonly influence the choices educators make in relation to their responsibilities.

Societal Variables

From a rational perspective, decisions should be value-free and unemotional. However, theorists (e.g., Simon, 1957) have long recognized that tensions between facts and values have been prevalent in organizational behavior. In the case of public education, history suggests that decision making "has been closely aligned with societal expectations, where a value-based position dominated" (Glasman & Nevo, 1988, p. 20). Yet the influence of societal values on national and state reforms received little attention during the 1980s. Since then, however, analysts have focused more directly on how and why local school officials make decisions that restructure governance, refashion curriculum, and improve instruction (Bauman, 1996). Especially in public schools, the choices made by administrators and teachers are almost always influenced by a combination of legal, philosophical, political, and economic forces.

Legal Requirements

Federal and state statutes and major court decisions establish parameters for decision making in schools; laws pertaining to civil rights, disabled citizens, and equal opportunity employment are clear examples. Even though these laws are relatively explicit, school boards at the direction of superintendents usually promulgate corresponding policy to assure that employees will make legal decisions correctly (Kowalski, 2006). Thus public policy usually has a legal base and is authoritative (Anderson, 1990); that is, it provides direction for employee decisions.

School reform has made legal influences even more relevant to decision making. During much of the 1980s, state legislatures had the most prominent role in establishing school improvement laws. Subsequently, the center of legal activity shifted to the courts because both state statutes and local policies were being challenged (Heise, 1995). Disputes over state standards for district accreditation and over testing for high school graduation exemplify issues that sparked lawsuits. More recently, the federal government has taken an aggressive role in setting laws affecting school improvement through NCLB.

Meta-Values

Historically, the development of public education has been influenced by three seemingly competing purposes: preserving the values and beliefs of a dominant culture, preparing individuals for the workforce, and compensating for injustice and inequity (Schlecty, 1990). Education goals are rooted in values, and societal values are enduring beliefs (meta-values) that are widely accepted (Razik & Swanson, 2001). Historically, education policy in the United States was guided by four such values:

1. *Liberty:* the deeply rooted value pertaining to "the right to act as one chooses" (Swanson, 1989, p. 274).

2. *Equality:* defined politically as the equal right to participate in a political system (Fowler, 2000), defined economically as equal wealth and spending on public education (Kowalski & Schmielau, 2001b), and defined educationally as equal opportunities (Fowler, 2000).
3. *Adequacy:* a relative value typically defined in terms of minimally acceptable levels (e.g., how much education is sufficient?) (King, Swanson, & Sweetland, 2003).
4. *Efficiency:* typically defined as a relationship of inputs to outputs and manifested through accountability measures (King et al., 2003).

Since the middle of the last century, two other values have been widely embraced. *Fraternity* pertains to developing a sense of community in the context of a diverse society. Tolerance for diversity, multiculturalism, and multicultural educaton are expressions of this value. For example, multicultural education is an expression of this value. Finally, *economic growth* focuses the belief that education should directly and indirectly contribute to the nation's economic strength. Programs such as Tech Prep and Schools That Work are expressions of this value (King et al., 2003). The six values are shown in Figure 2.2.

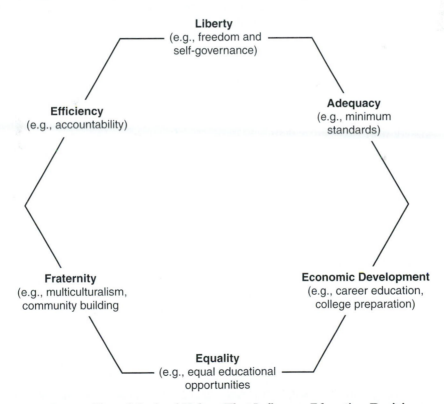

FIGURE 2.2   **Shared Societal Values That Influence Education Decisions**

Though these values continue to guide educational policy, they are not always conceptually consistent (Bauman, 1996). As a result, educators face the persistent dilemma of trying to balance conflicting beliefs when making decisions (Cuban, 1988). Consider, for instance, the decision facing educators in a district in which parents are demanding an open enrollment policy (i.e., allowing district residents to attend any school in the district) and the school board and superintendent are pushing principals and teachers to take an opposing position on the matter. From a liberty perspective, the proposed policy is positive because it broadens individual freedom; from an equality perspective, the policy is potentially negative because it is likely to reduce equal educational opportunities (e.g., choices made by parents could result in a situation in which special needs students are highly concentrated in several schools). Legal disputes involving school funding clearly demonstrate that excessive liberty almost always produces inequities. For example, wealthy school districts will generate and spend more money for education than poor school districts if they are permitted to do so (Kowalski & Schmielau, 2001a).[1] Despite such inherent tensions, neither the court of public opinion nor state courts have been willing to sacrifice one value in order to make another dominant in public education. Instead, the courts have tended to reach a compromise; for instance, judges have often ruled that some degree of inequity is acceptable in order to preserve liberty (King et al., 2003).

With respect to educator decision making, administrators and teachers also struggle when weighing liberty and equality or excellence and equality. Though they admit that the six values identified previously are noble, they often are divided when it comes to determining their order of importance. Those who believe that equal educational opportunities trump liberty or excellence tend to favor ideas such as equalized state funding and centralized controls; those who believe that liberty and excellence trump equality tend to favor ideas such decentralization and school choice. Therefore, these six meta-values are primarily a societal influence but they are interpreted and applied by individuals as they make decisions (Kowalski, 2006).

Politics

Politics is about authority and control, including the distribution and limitations of power (Knezevich, 1984), as well as the manner in which individuals and groups compete for power (King et al., 2003). Legally, public education is part of state government and more indirectly connected to the federal government. These linkages ensure that coalitions outside of schools can and will exert political influence on schools (Wirt & Kirst, 2001).

---

[1]Wealth in school districts is defined as assessed valuation per pupil—a statistic derived by dividing a district's taxable wealth by the number of pupils.

The nature of public schools as political organizations is anchored in three realities:

1. An organization's members and clients rarely possess identical values, beliefs, needs, preferences, perceptions, and wants.
2. Organizations rarely possess sufficient resources to satisfy all their members and clients.
3. Organizational goals and decisions emerge from an ongoing process of negotiations in which the various individuals and coalitions exercise power (Bolman & Deal, 2003).

In this context, educators are expected to make decisions in accordance with two standards:

1. *Professionalism,* meaning that their choices are made objectively and guided by professional knowledge.
2. *Public spirit,* meaning that their choices are made altruistically via a combination of emotional attachment (to others and the community) and a rational commitment to duty (Mansbridge, 1994).

As communities become more diverse, however, political pressures placed on educators intensify (Björk & Keedy, 2001; Kowalski, 1995), largely because politics is rooted in philosophical dissonance (Stout, Tallerico, & Scribner, 1994).

A disjunction between espoused values and reality is captured by conflicting demands most citizens place on educators. On the one hand, they expect principals and teachers to make decisions professionally and objectively (i.e., to use professional knowledge and to rise above political influence); on the other hand, they expect them to be respectful of and responsive to the public's authority over schools (Wirt & Kirst, 2001).

Experiences with political-coercive school reform initiatives demonstrate that tensions between democracy and professionalism are virtually unavoidable (Kowalski, 2004). For example, government officials have repeatedly promulgated legislation and then forced teachers to implement their ideas. In so doing, they relegated teachers to an instrumental role—that is, educators were told to implement the mandates without making important decisions about them (St. John & Clemens, 2004). Such action repeatedly resurrects a consequential question: How does the public's authority over schools interface with a profession's right to influence policy and control practice?

Economics

Economics entails the allocation of scarce resources. Public schools receive their fiscal resources from a combination of local, state, and federal revenues, with the largest percentage of funding typically coming from state government and lowest level coming from the federal government. Allocations to elementary and secondary education have been determined primarily in political contexts in which public education officials have historically had relatively little power (King et al., 2003; Wirt & Kirst, 2001). Thus it is not surprising that studies of school superintendents have consistently identified a lack of adequate funding as the most serious problem facing public schools (Glass, Björk, & Brunner, 2000; Kowalski, 2006; Kowalski & Petersen, 2005).

The relationship between important decisions and resources would appear axiomatic but this association is often ignored by policymakers and the general public. For instance, educators during the early 1980s were often criticized for not deploying microcomputers immediately after they became available. Rarely did the critics note that many school districts lacked (a) money to buy hardware, (b) space to develop labs or to put computers in classrooms, and (c) expertise (most teachers and administrators at that time were not computer literate).

In fact, unfunded mandates[2] have been rather common in public education as exemplified by the *1986 Asbestos Hazard Emergency Response Act* and the *Individuals with Disabilities Education Act* (Penning, 1994). More recently, educators have charged that NCLB includes several additional unfunded mandates (Blair & Keller, 2003). When principals and teachers have inadequate human and material resources, their choices are obviously constrained.

Organizational Variables

Districts and schools are organizations, meaning that they are social and political systems deliberately designed to achieve specific goals (Reitz, 1987). As systems, schools are somewhat like the human organism in that groups and individuals within them function much like cells and molecules in our bodies (Owens, 2001). Thus, there is some degree of interdependency among the subsystems; for example, every decision made in the English department of a high school has the potential of affecting all the school's other departments and programs. Thus, institutional pressures almost always exist when principals and teachers make choices, because the outcome of their decision can affect the entire school. Four factors are used here to demonstrate organizational influence on decision making.

School Climate and Culture

Organizational climate is a descriptive metaphor that provides a conceptual framework for understanding a school's distinguishing characteristics (Miskel & Ogawa, 1988) and employee perceptions of role expectations (i.e., perceptions of how they should behave while meeting their responsibilities (Hoy & Miskel, 2005). The concept has often been confused with *organizational culture;* however, texts in school

---

[2]*Unfunded mandates* is a term used to refer to federal or state government programs for which funding either is not provided or is provided only at a minimal level.

administration (e.g., Hanson, 2003; Kowalski, 2003; Owens, 2001) contain Renato Tagiuri's definition of climate that identifies culture as one of climate's four elements (the other three being ecology, milieu, and organizational structure (Hanson, 2003).[3]

For purposes of decision making, climate is especially useful in understanding how *organizational openness* affects the behavior of principals and teachers. Standardized instruments (e.g., the *Organizational Climate Description Questionnaire*) can be deployed to assess climate and determine the degree to which it is open or closed. The quality of openness has been applied to two associations: those occurring inside the school among educators, and those occurring between educators and the external environment (e.g., parents, community officials, and pressure groups). An open school climate is characterized by "cooperation and respect within the faculty and between the faculty and principal" (Hoy & Miskel, 2005, p. 187) and by a desire to have continuous information exchanges with the external environment (Hanson, 2003). In a closed climate, one finds opposite conditions. For example, there is a minimal level of collaboration with the principal "stressing routine trivia and unnecessary busywork" and the teachers responding by "exhibiting little commitment" (Hoy & Miskel, 2005, p. 188); collectively, school personnel avoid contact with the broader community (Hanson, 2003). Obviously, degrees of openness affect decision-making behavior. In an open climate, for example, teachers are encouraged to collaborate with colleagues to make decisions (Timperley & Robinson, 1998), and parents and other community members are encouraged to participate in important decisions (Sheldon & Epstein, 2002).

As discussed in the previous chapter in relation to school reform, organizational culture has emerged as the most critical element of climate because those studying organizational change (e.g., Fullan & Stiegelbauer, 1991; Hall & Hord, 2001; Sarason, 1996) have concluded that meaningful improvements are unlikely unless the underlying values and beliefs of educators are identified, evaluated, and altered. In large measure, values shared by educators have been judged to be inherently defensive of either professional interests or bureaucratic interests (Kogan, 1975).

Organizational culture is composed of shared beliefs, expectations, values, and norms of conduct for individuals and groups within a school. In this vein, it is a normative structure delineating "both 'what is'—knowledge, beliefs, and technology—and 'what ought to be'—values and norms—for successive generations" (Firestone & Corbett, 1988, p. 335). A school's culture is shaped by its external environment (e.g., community needs and wants, competition, prevailing practices), values (shared basic concepts and beliefs), heroes (individuals who personify the shared values), rites and rituals (systematic and programmed routines), and a mechanism for disseminating shared values (network) (Deal & Kennedy, 1982). As Razik and Swanson (1995) noted, "Culture is a part of the organization, and it is the organization" (p. 211). While part of culture is factual, other aspects are mythical

---

[3]For a detailed description of organizational climate, see Hanson (2003).

because individuals and groups establish meaning for themselves by interpreting the conditions around them (Bates, 1984).

District and school cultures can be described on the basis of strength (i.e., the degree to which organizational members adhere to the same set of values and beliefs). Philosophically, a *strong culture* is characterized by cohesiveness and a *weak culture* by fragmentation (Kowalski, 2006). Cultures may also be described based on the degree to which their underlying assumptions are congruous with the profession's knowledge base. In a *positive culture* there is congruence and in a *negative culture* there is incongruence (Kowalski, 2006). An interface of cultural strength and congruence with the professional knowledge is illustrated in Figure 2.3. A strong-positive culture is arguably the ideal because the principal and teachers share values and beliefs that promote effective practices (e.g., accepting professional responsibilities, accountability, and individualized approaches to instruction). Conversely, a strong-negative culture typically presents the most difficult situation because the principal and teachers share values and beliefs that deter effective practices (e.g., rejecting professional responsibilities, accountability, and individualized approaches to instruction).

Accurately assessing culture, however, is difficult and time consuming because underlying assumptions are not readily apparent—even to the principal and teachers. Schein (1992) identified three layers of culture:

1. *Artifacts.* This layer includes visible structures and processes. Although easy to identify, they can be misleading. For example, a crucifix on the wall of a classroom would indicate that a school is Catholic but it does not ensure that the staff embraces neo-Thomism as a guiding educational philosophy. Or having trophies and pictures of sporting events throughout the school would indicate that athletics are important but it does not ensure that all employees share this conviction.
2. *Espoused values.* This layer includes statements indicating what school personnel profess to value. They are found in documents containing philosophical statements, visions, and planning goals, and they are routinely repeated by organizational members. Even so, they may or may not depict real values. For example, a school philosophy may emphasize student self-discipline but a myriad of policies and rules and the behavior of school employees may contradict that claim.
3. *Basic assumptions.* This layer includes explicit assumptions that guide behavior and typically are not confronted or debated. Over time, they determine how educators deal with problems, and hence how they make decisions. If these beliefs are professionally or politically unacceptable, however, they are suppressed. For example, a school's staff may believe that 40 percent of the students will fail regardless of their interventions, and even though they deny they embrace this belief, their behavior strongly suggests that they do.

Unquestionably, culture is a powerful organizational force in determining decision-making behavior (Clemen, 1996). For example, a school culture may sanc-

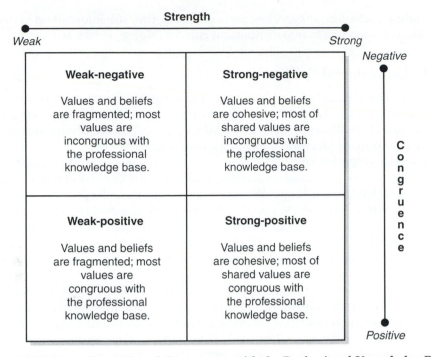

FIGURE 2.3   Strength and Congruence with the Professional Knowledge Base

tion a teacher for making a decision independently and in subtle and direct ways discourage any employee from taking risks. Consider the following examples of how culture influences both dispositions toward making decisions and decision-making behavior.

- Risk taking and the opposite behavior, failure avoidance, are typically embedded in organizational culture (Schein, 1996). In the case of public schools, failure avoidance has been the norm for administrators and teachers as evidenced by the fact that they rarely are given incentives to take risks but almost always are penalized for failure (Kowalski, 2003).
- Negative school cultures are one of the primary deterrents to decentralizing authority. Hence, they prevent important decisions from being made at the school level (Guskey & Peterson, 1996).
- Culture influences creativity. Studies (e.g., Amabile, 1988) demonstrate that manifestations of institutional culture, such as a lack of trust, competition, and having limited choices (by virtue of tight controls through policy and rules), push people toward routine behavior.

If data-driven decision making is to become the norm in elementary and secondary education, then elements of school climate, and especially cultural assumptions, must be altered. In a data-driven culture, the principal and teachers embrace scientific approaches; more precisely, they use information systematically and continuously to make important choices (Noyce, Perda, & Traver, 2000).

Organizational Politics

Institutional politics is not about the manner in which schools are structured but rather the topic relates to the distribution of power, both between society and schools and within schools (Hoy & Miskel, 2005). Studies of educator behavior reveal that many decisions, including important ones, are shaped either by self-interests or the interests of formal (e.g., an academic department in a high school) or informal (e.g., a group of teacher seeking the dismissal of the principal) groups (Estler, 1988). Accordingly, Wirt and Kirst (2001) describe public schools as miniature political systems. Despite the obvious political aspects of schooling, educators usually have been reluctant to discuss politics primarily because they have been socialized to believe that such discourse is unprofessional. In the eyes of many, politics is generally characterized by corruption, strong-arm tactics, and other unethical behaviors (Bauman, 1996).

Though the influence of external coalitions on public education is readily recognized, especially in the realm of school reform, much less attention has been given to internal politics. This neglect is noteworthy because internal tensions also affect decision behavior. Hoy and Miskel (2005), adapting the work of Mintzberg (1983) to education, described the following types of internal political systems.

- *Personalized internal coalition.* Power is concentrated in the hierarchy of authority. For example, the superintendent makes important decisions, and as a result, political activity is very low.
- *Bureaucratic internal coalition.* Power is concentrated in policy, rules, and regulations, and enforcement authority is divided among administrative divisions (e.g., between district and school administration or between the district's instructional and business divisions). Though the intent is to limit teacher power, political activity is usually moderate to high as teachers seek to acquire resources and influence.
- *Ideologic internal coalition.* Power is determined by a strong culture; that is, educators make decisions on the basis of shared values and beliefs. As a result of philosophical harmony, political activity is low.
- *Professional internal coalition.* Power is determined by expertise, and political activity is typically high because of tensions between legitimate (position-based) power and professional (knowledge-based) power.
- *Political internal coalition.* Power is distributed among one or more groups that either compete with or dominate administrators. Political activity is extremely high.

Given the differences among these possible configurations, the extent to which politics influences educator decisions depends on the type of political system existing within districts and schools. Of special note, however, is the professional internal coalition because it demonstrates that when knowledge is treated as a source of power, political activity often increases as conflict emerges between organizational authority (e.g., the position power of principals) and professional authority (e.g., the knowledge and skills possessed by teachers).

Threat and Risk

Threat is a challenge either to an organization's or a society's future. It typically results from a perceived or real deficiency or lack of equilibrium. Public dissatisfaction leading to a myriad of school reform initiatives during the last two decades of the twentieth century is a good example. When confronted with evidence that schools were not performing well and thus needed to improve, educators exhibited a proclivity to focus on the direct threats to schools (i.e., the possible negative consequences that change could have on them and their students). Conversely, the general population had a tendency to focus on societal threats (i.e., the possible negative consequences of ineffective schooling on the nation's welfare). Though threats can and often do generate anxiety and stress, they also may serve a positive purpose. Both vouchers and parental choice provisions in NCLB provide examples. Forced to compete for students, policymakers and employees in public schools often become more amenable to risk taking and experimentation. Even when threats are only perceived as being real, they increase tolerance for risk-taking behavior (Bassett, 1970).

Related to decisions, risk entails situations in which choices have more than one consequence, and although none occurs with certainty, each has a probability of occurring (Razik & Swanson, 2001). For example, an after-school tutoring program intended to help students in mathematics may increase, decrease, or have no effect on achievement test scores. Though none of these outcomes is certain, their probabilities of occurring are not identical. Therefore, the principal can reduce risk associated with his or her decision by determining the probabilities of each possible outcome (e.g., by conducting a pilot study or by accessing data from research conducted in other schools) prior to implementing the program.

A potential loss and the value of a potential loss are also notable elements of risk (Yates & Stone, 1992). Using the example of the after-school tutoring program, assume that it does not increase achievement test scores. The school will have lost resources in terms of salaries, materials, and so forth. The value of the loss is determined by the effect it has on school stability (Hanson, 2003). In general, therefore, the greater the probability of a loss and the greater the level of significance placed on a loss, the greater the level of perceived risk associated with making a decision (Ponticell, 2003).

By requiring educators to make decisions about school improvement at the local level, policymakers have essentially increased demands for risk taking in schools (Kowalski, 2006). For many educators, the strategy of setting broad state reform goals and then holding them accountable for determining how to achieve them has produced considerable conflict for at least two reasons. First, most educators have not been socialized to value risk taking (Darling-Hammond, 1989);

second, rewards and sanctions in public schools favor failure avoidance rather than risk taking (Kowalski, 2006). For example, there are few if any incentives in most schools for teachers to experiment with new instructional paradigms, yet there are definite consequences if they do so and fail. In essence, current reform policy and prevailing school cultures are incompatible; the former encourages risk-taking behavior and the latter discourages it. This is a primary reason why restructuring school culture has become the quintessential challenge for school leaders (Sarason, 1996). Relationships among risk, threat, and school culture are summarized in Table 2.1.

Uncertainty, Ambiguity, and Conflict

Scholars studying organizational life discovered decades ago that two common problems plague administrative work: uncertainty and inadequate coping strategies for dealing with uncertainty (Thompson, 1967). Uncertainty arises when school leaders cannot predict the future accurately, either because they lack critical information or because they cannot discern which types of information are cogent (Nutt, 1989). According to Milliken (1987), uncertainty has three environmental dimensions: future conditions, effects of future conditions, and responses to future conditions. Assume that a principal is considering four options for improving the academic performance of students scoring below grade level on the state achievement test. Using this scenario, the following examples of uncertainties could exist with respect to each environmental dimension:

- *Future conditions level.* The principal does not know if new instructional materials will be adopted or if the state will alter its policy on achievement tests.
- *Effects of future conditions level.* The principal does not know what effects either new instructional materials or new state policy will have.

TABLE 2.1   Threat, Risk, and Organizational Culture in Public Schools

Threat level	Demand for risk	Cultural disposition toward risk
(extent to which the stability of public schools is jeopardized)	(extent to which society expects educators to take risks in an effort to improve schools)	(social pressures expressed through norms and sanctions that either encourage or discourage risk taking)
Low	Low (demand is inconsequential)	Negative (behavior discouraged)
Moderate	Moderate (demand is isolated to selected areas of decision making)	Negative (behavior discouraged)
High	High (demand is broad and pervasive)	Negative (behavior discouraged)

■ *Response level.* If new materials are adopted or if the state changes its policy, the principal does not know what effects these alterations will have on each of his or her possible choices.

Decision makers who have low tolerance for uncertainty usually make subjective estimates about the future, about the effects of the future, and about the value of their alternative choices. Consequently, they typically select the option they personally favor rather than the option that has been found to have the highest probability of solving the problem. By acting on emotion or intuition, they have increased risk; that is, they have increased the likelihood that their decision will result in a significant loss that will have a negative effect on the school's stability.

Ambiguity occurs when the elements of a decision are "unclear or unknown, as contrasted with uncertainty, in which important factors are clear but making prediction using a factor is not" (Nutt, 1989, p. 6). In the case of public education, ambiguity has been produced primarily by philosophical dissonance. Some elements of society, for instance, believe that the primary mission of public schools is preparing students for the workforce. Others believe that it is preparing good citizens. And still others believe it is preparing students for college. As a result, educators are often unclear about their primary objectives and the preferred strategies for achieving them. And the greater the level of ambiguity, the more employees question the organization's motives and the value of their own work (March & Simon, 1958).

Conflict is inevitable in all organizations (Hanson, 2003). In relation to decisions, it typically occurs when key stakeholders disagree with respect to option preferences or with respect to risk levels associated with options (Nutt, 1989). Ambiguity also is a source of conflict, especially in public schools. For example, educators are often confused by parents who demand reform until change initiatives affect them or by parents who demand higher academic standards but protest when athletic budgets are curtailed so that more resources can be allocated to adademic programs. Since public schools are political institutions, compromise has become a common conflict-resolution strategy (Fowler, 2000; Wirt & Kirst, 2001). Nutt (1989) concluded, however, that decision makers who focus entirely on conflict "make assumptions that sweep away ambiguity and uncertainty, treating tough decisions as if they were easy" (p. 12). In essence, conflict in schools discourages rational decisions because problems are often framed politically. As an example, after studying reasons why teachers did not engage in data-driven decision making, Ingram, Louis, and Schroeder (2004) concluded that the political nature of schools was a primary deterrent.

Personal Variables

Over the last half century, the model developed by Getzels and Guba (1957) has been used to demonstrate how personal characteristics affect organizational behavior. Applied to education, a school is viewed as a social system in which expectations are divided into two dimensions—the nomothetic and the idiographic.

The former represents the school's normative expectations shaped by institutional history and culture, formal roles, and resultant role expectations; the latter represents personal dispositions that include the person (e.g., education, experience, and intelligence), the person's personality (e.g., being extroverted or introverted), and the person's need dispositions (i.e., the individual's need dispositions toward work). According to the model, behavior, including decision making, is explained by an interface of these two dimensions that results in a mixture of influences that may vary from employee to employee. The Getzels and Guba model was subsequently expanded to include two additional dimensions: organizational culture (Getzels & Thelen, 1960) and communities (Getzels, 1978). The former was explained previously as an organizational variable; the latter was addressed here as a social variable.

Compared to organizational and societal variables, much less research has been conducted on characteristics of decision makers that influence choices (Scott & Bruce, 1995). Because teaching is a profession in which most practitioners work in relative isolation, it seems logical that teachers have a myriad of opportunities to make decisions based largely or entirely on personal preferences. Thus, knowing and understanding personal variables that can influence choices are important. However, providing an exhaustive discussion of personal variables is not feasible here. Instead, the purpose in this chapter is to demonstrate how the more salient factors serve to constrain or broaden the choices educators make.

Knowledge and Skills

Decision making is affected by a person's knowledge and skills, both in terms of process (i.e., knowing how to make good decisions) and substance (i.e., the nature of a specific decision). Most educators, including administrators, probably have not studied decision making formally. Even those who have had a course in tests and measurements or basic research methodology are not really prepared to use data in relation to decision analysis, often because their courses had little relevance to their practice (Holcomb, 1999). Yet principals and teachers are expected to possess the ability to collect and manage information about students and to use these data to determine the reasons why students are not achieving at proficiency levels (Price & Burton, 2004).

In addition to having varying levels of expertise in data-driven decision making, educators differ considerably in their knowledge of subject matter. This may be due to differences in: (a) levels of formal education, (b) quality of formal education, (c) levels of experience, (d) personal interests and commitment, and (e) application skills (e.g., cognitive reasoning). However, one can generally conclude that levels of education and experience are almost always important factors in decisions. For example, a first-year teacher in third grade who has completed only one methods course in mathematics is likely to have limited insights regarding improving instruction in this subject. Moreover, simply possessing knowledge does not ensure that it will be deployed or deployed correctly. Some educators with advanced academic degrees still rely on intuition and routine.

Personality

Personality is composed of a complex of characteristics that distinguish a person. Some of these characteristics are pivotal to decision making. The following are arguably the most important:

- *Tolerance for uncertainty.* Uncertainty refers to unknown future conditions. Individuals with low tolerance dismiss the consequences of uncertainty and rely on simplistic and often erroneous assumptions (Nutt, 1989).
- *Tolerance for ambiguity.* Ambiguity occurs when important factors related to a decision are unclear or unknown. Individuals with low tolerance are prone to make quick decisions in order to reduce anxiety (Nutt, 1989).
- *Risk-taking preference.* Risk pertains to consequences of decisions, either for the organization or the decision maker. Individuals with an aversion to taking risks seek to avoid failure (Bassett, 1970); for example, teachers with an aversion to risk prefer to be closely supervised by highly directive principals (Kowalski, 2005). The extent to which this disposition is innate or cultural (i.e., produced by an organization's culture) is not always clear.
- *Readiness for change.* Individuals differ in their readiness to deal with change (Kowalski, Robinson, & Weaver, 1997). Since many decisions involve improving instruction, an aversion to change deters effective decisions. For example, teachers opposed to new graduation requirements may make conscious choices that are intended to make new requirements ineffective.
- *Tolerance for conflict.* Conflict is inevitable in all organizations but individuals differ in their ability to deal with conflict. Conflict occurs when there are two or more competing interests. It can occur at four levels: intrapersonal, interpersonal, intragroup, or intergroup (Hanson, 2003). Individuals with an aversion to conflict have a tendency to make accommodations instead of effective decisions (Kowalski, 2003).

Values

Rokeach (1972) observed, "an adult probably has tens or hundreds of thousands of beliefs, thousands of attitudes, but only dozens of values" (p. 124). Personal values represent principles that really matter to the individual (Clemen, 1996). They are conceptions of desirable conduct (Razik & Swanson, 2001) that affect the pursuit of instructional objectives. For example, a teacher's goal is to raise achievement test scores in her classroom by 5 percent during the current school year. In pursuing this goal, however, her decisions are guided by a commitment to spend a reasonably equal amount of time working with each student. Thus, her commitment to this value guides decisions in her professional practice, including those related to the goal of raising test scores.

The importance of values and beliefs in decision making is critically important. A principal, for example, usually is influenced to varying degrees by four philosophical frames:

1. Personal values and beliefs
2. Values and beliefs embedded in the culture of the education profession
3. Values and beliefs embedded in the workplace culture (i.e., school culture)
4. Values and beliefs embedded in the community served by the school

Predictably, an educator experiences conflict if his or her personal values are incongruous with the dominant values of the education profession, the school's culture, or the local community culture (Nyberg, 1993).

Studies reveal that personal values almost always influence administrative decisions (e.g., Willower, 1994) and teacher decisions (e.g., Willemse, Korthaven, & Lunenberg, 2005). In some instances, personal and professional values may be compatible but both may be inconsistent with community values. As an example, McMillan (2003) reported that student assessment decisions regularly spawned conflict for teachers because personal and professional values about student assessment were not in agreement with societal demands for assessment. Perhaps the most common case is forcing teachers to comply with mandates for conducting large-scale and high-stakes testing.

Because educator decisions are influenced by personal values, the integration of rationality (e.g., data, evidence) and moral reasoning (e.g., exhibiting a concern for students and ensuring that they are treated justly) is considered essential. Contrary to what some may believe, rationality and values do not have to be mutually exclusive. Hoy and Miskel (2005) remind us that "values and rationality are symbiotic, not antithetical" (p. 303). For example, values play a central role in determining if teachers and principals use data appropriately rather than using them to distort the truth.

Bias

Bias involves partiality or prejudice in interpreting data and applying flawed interpretation to a decision situation (Nutt, 1989). There are at least two reasons why teachers should understand bias. First, teachers need to identify and control their personal bias; second, they need to identify and avoid bias that may exist in instruments used to collect data (e.g., test bias) (Popham, 2006).

Bias can be a serious barrier to experiential learning because individuals "form an emotional attachment to their beliefs and will often regard ideas or experiences that challenge those beliefs as threats to the self" (O'Looney, 2003, p. 164). This is one reason why simply providing information that contradicts one's biases is typically ineffective in eliminating the bias (Head & Sutton, 1985). In the case of teachers, biases about effective teaching are often anchored in personal experiences that were initially acquired when the educators were students (Kagan, 1992).

Bias is especially cogent in probability assessment—the process of determining the likelihood of the success of alternative choices. Clemen (1996) argues that individuals can learn to control bias when assessing probabilities, especially if they are aware of heuristics and biases. Several of the more common ones are described below:

- *Availability heuristic.* An individual remembers an event and then overestimates how often the event recurred. The judgment then guides assessment of alternative choices. For example, a teacher remembers giving a student additional homework in an effort to raise his test score. The student's parents objected by writing a negative letter to the principal. When considering assigning additional homework to other students, the teacher focuses on the one negative experience and concludes that the outcome was indicative of other situations where he assigned additional homework. Therefore, he decides not to assign the homework.

- *Representativeness bias.* An individual attempts to predict the future based on memory of the past. Cause and effect are misinterpreted, and a choice is based on the assumption that what worked in the past will work in the future. For example, a teacher threatens a student with a failing grade in hopes of motivating her to a higher level of performance. The student does work harder in the course, and the teacher concludes that the threat caused the positive effect. Rather than determining if the incident was typical or if other variables may have been responsible for the behavior change, the teacher concludes that threats will be equally successful in the future.

- *Anchoring and adjustment bias.* An individual makes an immediate judgment (the anchor) and then examines additional information (the adjustment). However, the initial judgment takes precedent and adjustment data are not assessed objectively. For example, a teacher forms an opinion after the first day of class that Johnny is a lazy student. Subsequently, the teacher takes the time to review Johnny's file. In deciding whether to devote more personal time to Johnny, the teacher ignores data in his file that conflicts with his first impression of the student. Therefore, he decides that Johnny does not deserve his added attention.

- *Hindsight bias.* An individual assumes a fatalistic posture that certain conditions or outcomes were unavoidable. The posture is projected to the future and influences choices. For example, a geometry teacher usually fails about 20 percent of the students. She attributes the failure rate to students concluding that they were "doomed" to fail. Therefore, she opts not to provide additional help to students having difficulty because she believes her interventions are inconsequential.

- *Law of small numbers bias.* An individual examines a small group and assumes the group is typical of a population. Probability assessment is based on the small group even though it is not representative of the population. For example, a principal is promoting an in-school suspension program. He conducts a pilot study with students who have been late to class. Based largely on anecdotal evidence, he concludes that the in-school suspension program was successful. He then elects to use the program for all suspensions regardless of the nature of the infraction.

■ *Gambler's fallacy.* An individual relies on a "law" of averages to make decisions. For example, the principal asks a teacher to volunteer to be on a committee. The teacher declines. He asks another teacher, who also declines. Rather than assessing why the teachers have declined, he opts to keep asking others, believing that someone will agree to serve. This is like a gambler noting that after rolling dice, the number 6 has not appeared ten consecutive times. He then bets that a 6 will appear believing that law of averages will take effect. In truth, the probability of rolling a 6 is no greater the eleventh time than it was the first time.

These biases demonstrate how easy it is to be subjective and to ignore evidence when assessing the probability of decision choices.

Decision-Making Style

Style refers to the habitual patterns exhibited by a decision maker when making choices (Driver, 1979) and is characterized by the quantity and quality of information gathered and the scope of alternative choices that are considered (Driver, Brousseau, & Hunsaker, 1990). Some authors (Hunt, Krzystofiak, Meindl, & Yousry, 1989; Mitroff, 1983) have described decision-making style in relation to the manner in which individuals interpret data available to them. And still others (e.g., Selby, Isaksen, & Treffinger, 2004) have associated style with orientation to change, a preferred manner of processing data, and a preferred method of making a decision. Collectively, the definitions focus on how individuals make decisions.

Some authors who have studied decision-making styles (e.g., Hunt et al., 1989) have reduced the number of possible styles to two: analytics and intuitives. The former gather and analyze data to guide their choice; the latter rely on instinct to make a choice. Other authors have narrowed the number of basic styles to three. For example, Harren (1979) identified a dependent style (individuals attempt to transfer some responsibility for decisions by seeking advice from others), a rational style (individuals use a rational model to make logical and objective choices), and an intuitive style (individuals act on instinctive hunches and feelings). Scott and Bruce (1995) extended the number of categories to five by adding an avoidance style (simply avoiding making the decision) and a spontaneous style (making a decision immediately without deliberation or consultation). The avoidance category is especially noteworthy with respect to teachers because of the nature of their work. As an example, professors using open-ended case studies (i.e., cases not taken to their conclusion so that the reader can assume the responsibility of making a decision) in undergraduate teacher education courses reported rather consistently that about one-third of their students either avoided making decisions or they requested their professor or other students to direct them to make a decision (Sudzina & Kowalski, 1999). One explanation for this finding is career selection. That is, a highly controlled profession, such as teaching, may attract individuals with avoidance or dependent styles (Kowalski, 2005). Authors who have studied decision-making behavior (e.g., Driver, 1979; Driver et al., 1990; Scott & Bruce, 1995) conclude style is a learned behavior.

SUMMARY

Decision-making behavior and ultimately decisions can be affected by a myriad of societal, organizational, and individual variables. The most common were described in this chapter. These factors are reflective of demands and constraints that limit options educators have in making effective decisions. Demands represent job requirements that society, the school, and the individual establish; examples include policy, laws, rules, a need to help students, and planning goals. Constraints are restrictions that serve to limit choices available to meet demands; examples include ethics (professional and personal), human and material resources, political pressure, and a lack of community support.

In responding to decision situations, educators could ignore demands and constraints, either by not making important decisions or by making them as if demands and constraints were irrelevant. Those who pursue this precarious course of action, especially principals, risk a loss of job security. A preferred alternative, therefore, is to increase choice opportunities so that the effects of demands and constraints are reduced (Sergiovanni, 2006). Doing this requires an understanding of the variables discussed in this chapter.

QUESTIONS AND SUGGESTED ACTIVITIES

Case Study Questions

1. How did Wendy acquire knowledge about the effects of retaining students in first grade?

2. Why is Wendy troubled by this knowledge?

3. What are some possible values that may influence Wendy's decision to apply or ignore research on the effects of first-grade retention?

4. Are there any demands and constraints apparent in the case study? If so, what are they?

5. What choices does Wendy have regarding a decision about the two students who are not doing well in her class?

Chapter Questions

6. How can community politics influence decisions made by principals and teachers?

7. What is the difference between school climate and school culture?

8. Why is school culture highly relevant to decision making?

9. What is decision-making style? Which style is least desirable for educators?

10. What are uncertainty and ambiguity in relation to decision making?

11. What are some factors that may deter educators from engaging in data-driven decision making?

12. How do goals and values intersect in decisions?

13. What is bias? How does bias affect probability assessment?

REFERENCES

Amabile, T. (1988). A model of creativity and innovation in organizations. *Research in Organizational Behavior, 10,* 123–167.

Anderson, J. E. (1990). *Public policymaking: An introduction.* Boston: Houghton Mifflin.

Bassett, G. A. (1970). Leadership style and strategy. In L. Netzer, G. Eye, A. Graef, R. Drey, & J. Overman (Eds.), *Interdisciplinary foundations of supervision* (pp. 221–231). Boston: Allyn and Bacon.

Bates, R. J. (1984). Toward a clinical practice of educational administration. In T. J. Sergiovanni & J. Corbally (Eds.), *Leadership and organizational culture* (pp. 64–71). Urbana: University of Illinois Press.

Bauman, P. C. (1996). *Governing education: Public sector reform or privatization.* Boston: Allyn and Bacon.

Björk, L. G., & Keedy, J. L. (2001). Politics and the superintendency in the U.S.A.: Restructuring in-service education. *Journal of In-service Education, 27*(2), 275–302.

Blair, J., & Keller, B. (2003, August 6). NEA seeks allies to bring lawsuit on ESEA funding. *Education Week, 22*(43), 1, 22–23.

Bolman, L. G., & Deal, T. E. (2003). *Reframing organizations: Artistry, choice, and leadership* (3rd ed.). San Francisco: Jossey-Bass.

Clemen, R. T. (1996). *Making hard decisions: An introduction to decision analysis* (2nd ed.). Belmont, CA: Duxbury Press.

Cuban, L. (1988). Why do some reforms persist? *Educational Administration Quarterly, 24*(3), 329–335.

Darling-Hammond, L. (1989). Accountability for professional practice. *Teachers College Record, 91,* 59–80.

Deal, T. E., & Kennedy, A. A. (1982). *Corporate cultures: The rites and rituals of corporate life.* Reading, MA: Addison-Wesley.

Driver, M. J. (1979). Individual decision making and creativity. In S. Kerr (Ed.), *Organizational behavior.* Columbus, OH: Grid Publishing.

Driver, M. J., Brousseau, K. E., & Hunsaker, P. L. (1990). *The dynamic decision maker.* New York: Harper and Row.

Estler, S. (1988). Decision-making. In N. J. Boyan (Ed.), *Handbook of research in educational administration* (pp. 305–319). White Plains, NY: Longman.

Firestone, W. A., & Corbett, H. D. (1988). Planned organizational change. In N. Boyan (Ed.), *Handbook of research on educational administration* (pp. 321–340). New York: Longman.

Fowler, F. C. (2000). *Policy studies for educational leaders.* Upper Saddle River, NJ: Merrill, Prentice Hall.

Fullan, M., & Stiegelbauer, S. (1991). *The new meaning of educational change.* New York: Teachers College Press.

Getzels, J. W. (1978). The communities of education. *Teachers College Record, 79,* 659–682.

Getzels, J. W., & Guba, E. G. (1957). Social behavior and the administrative process. *School Review, 65,* 423–441.

Getzels, J. W., & Thelen, H. A. (1960). The classroom as a social system. In N. B. Henry (Ed.), *The dynamics of instructional groups* (pp. 53–83). Chicago: University of Chicago Press.

Glasman, N. S., & Nevo, D. (1988). *Evaluation in decision making: The case of school administration.* Boston: Kluwer.

Glass, T., Björk, L., & Brunner, C. (2000). *The 2000 study of the American school superintendency.* Arlington, VA: American Association of School Administrators.

Guskey, T. R., & Peterson, K. D. (1996). The road to classroom change. *Educational Leadership, 53*(4), 10–14.

Hall, G. E., & Hord, S. M. (2001). *Implementing change: Patterns, principals, and potholes.* Boston: Allyn and Bacon.

Hanson, E. M. (2003). *Educational administration and organizational behavior* (5th ed.). Boston: Allyn and Bacon.

Harren, V. A. (1979). A model of career decision making for college students. *Journal of Vocational Behavior, 14,* 119–133.

Head, J. O., & Sutton, C. R. (1985). Language, understanding, and commitment. In L. West & A. Pines (Eds.), *Cognitive structure and conceptual change* (pp. 91–100). Orlando, FL: Academic Press.

Heise, M. (1995). The courts vs. educational standards. *Public Interest, 120,* 55–63.

Holcomb, E. L. (1999). *Getting excited about data: How to combine people, passion, and proof.* Thousand Oaks, CA: Corwin Press.

Hoy, W. K., & Miskel, C. G. (2005). *Educational administration: Theory, research, and practice* (8th ed.). New York: McGraw–Hill.

Hunt, R. G., Krzystofiak, F. J., Meindl, J. R., & Yousry, A. M. (1989). Cognitive style and decision making. *Organizational Behavior and Human Decision Processes, 44,* 436–453.

Ingram, D., Louis, K. S., & Schroeder, R. G. (2004). Accountability policies and teacher decision making: Barriers to the use of data to improve practice. *Teachers College Record, 106*(6), 1258–1287.

Kagan, D. M. (1992). Implications of research on teacher belief. Eduational Psychologist, 27(1), 65–90.

King, R. A., Swanson, A. D., & Sweetland, R. G. (2003). *School finance: Achieving high standards with equity and efficiency* (3rd ed.). Boston: Allyn and Bacon.

Knezevich, S. J. (1984). *Administration of public education: A sourcebook for the leadership and management of educational institutions* (4th ed.). New York: Harper & Row.

Kogan, M. (1975). *Educational policy-making.* Hamden, CT: Linnet Books.

Kowalski, T. J. (1995). *Keepers of the flame: Contemporary urban superintendents.* Thousand Oaks, CA: Corwin Press.

Kowalski, T. J. (2003). *Contemporary school administration: An introduction* (2nd ed.). Boston: Allyn and Bacon.

Kowalski, T. J. (2004). The ongoing war for the soul of school administration. In T. J. Lasley (Ed.), *Better leaders for America's schools: Perspectives on the Manifesto* (pp. 92–114). Columbia, MO: University Council for Educational Administration.

Kowalski, T. J. (2005). *Case studies on educational administration* (4th ed.). Boston: Allyn and Bacon.

Kowalski, T. J. (2006). *The school superintendent: Theory, practice, and cases* (2nd ed.). Thousand Oaks, CA: Sage.

Kowalski, T. J., & Petersen, G. J. (2005, November 12). *School reform strategies and normative expectations for democratic leadership in the superintendency.* Paper presented at the annual conference of the University Council for Educational Administration, Nashville, TN.

Kowalski, T. J., Robinson, W. Y., & Weaver, R. A. (1997). The relationship between social work environment, personal characteristics, and administrator propensity for change. *Planning and Changing, 28*(4), 203–219.

Kowalski, T. J., & Schmielau, R. E. (2001a). Liberty provisions in state policies for financing school construction. *School Business Affairs, 67*(4), 32–37.

Kowalski, T. J., & Schmielau, R. E. (2001b). Potential for states to provide equality in funding school construction. *Equity and Excellence in Education, 34*(2), 54–61.

Mansbridge, J. (1994). Public spirit in political systems. In H. Aaron, T. Mann, & T. Taylor (Eds.), *Values and public policy* (pp. 146–172). Washington, DC: Brookings Institute.

March, J. G., & Simon, H. (1958). *Organizations.* New York: John Wiley.

McMillan, J. H. (2003). Understanding and improving teachers' classroom assessment decision making: Implications for theory and practice. *Educational Measurement, 22*(4), 34–43.

Milliken, F. J. (1987). Three types of perceived uncertainty about the environment: State, effect, and response. *Academy of Management Review, 12*(1), 133–143.

Mintzberg, H. (1983). *Power in and around organizations.* Englewood Cliffs, NJ: Prentice Hall.

Miskel, C., & Ogawa, R. (1988). Work motivation, job satisfaction, and climate. In N. Boyan (Ed.), *Handbook of research on educational administration* (pp. 279–304). New York: Longman.

Mitroff, I. I. (1983). *Stakeholders of the organizational mind.* San Francisco: Jossey–Bass.

Noyce, P., Perda, D., & Traver, R. (2000). Creating data-driven schools. *Educational Leadership, 57*(5), 52–56.

Nutt, P. C. (1989). *Making tough decisions: Tactics for improving managerial decision making.* San Francisco: Jossey-Bass.

Nyberg, D. (1993). *The varnished truth: Truth telling and deceiving in ordinary life.* Chicago: University of Chicago Press.

O'Looney, J. (2003). Applying learning principles to development of multimedia for addressing bias in street-level public decision-making. *Journal of Educational Multimedia and Hypermedia, 12*(2), 163–183.

Owens, R. G. (2001). *Organizational behavior in education* (6th ed.). Boston: Allyn and Bacon.

Penning, N. (1994). The folly of unfunded mandates. *School Administrator, 51*(9), 38.

Ponticell, J. A. (2003). Enhancers and inhibitors of teacher risk taking: A case study. *Peabody Journal of Education, 78*(3), 5–24.

Popham, W. J. (2006). *Assessment for educational leaders.* Boston: Allyn and Bacon.

Price, W. J., & Burton, E. M. (2004). Leadership skills for supporting learning. *Leadership, 34*(2), 20–22.

Razik, T. A., & Swanson, A. D. (1995). *Fundamental concepts of educational leadership and management.* Upper Saddle River, NJ: Merrill, Prentice Hall.

Razik, T. A., & Swanson, A. D. (2001). *Fundamental concepts of educational leadership* (2nd ed.). Upper Saddle River, NJ: Merrill, Prentice Hall.

Reitz, H. J. (1987). *Behavior in organizations* (3rd ed.). Homewood, IL: Irwin.

Rokeach, M. (1972). *Beliefs, attitudes, and values: A theory of organization.* San Francisco: Jossey-Bass.

Rozycki, E. G. (1994). Values education or values confusion? *Educational Horizons, 72,* 111–113.

St. John, E., & Clemens, M. M. (2004). Public opinions and political contexts. In T. J. Kowalski (Ed.), *Public relations in schools* (3rd ed., pp. 47–67). Upper Saddle River, NJ: Merrill, Prentice Hall.

Sarason, S. B. (1996). *Revisiting the culture of the school and the problem of change.* New York: Teachers College Press.

Schein, E. H. (1992). *Organizational culture and leadership* (2nd ed.). San Francisco: Jossey-Bass.

Schein, E. H. (1996). Culture: The missing concept in organization studies. *Administrative Science Quarterly, 41*(2), 229–240.

Schlechty, P. C. (1990). *Schools for the twenty-first century: Leadership imperatives for educational reform.* San Francisco: Jossey-Bass.

Scott, S. G., & Bruce, R. A. (1995). Decision making style: The development of a new measure. *Educational and Psychological Measurements, 55,* 818–831.

Selby, E. C., Isaksen, S. G., & Treffinger, D. J. (2004). Defining and assessing problem-solving style: Design and development of a new tool. *Journal of Creative Behavior, 38*(4), 221–243.

Sergiovanni, T. J. (2006). *The principalship. A reflective practice perspective.* Boston: Allyn and Bacon.

Sheldon, S. B., & Epstein, J. L. (2002). Improving student behavior and school discipline with family and community involvement. *Education and Urban Society, 35*(1), 4–26.

Simon, H. A. (1957). *Administrative behavior* (2nd ed.). New York: Macmillan.

Stout, R. T, Tallerico, M., & Scribner, K. P. (1994). Values: The "what?" of the politics of education. *Journal of Education Policy, 9*(5–6), 5–20.

Sudzina, M., & Kowalski, T. J. (1999, October). *Strategies for evaluating work with case studies.* Paper presented at the Midwest Educational Research Association, Chicago.

Swanson, A. D. (1989). Restructuring educational governance: A challenge of the 1990s. *Educational Administration Quarterly, 25*(3), 268–293.

Thompson, J. D. (1967). *Organizations in action.* New York: McGraw-Hill.

Timperley, H. S., & Robinson, V. M. (1998). Collegiality in schools: Its nature and implications for problem solving. *Educational Administration Quarterly, 34,* 608–629.

Willemse, M., Korthaven, F., & Lunenberg, M. (2005). Values in education: A challenge for teacher educators. *Teaching and Teacher Education, 21*(2), 205–217.

Willower, D. J. (1994). Values, valuation and explanation in school organizations. *Journal of School Leadership, 4,* 466–483.

Wirt, F. M., & Kirst, M. W. (2001). *The political dynamics of American education* (2nd ed.). Berkeley, CA: McCutchan.

Yates, J. F., & Stone, E. R. (1992). The risk construct. In J. F. Yates (Ed.), *Risk-taking behavior* (pp. 1–25). New York: Wiley.

Decision Complexity, Models, and Action Theories

Chapter Focus

As explained in the previous chapter, educators can elect to make decisions subjectively or objectively, irrationally or analytically. This chapter has two related purposes. First, it is intended to demonstrate why objective and analytical choices are usually more effective than subjective and irrational choices. The second is to demonstrate why you should engage in *decision analysis*—a process that is exceedingly important in situations in which your knowledge is insufficient to make an informed choice. Decision paradigms, models that inform you of how decisions should be or actually are made, are essential to analysis because they provide a framework for assessing and evaluating alternatives.

The content in this chapter addresses the complexity of decision making; the intent is to describe different types of decisions and to explain decision analysis more fully. Next, categories of decision models are identified and examples of paradigms in these categories are explained. Then espoused theories are compared to action theories, and the critical role of reflection in developing action theories is detailed. After reading this chapter, you should be able to address the following queries:

1. What types of decisions do educators make?
2. What is decision analysis?
3. What are differences among normative, prescriptive, and descriptive decision models?
4. In what ways do popular paradigms differ?
5. How do educators use reflection to develop action theories that can be applied to decision making?

CASE STUDY

The Randolph Township School District was formed in 1962 as a result of the consolidation of the Blueberry City Schools and East Randolph Township Schools. Today, the district enrolls 2,340 students in three elementary schools, a middle school, and a high school.

The high school is housed in an old three-story structure located in the business section of Blueberry. The facility was built in 1923 and has been remodeled four times, the most recent occurring about sixteen years ago. Superintendent Edward Bohling has repeatedly urged the school board to conduct a referendum to gain voter approval to replace the antiquated facility. However, three of the five board members had opposed the idea.

The issue of replacing the high school became a major issue in the last school board election. Jack Conway, a farmer and three-term incumbent, was challenged by Brent Lowry, an attorney and proponent of building a new school. Neither of the other two members who opposed construction was up for reelection. The local newspaper characterized the school board contest between Conway and Lowry as a "referendum" for a new high school. When the votes were counted, Lowry won by a two to one margin.

After Mr. Lowry took his oath of office and joined the school board, the two remaining dissenters attempted to forge a compromise. They told the superintendent and the other three board members that they would support a combination of remodeling and additions to the existing structure provided the cost did not exceed $15 million. Mr. Bohling countered by suggesting that the board approve a feasibility study to determine available options for meeting facility needs and the projected costs of those options. Reluctantly, the two dissenters agreed to support the superintendent's suggestion, partially because the study would delay a decision on the building project.

The superintendent, with board approval, selected a highly respected architectural firm and educational consultant to complete the study. The firm had a long and distinguished history of designing school buildings, and the consultant, a professor at one of the state universities, had worked with dozens of school systems in the state. The feasibility study was completed four months later.

The study identified three options for solving facility needs at the high school.

1. The building could be replaced at an estimated cost of $32 million.
2. The current facility could be renovated and additions constructed at an estimated cost of $18 million.
3. The oldest sections of the current facility could be razed and replaced, with the remaining portions of the building renovated at an estimated cost of $26 million.

The architects and educational consultant pointed out the advantages and disadvantages of the three options and then concurred that Option 1 provided the best educational solution—and in the long term, the most efficient alternative. They concluded that Option 2 was not an effective solution because it would not resolve flexibility and adaptability problems that were restricting curriculum, instruction, and extracurricular activities. They concluded that Option 3 was not an effective solution because it cost nearly as much as Option 1 and would retain the school in a downtown area where the site lacked acreage. Over 150 pages of evidence were included in the study.

Superintendent Bohling was ecstatic when he read the report. The document not only proved that he was right all along, but the evidence was so compelling he could not envision board resistance. After the report was released to the board, the media, and the public, however, he realized he was wrong. Neither of the board members who had been opposing building a new high school were dissuaded by the report. In an executive session (which is allowed under state law for issues involving the acquisition or disposal of property), both of them criticized the document, arguing that the architects and consultant merely wrote what Superintendent Bohling wanted them to write. They urged the other board members to support Option 2.

Over the next few days, Superintendent Bohling met privately with each of the three board members who supported Option 1. Two of them remained adamant that Option 1 was the only alternative they would support. The third board member, however, said he was leaning toward a compromise after having lunch the previous day with the two board members favoring Option 2. They told him they would support Option 3 if it meant board harmony—that is, they would support Option 3 if three other board members agreed to do so.

As he drove back to his office, Superintendent Bohling was dismayed. How could reasonable and educated individuals be so closed minded? If he decided to stand firm and recommend approval of Option 1, he would probably receive three positive votes, but the two dissenters would be angry. If he decided to broker a compromise, he might alienate the two board members supporting Option 1, and he would have to live with the fact that he pursued an action he did not believe to be acceptable professionally.

Complexity and Analysis

More than a few administrators have discovered that rationality does not rule when it comes to making decisions about public education—even when the decisions are pivotal to program quality and involve millions of dollars. Choices involving building new schools, closing existing schools, and changing school boundaries are almost always controversial, regardless of the quantity and quality of pertinent evidence. This is because emotion and politics are pervasive in public policymaking. The Randolph Township School District case study exemplifies this fact. Armed with findings and a recommendation from architects and an educational consultant, the superintendent still faces an uphill battle in gaining approval for a new high school building. Many residents may ignore or reject evidence, especially if the facts conflict with their interests. Consequently, the superintendent should expect resistance in the form of objections to higher taxes, relocating the school, and change in general.

Unlike most other scientific professions, where practitioners have complete or considerable autonomy to make decisions, district and school administrators must apply their professional knowledge in highly political contexts (Kowalski, 2003). As noted in the previous chapter, educators are burdened with the conflicting expectations that their practice is guided both by a professional knowledge base and by the will of the people (Wirt & Kirst, 2001). Consequently, decision making in public education typically involves an intricate mix of professionalism and democracy (Zeichner, 1991). Even more challenging, the elements of professionalism and democracy are neither uniform nor consistently balanced across districts and schools (Kowalski, 2005).

The political dimension of schooling increases the need for educators to have a correct understanding of decision complexity, decision analysis, and decision paradigms. And because conditions of practice are not constant, even in the same school district, effective decision making almost always depends on the practitioner's ability to deploy and integrate espoused and action theories and to identify and use various decision paradigms.

Decision Complexity

Noted scholar Herbert Simon (1993) described decision making as a three-stage process (see Figure 3.1). The first involves finding a problem that requires attention and accurately framing it. The second and more readily recognized phase entails identifying possible solutions to the problem. Finally, decision making involves the evaluation of alternative solutions and selection of one of them. Though this

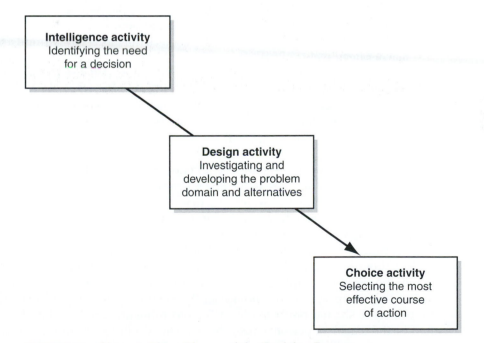

FIGURE 3.1   Simon's Three Phases of the Decision Process

process appears uncomplicated, pursuing a rational, ordered approach to making a decision is an intricate process—especially when the problem is mired in uncertainty and risk.

Decisions made by educators are characterized by three variables. The first is *frequency,* which is commonly described on a continuum ranging from *routine* to *unique.* Routine decisions are made daily, whereas unique decisions have not been encountered previously. The second variable is *configuration,* which is commonly described on a continuum ranging from *structured* to *unstructured.* Structure is determined by the extent to which the problem in question is clear and easily defined (or framed). The third variable is *significance,* which is commonly described on a continuum ranging from *unimportant* to *important.* Significance is determined by potential consequences of decisions.

Collectively, frequency, configuration, and significance determine the extent to which a decision can be classified as being *programmed* or *unprogrammed.* A programmed decision is one that can be made using preestablished policy or procedures. According to Simon (1960), programmed decisions are routine, structured, and relatively unimportant, whereas unprogrammed decisions have no prescribed course of action, and are uncommon, unstructured, and relatively important. The range of the three variables and their relationship to programmed decisions is illustrated in Figure 3.2.

Clearly, unprogrammed decisions are more difficult to make. However, they also are more threatening for administrators and teachers for four reasons:

1. They involve high levels of uncertainty; that is, the precise outcome of each possible choice on the district or school is unknown.
2. They involve high risk; that is, some choices may affect an administrator or teacher negatively.
3. They typically have profound organizational consequences; that is, they almost always influence district or school effectiveness.
4. They are extremely challenging; that is, they involve unknown information requirements (Simon, 1960), and require general problem-solving strategies (Cray, Haines, & Mallory, 1994).

Differences between programmed and unprogrammed decisions are exhibited in the following two examples. In the first scenario, a principal must decide whether to order additional art materials. She has made this decision numerous times in the past, and in each instance she has acted after the art teacher informed her that the existing materials would be depleted within 45 days. In the past, she always has followed existing school district policy and ordered the same quantity from the same vendor. Therefore, the decision she must make is highly programmed.

In the second example, the same principal must make a recommendation regarding the reemployment of a novice teacher. Having just two years of experience as a principal, she has never made such a recommendation. Based on her assessment of the teacher's performance, she is inclined not to recommend reemployment. She recognizes, however, that making this decision could produce negative consequences—for her and for the school. Her fears are exacerbated by the fact

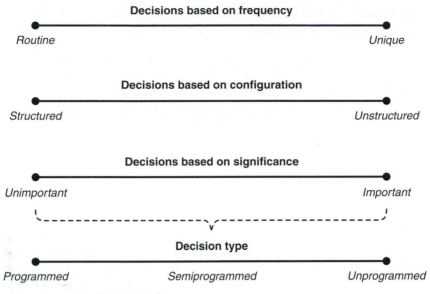

Decisions based on frequency

Routine   Unique

Decisions based on configuration

Structured   Unstructured

Decisions based on significance

Unimportant   Important

Decision type

Programmed   Semiprogrammed   Unprogrammed

FIGURE 3.2   Decision Continua

that district policy on this matter is vague and by an awareness that no principal in the district has made such a recommendation in the past five years. Uncertainty, uniqueness, risk, and potential consequences make this decision highly unprogrammed.

Unstructured, nonroutine decisions require an educator to provide judgment, evaluation, and insights when framing the problem (Simon, 1976) because there is no well-known agreed-upon choice. As shown in Figure 3.2, decisions also can be described as "semiprogrammed." These are situations in which only part of the problem can be addressed with a proven decision. For example, assume a principal has an opportunity to buy a large quantity of art supplies at a 40 percent discount. She knows that based on past history, all of the supplies would be consumed during the school year; however, she does not know the repercussion of having to find storage space if she makes this choice.

In the course of a normal school day, educators make hundreds of decisions, most of which are relatively routine and unimportant. Little concern is expressed with regard to these situations, in large measure because the choices are predictable and acceptable. Unprogrammed decisions, however, require analysis and as noted earlier, an understanding of models and the ability to apply them are integral to this procedure.

Decision Analysis

Decision making is shaped by two critical variables that were discussed previously in Chapter 1: *problems* (statements that frame the situation requiring a decision) and *objectives* (what is to be accomplished in making a decision) (Clemen,

1996). After a problem and objective are determined, the decision maker should complete three essential tasks:

1. Identify criteria that determine what constitutes an acceptable decision.
2. Identify alternatives for achieving the objective.
3. Assess and evaluate the alternatives using the criteria.

Bad decisions can stem from errors at any of these stages. Consider the following examples:

- Selected criteria may be inappropriate, deployed incorrectly, or not subject to assessment.
- Identified alternatives may not be plausible or relevant.
- Assessment or evaluation of the alternatives may be affected by bias or errors.

The importance of decision analysis is defined by the potential for making poor decisions. The process is intended to provide prescriptive advice, especially when the individual's expertise is insufficient to make an informed choice (Clemen, 2001). Decision analysis "provides structure and guidance for thinking systematically about hard decisions" (Clemen, 1996, p. 2). More precisely, it is a course of action requiring you to (a) frame the problem, (b) scrutinize pertinent values and objectives, and (c) make the most appropriate choice from the list of alternative actions. Decision theories or models[1] provide essential knowledge for conducting analysis.

The need to engage in analysis is determined primarily by three variables defined earlier in the book: uniqueness, uncertainty, and risk. When decisions pertain to unusual or uncommon problems, when the consequences of alternative choices to managing the problem are unknown, and when some alternative choices have the potential of seriously damaging the organization or individuals, the need for analysis is high. Since neither administrators nor teachers have the time to analyze every decision before it is made, they must learn to discern which decisions require analysis.

Decision-Making Models

Decision paradigms are typically dichotomized as being normative or descriptive (Grandori, 1984). More accurately, Dillon (2006) points out that there are three categories:

1. *Normative models:* paradigms stipulating in theory what the decision maker should do
2. *Prescriptive models:* paradigms stipulating what the decision maker should and can do
3. *Descriptive models:* paradigms describing what decision makers have actually done

[1]Although distinctions are commonly made between theories and models in the physical sciences, much of the literature on decision making does not recognize such dissimilarities.

The literature on decision making contains dozens of models, and though some are clearly normative and prescriptive, most are descriptive. Across all three categories, scholars agree on two critical points:

1. Models are highly useful when an individual has to make a nonprogrammed decision.
2. Models have no value if they are unknown to or misused by the decision maker.

In the case of decision paradigms, familiarity is critical. Slovic and Tversky (1974), for example, described an *understanding/acceptance principle,* a belief that the deeper the understanding of a normative principle, the greater the inclination to respond in accord with it. Subsequent research (e.g., Stanovich & West, 1999) generally supports this principle. Because decision models are principle-based, we therefore can deduce that understanding these paradigms correctly is a critical factor in determining if they will actually influence behavior as intended.

Though there are a myriad of decision-making theories and models, a handful recur in the literature and are considered the dominant paradigms. The purpose here is to summarize these approaches in order to provide you with an understanding of how they can facilitate making difficult decisions in schools.

Classical Model

Traditionally, decision-making research has been predicated on the dual assumptions that it is an orderly rational process of choosing from alternative means of accomplishing objectives and that the process is logical and sequential (Owens, 2001). The classical approach, the quintessential example of a normative model, advocates a "scientific" approach intended to produce the "ideal" decision. It is rooted in technical efficiency principles associated with the classical theory of organizations.[2] For example, administrators and teachers are expected to be unbiased and totally objective when making decisions. Rational models have been popular because they are thought to provide (a) rules for a potentially disorderly process, (b) a deductive approach to problem solving, and (c) predictability, order, technical competence, impersonality, and objective reasoning (Tanner & Williams, 1981).

Though there are multiple rational models, Griffiths (1959) suggested that they share the following elements:

- Recognizing, defining, and limiting a problem
- Analyzing and evaluating the problem
- Establishing criteria or standards for judging whether a solution is acceptable
- Collecting data
- Formulating and selecting a preferred solution and testing it
- Putting a preferred solution into effect

[2]Classical theory is also known as bureaucracy. It is a normative theory that is intended to produce technical efficiency in organizations. Its most readily identifiable characteristic is the pyramid-shaped structure in which most authority is vested in a few executives at the top of the pyramid.

The illustration shown in Figure 3.3 is a seven-step classical model applied by a principal in a high school in which a high percentage of students has failed the state-required graduation examination.

The classical model for decision making was initially designed and deployed in economics in a context in which the decision maker acted as a "maximizer" (Razik & Swanson, 2002); that is, a person who quantified alternatives to determine the absolute best one. Simon (1960) noted that this approach requires the decision maker to (a) identify all decision alternatives, (b) view every alternative in a panoramic fashion before choosing one of them, (c) know all consequences that would follow each choice, (d) assign values to each alternative, and (e) select one based on its quantitative superiority. In order to complete these tasks, the decision maker must have access to complete information, be totally free of bias and political influence, and be able to assign parametric measures to items that may not be readily quantifiable.

Consider another example in which a group of more than 100 parents presents the superintendent and school board with a petition demanding that Spanish be offered as a foreign language in the elementary schools. The superintendent perceives this demand to be a problem rather than an opportunity for at least two reasons: The demand has created conflict that is reducing operational efficiency (e.g., school employees are spending time dealing with the parents instead of performing their normal duties), and the demand is producing discord between parents and school personnel (e.g., some of the parents have decided to openly criticize the superintendent and school board for their lack of attention to this matter). The superintendent's objective is to eliminate the conflict and discord. If he deploys the classical model, it is improbable that he will have the time, information, and resources necessary to do so appropriately. For instance, he is unlikely to identify all the possible alternatives for achieving his objective, his own biases make rationality and objectivity unlikely (remember that he already is the primary target of parental criticism), and limited resources may prevent him from considering alternatives that could be effective.

Critics of the classical approach, such as March (1978), argue that decision makers either are unaware of their preferences or they avoid them, suppress them, or change them when selecting a preferred alternative. Simon (1997) adds that in most situations, decision makers are unable to implement the classical model as intended because of three pervasive obstacles:

1. Only a few of the alternatives can actually be identified.
2. Knowledge of consequences for each alternative is only fragmentary.
3. Values attached to consequences can only be imperfectly anticipated.

Moreover, a quest for the perfect decision can be sidetracked by faulty problem statements, the inability to access necessary information, and time restrictions (i.e., the amount of time the decision maker could devote to the quest) (Zey, 1992).

In districts and schools, the essential assumptions of rational models have to be considered in light of pervasive circumstances that are less common in private organizations. For example, the political nature of contextual variables, an ob-

FIGURE 3.3   **Application of a Classical Model to a High School Problem**

Step 1: Identifying the problem. Approximately 35 percent of the sophomores failed the state competency examination, resulting in the state's placing the school on academic probation.

Step 2: Analyzing the problem. The current curriculum is not aligned with the content being covered on the state competency test; the school does not provide sufficient remedial services for students who are having difficulty in English and mathematics; recent budget reductions have eliminated voluntary test-preparation courses during the summer.

Step 3: Setting the objective. Improve student performance so that the percentage of students failing the examination will be reduced by at least 10 percent in each of the next three years.

Step 4: Developing alternatives.
  a. Complete a curriculum audit and realign course content to ensure that material included on the state examination is covered in required courses.
  b. Employ a minimum of five teacher aides to assist teachers in freshman English and mathematics classes.
  c. Require eighth-grade students to take achievement examinations in English and mathematics and mandate ninth-grade remedial courses in these subjects for students who score one or more years below grade level.
  d. Provide funding to ensure that a sufficient number of remedial courses and voluntary test preparation courses are offered in the summer.
  e. Require all incoming freshmen to have individualized education programs.
  f. Require all students who receive a grade below C in English or mathematics to attend summer school between the ninth and tenth grade and in subsequent summers until they pass the state competency examination.

Step 5: Evaluating the alternatives. Each of the six alternatives is assessed in relation to its potential to affect student performance and to its cost. Moreover, they are evaluated with regard to their potential to achieve the stated objective and with regard to their potential consequences on the school (including employees) and students.

Step 6: Picking the best solution. After the alternatives are evaluated, one or a combination of two or more are identified as the preferred solution to the problem.

Step 7: Implementing the preferred solution. Once the preferred solution is known, action is taken to ensure proper implementation (e.g., establishing or revising policy and regulations and providing adequate human and material resources).

struction referred to as *contextual rationality* (March & Simon, 1993), diminishes rationality and objectivity (Slater & Boyd, 1999). Especially in public schools, educator decisions are affected by the interests of internal and external individuals and groups. Moreover, administrators rarely have complete information, an exhaustive list of alternative solutions, or totally unbiased dispositions (Browne, 1993). Thus, their decisions are usually made in the context of mixed motives, ambiguity, and limited information.

Expected Utility Model

Recognizing that making the ideal decision for an unstructured, complex, and non-routine problem is impractical, scholars developed more realistic (prescriptive) models. One of them is the expected utility model. The purpose of this paradigm is to produce a "good" decision—that is, to select the known and plausible alternative that best achieves the decision maker's objective (Baron, 1996). It differs from the classical model in that alternatives are evaluated on the basis of their utility rather than quantified value.

The concept of utility is based on *transitivity* and *connectedness* (Baron, 2000). The former refers to the relative value of alternatives in relation to each other. For example, if a teacher identifies three alternatives for increasing a student's participation in class, she would make paired comparisons—that is, the first alternative (A) would be compared with the second alternative (B), the second alternative (B) with the third alternative (C). Connectedness means that in each paired comparison, one alternative is found to be better (in which case, it has more utility) or to be equally good. The model stipulates that there is no such thing as a nonanswer for a comparison (i.e., concluding the utility relationship cannot be established). Determining the best alternative, therefore, results from judgments about the utility of each option to meet the decision maker's objective. If executed properly, the decision maker selects the best alternative from those that are known (Baron, 2000).

In addition, the *expected utility model* addresses uncertainty by having the decision maker identify multiple possible futures (referred to as "states of the world"). Assume, for example, that the superintendent who has been given a petition demanding Spanish instruction in elementary schools works in a district with unstable enrollment patterns. If he applied the expected utility model, each of the alternative decisions would have to be evaluated in relation to possible future states. Since enrollments have fluctuated, this would mean each alternative would have to be examined in the context of three scenarios: increased, static, and decreased elementary school enrollments. An alternative is determined to be best when it has higher utility in one or more future states and is at least equal in utility in the remaining states.

Compared to the classical model, expected utility does not purport to establish the ideal decision; rather, it is intended to identify the alternative that has the greatest utility from among the known alternatives. Though arguably more realistic than the classical model, at least in relation to applicability to education decisions, studies (e.g., McNeil, Pauker, & Tversky, 1988; Tversky & Kahneman, 1988) have found that much like the classical model, its axioms are commonly violated.

Behavioral Model

The behavioral model provides insights into adjustments administrators and others make as a result of flawed assumptions in rational models. Also linear, the following four convictions distinguish it from the classical model:

1. Decision makers are not unbiased.
2. Decision makers do not have access to all pertinent information.
3. Decision makers rarely, if ever, identify all plausible alternatives.
4. Decision makers rarely, if ever, identify and choose the ideal decisions.

The behavioral model is guided by the principle of *bounded rationality*—a standard that recognizes that totally rational and perfect decisions are unrealistic. This principle's primary characteristic is *satisficing*. March and Simon (1958) described this concept as "the difference between searching a haystack to find the sharpest needle in it and searching the haystack to find a needle sharp enough to sew with" (pp. 140–141). In essence, satisficing involves the tendency of decision makers to select something less than ideal (Hellreigel & Slocum, 1996). In addition to the four previously stated convictions, bounded models are predicated on two additional beliefs.

1. Decisions are made in the context of conflicting values and interests (i.e., in political contexts).
2. Decision makers such as administrators and teachers often select the first available satisfactory course of action instead of endlessly pursuing the ideal course of action.

Behavioral decision making emerged from descriptive studies examining how decisions were actually made in various types of organizations. Consequently, the model is considered both descriptive and prescriptive (i.e., it describes actual behaviors and provides a realistic but structured course of action that practitioners can follow). If applied to the example in Figure 3.3, the principal would evaluate the alternatives in the order they were identified and select the first one that appeared to provide an acceptable response to the test score problem.

Ethical Model

Ethical models are normative in that they are value-based and prescribe a code of conduct and values for making decisions. Instead of relying on rationality and objectivity, they depend on moral and professional standards (Hitt, 1990). They are premised on the belief that administrative decisions are more than factual propositions in that they include preferences for achieving desired conditions (Simon, 1997). For example, eliminating prejudice from public schools and promoting social justice prompts administrators to meld moral judgments (e.g., treating every one as equals) and factual information (e.g., achievement test scores).

Values are pivotal to ethical decision making, and in education they are found in professional codes of conduct for administrators, counselors, and teachers. They constitute a structured rationale for educator decisions (Hitt, 1990). In an ethical framework, for example, administrators are expected to balance societal, student, employee, and organizational interests rather than acting politically to advance personal or special group interests.

The topic of ethics is complex across professions because it de facto requires the integration of general and profession-specific values. A number of authors have addressed administrative ethics generally. Blanchard and Peale (1988), for example, offer a simple three-part test for determining whether a choice you make is ethical.

1. Is the decision legal?
2. Is the decision balanced?
3. How will the decision make me feel about myself? (p. 27)

One of the most widely used ethics typologies deployed in education was developed by Starratt (1991). It includes three foundational themes:

1. *Ethic of critique:* includes issues of power and control that relate to how administrators treat teachers, parents, and students
2. *Ethic of justice:* includes issues related to fundamental values such as democratic participation and equality (e.g., ensuring reasonably equal educational opportunities)
3. *Ethic of caring:* includes issues pertaining to relationships such as cooperation, shared commitment, and friendship

Though the first two themes have received some attention in school administration, the third has been largely ignored (Starratt, 2003).

According to Balachandran (2002), three factors traditionally have determined the boundaries of ethical behavior:

1. Laws
2. The decision maker's organization (e.g., the school in which you work)
3. The decision maker's profession

As an example, a school principal's decision was deemed to be ethical if it (a) complied with the law; (b) complied with district policy; and (c) complied with the education profession's code of ethics. Today, ethical behavior is viewed more broadly to include moral leadership/practice and social justice. Moral leadership requires attention to the nature of schools, what schools do to and for students, how decisions are made, and the types of decisions that are made. Sergiovanni (2001) refers to the moral leadership dimension of administration as *purposing.* By engaging in moral leadership, the administrator allows members of the entire school community to identify goals and strategies that can be widely supported.

In school administration, ethical decisions extend beyond legal considerations to include issues such as abuses of power, discrimination, violating confidentiality, and playing politics for purposes of self-interest (Howlett, 1991). Ethical decision models encourage administrators to examine their thoughts and feelings about the nature of schools and their work in them (Mitchell & Tucker, 1992). That is, leaders are encouraged to direct their attention to thinking about what schools are and should be in a democratic society. The paradigms emphasize the common good and equal treatment of all citizens. In this vein, ethical decision making can be viewed as the antithesis of political decision making (Kowalski, 2003).

Participatory Model

Just as in ethical decision making, values and beliefs drive participatory models. The following four are especially prominent:

1. Participation leads to increased productivity.
2. Administrators need to consider both ethics and individuals when making decisions.
3. The decision-making process of a school should reflect the values of a democratic society.
4. Participation increases employee consciousness with respect to their rights (Estler, 1988).

In addition, group decision making can broaden information, knowledge, and skills that affect the problem in question (Kowalski, 2006).

During the 1980s, participatory decision making was popularized by the concept of site-based management (SBM), an organizational and political initiative intended to give parents, teachers, and others a greater voice in school governance. This topic is the focus of the next chapter.

Political Model

Because school districts operate in political environments and because they are political organizations (Sergiovanni & Carver, 1980), decisions made in them and for them are often influenced by the interventions of competing forces. Giesecke (1993) identified the following as the most common characteristics of a political approach to decision making:

- *Interdependency of decision participants.* No single individual or group typically has sufficient power to act unilaterally.
- *Dispersal of power.* Unlike the ideal bureaucracy, power is not concentrated; some of the most influential individuals and groups (e.g., a parent coalition, the local chamber of commerce) have no legitimate (i.e., organization-based) authority within the district or school.
- *Coalition building.* As individuals and groups pursue their interests, they form coalitions in order to be competitive.
- *Bargaining.* Bartering between and among coalitions is prevalent.
- *Compromise.* Decisions reflect accommodations; achieving consensus among members of a diverse group is a prime example.

Decisions made by school administrators potentially affect the interests of four entities: students, school employees, the school or district as an organization, and the community at large. Normative approaches suggest that administrators should make rational decisions and not be swayed by either emotion or politics. But in reality, many practitioners care deeply about students, and they often feel compelled to be submissive to powerful groups and individuals (Kowalski, 2006). Consider a principal who has to decide whether to make an exception to policy for a teacher who has requested a personal leave day the Friday before spring break. District policy prohibits personal leave either on the day before or the day after scheduled vacations. The teacher making this request, however, is president of the teachers' union. The principal's objective is to resolve the matter as soon as possible, and his only criterion for making a decision is to protect his own interests. Without regard for organizational precedent or the interests of the teacher's students, he advises the teacher to sidestep the policy by "getting sick" on that day.

Districts and schools are social and political entities in which power and authority are shared and distributed among various formal and informal groups (Hanson, 2003). They also are loosely coupled systems (Weick, 1976), meaning that individuals and groups often act independently. Astute administrators recognize the distribution of power and use this knowledge to determine when and with whom they can bargain (Giesecke, 1993).

Incremental decision making, sometimes referred to as "muddling through," is a pragmatic approach reflective of political influences in organizations (Lindblom, 1993). The intent is to minimize the amount of organizational change produced by decisions. Consequently, analysis is restricted to determining differences between existing situations and alternative decisions. The quality of alternatives also is based on the degree to which they are acceptable. Critics argue that this approach is overly restrictive and basically aimless (Hoy & Tartar, 1995).

Garbage Can Model

Observing how decisions are really made, researchers have noted that in many instances the traditional decision-making model gets inverted; that is, solutions are already being proposed before problems are framed and addressed. How is this possible? Cohen, March, and Olsen (1972) used a garbage can as a metaphor to answer this question. They compared an organization to a garbage can containing three ingredients:

1. *Preferred solutions:* various actions, programs, and so forth that organization members wish to implement
2. *Problems:* pervasive conditions that hamper organizational productivity
3. *Fluid participation:* inconstant interest and involvement among organization members

When external or internal events create change opportunities or demands, a preferred solution and a particular problem find a sponsor. Hanson (1996) explained:

> . . . a participant, or a coalition of participants, decides to use extensive time and energy to promote a particular solution to a specific problem. That participant or coalition may prevail because other participants sponsoring other problems and solutions reduce their participation and drop out from involvement all together. (p. 144)

In essence, the decision maker is able to implement his or her preferred solution when a choice opportunity (an event or condition) generates an advantageous mixture of people and problems.

Imagine an elementary school principal who had unsuccessfully advocated cooperative learning over the past several years. Her proposal was rejected because influential faculty were unwilling to experiment with new instructional paradigms. After 55 percent of the third-grade students scored below grade level on the state proficiency examination, however, the principal and faculty were pressured by state officials and the public to improve the school's performance. This political force for change constituted a choice opportunity—that is, an occasion in which a previously rejected idea could be implemented. Recognizing that teachers previously opposed to change became silent as a result of public criticism, the principal was able to implement cooperative learning. Figure 3.4 illustrates what occurred in this example.

The garbage can model has often been described as a solution in search of a problem; more accurately, however, decisions result from the convergence of preferred solutions, problems, and fluid participation (Hoy & Miskel, 2005). Several prevalent conditions in districts and schools encourage decisions to be made in this manner. Foremost is the presence of ambiguous and often competing goals. As an example, interest groups typically have different priorities with respect to public education's purposes, and consequently, effectiveness and success, even within a single district or school, get defined in different ways (Kowalski, 2003).

Decisions reflective of the garbage can model are neither rational nor linear. Frequently, they are counterproductive for at least three reasons:

1. Unlike the example presented here in relation to adopting cooperative learning, preferred solutions often are unproven or ineffective initiatives (i.e., they are not supported by the profession's knowledge base) (Tartar & Hoy, 1998).
2. Decisions made in this manner typically are inconsistent; that is, they often conflict with previous decisions (Schmid, Dodd, & Tropman, 1987).
3. Decisions made in this manner are often poorly defined (Schmid et al., 1987).

Thus, it is important to realize that the garbage can model is neither normative nor prescriptive. However, it is an important paradigm that we should

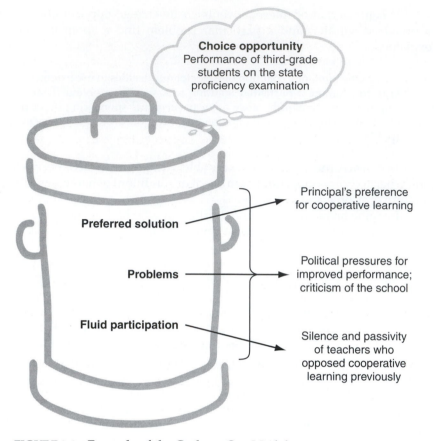

FIGURE 3.4   Example of the Garbage Can Model

understand because it provides insights into how personal, group, and political preferences often shape decisions, especially at times when schools are pressured to change.

Action Theories and Reflective Practice

According to Argyris and Schön, (1974), decisions are influenced by both *espoused* and *in-use theories*. The former exist at a conscious level and typically are altered as a result of exposure to new knowledge and experiences. However, espoused theories may not influence either decision-making behavior or decisions; for example, some administrators respond impulsively to most problems. Normative, prescriptive, and descriptive models found in the literature, and discussed to this point, exemplify espoused theories. In-use theories, commonly referred to as *action theories*, are learned from experiencing life—both inside and outside of the school (Osterman & Kottkamp, 1993). In essence they represent the decision maker's intuition about problems and their resolution.

Schön (1983, 1990) explains that the complexity and ambiguity of practice in all professions requires more than technical knowledge. He supports this conclusion by describing three intermediate zones of practice:

1. *Uncertainty.* Problems often do not occur as well-informed structures, and therefore the probability of alternatives succeeding or failing is unknown. For example, teachers may not know precisely how personal, social, and psychological factors are affecting a student, and consequently the effects of various interventions are not predicted accurately.
2. *Uniqueness.* Problems are often unfamiliar in that they were not addressed in textbooks, do not comply with the standards of espoused theories, and do not recur with regularity in practice. For example, a teacher may not have had experience trying to assist a student who has a particular type of learning disability.
3. *Value conflict.* Problem solving is complicated by the fact the decision maker usually must choose among alternative decisions supported not only by different values but values that may conflict with each other. Consider a situation experienced by a principal in relation to a divided site-based council. The members disagreed over the best way to improve discipline at the schoool. The council, consisting of eleven members, was divided six to five. The majority included all noneducators; the minority included four teachers and the principal. The majority preference is supported by the value of democracy; the minority preference is supported by the value of professionalism.

Schön adds that decisions may fall into more than one zone, and when this is true, making a choice is complex and difficult. For example, consider a novice superintendent who must eliminate proposed appropriations in order to balance the district's annual budget. He has never made such a decision previously (uniqueness zone); primarily because he is unfamiliar with the community and school district, he cannot accurately predict the ramifications of each alternative reduction (uncertainty zone); the administrators, teachers, and school board members have different priorities regarding budget appropriations (value conflict zone).

The art of reflective practice is the most effective tool for placing theoretical knowledge in perspective. Schön (1990) differentiated between "knowing-in-action" and "reflecting-in-action." The former is embedded in the socially and institutionally structured context shared by those who enter school administration and teaching. The latter represents a type of artistry that becomes important when problems and challenges are unique and less than rational. Educators develop an implicit repertoire of techniques and strategies that they apply to decisions—especially those that are routine. Using action theories, they form mental images of likely outcomes. When decisions produce expected results, there is little need to give further thought to the situation (in fact, experiences such as these serve to verify convictions already embedded in the administrator's tacit knowledge).

Occasionally, however, surprises trigger both reflection-in-action and reflection-on-action, causing them to think about unanticipated consequences as they are occurring and after the consequences are known (Kowalski, 2003). Without reflecting, decision makers do not come to understand how their behavior may be driven by implicit compliance with organizational cultural norms and their own work habits (Osterman & Kottkamp, 1993).

Decision making in professions provides a valuable opportunity for experiential learning. Kolb (1984) defined this process as being cyclical and having four stages:

1. An experience
2. An observation of and reflection about the experience
3. An abstract reconceptualization
4. Experimentation

Though experience provides a basis for learning; it alone does not guarantee learning. In the context of professional knowledge, learning occurs when a practitioner reflects on experiences, reshapes his or her knowledge based on reflection, and then applies the new knowledge when making future decisions. Thus in order to grow professionally, the practitioner must have (a) an understanding of the theoretical frame of the existing knowledge (i.e., approaches such as those discussed in this chapter), (b) the ability to engage in reflection, and (c) a commitment to continuously learn from experience.

SUMMARY

Educators make literally hundreds of decisions each day. Fortunately, most of them are routine and require little forethought. Some, however, are unique and immersed in uncertainty and risk. As you might expect, decisions involving uncertainty and risk are more difficult, frustrating, and threatening. One way to deal with this discomfort is to apply normative, prescriptive, and descriptive decision-making models.

Scientific approaches to making decisions were initially based on assumptions of rationality and complete information. Over time, scholars observed that most practitioners neither had the time nor the required data to make infallible choices. Consequently, new behavioral models emerged that described practitioners' inclinations to make satisfactory decisions.

In the case of schools, educators find decision making to be especially difficult because of conflicting expectations. On the one hand, administrators and teachers are expected to behave ethically, and on the other hand they are expected to be sensitive to the public's political will. Thus, many practitioners find themselves asking: Should my decision be morally correct or politically correct? Educators also find that their personal interests make some decisions difficult. That is, they often must choose between doing what is right and doing what is personally advantageous. As the garbage can metaphor demonstrates, organizational leaders often take advantage of threats and turmoil to advance their preferred solutions to prevailing problems.

The value of decision models is attenuated, however, if educators do not understand them or if they fail to engage in reflective practice. Learning from experience requires administrators and teachers to interface theoretical aspects of their knowledge base with actual outcomes so that they develop personal action theories.

QUESTIONS AND SUGGESTED ACTIVITIES

Case Study Questions

1. If you were the superintendent in the case study, what would you identify as your objective with respect to making a decision?

2. What alternatives can you identify in relation to meeting your objective?

3. To what degree do your alternatives entail uncertainty and risk?

4. What is the ethical dimension of the superintendent's decision?

5. What is the political dimension of the superintendent's decision?

Chapter Questions

6. What are the differences between routine and nonroutine decisions?

7. What are the differences among normative, prescriptive, and descriptive decision-making approaches?

8. Identify the assumptions underlying the classical approach to decision making. Which of them are unrealistic?

9. How does the expected utility approach differ from the classical approach?

10. What is the basis of ethical decision-making approaches?

11. To what extent are political and ethical approaches compatible?

12. What is decision analysis? Why does decision analysis require knowledge of various decision-making models?

13. What is experiential learning? Why does experiential learning require knowledge of various decision-making models?

REFERENCES

Argyris, C., & Schön, D. A. (1974). *Theory in practice: Increasing professional effectiveness*. San Francisco: Jossey-Bass.

Balachandran, M. E. (2002). Ethical decision making in business. *Business Education Forum, 57*(1), 26–28.

Baron, J. (1996). Norm-endorsement utilitarianism and the nature of utility. *Economics and Philosophy, 12*, 165–182.

Baron, J. (2000). *Thinking and deciding* (3rd ed.). New York: Cambridge University Press.

Blanchard, K. H., & Peale, N. V. (1988). *The power of ethical management*. New York: W. Morrow.

Browne, M. (1993). *Organizational decision making and information.* Norwood, NJ: Ablex.

Clemen, R. T. (1996). *Making hard decisions: An introduction to decision analysis* (2nd ed.). Belmont, CA: Duxbury Press.

Clemen, R. T. (2001). Naturalistic decision making and decision analysis. *Journal of Behavioral Decision Making, 14*(5), 359–361.

Cohen, M. D., March, J. G., & Olsen, J. P. (1972). A garbage can model of organizational choice. *Administrative Science Quarterly, 7*(1), 1–25.

Cray, D., Haines, G. H., & Mallory, G. R. (1994). Programmed strategic decision making: The view from Mintzberg's window. *British Journal of Management, 5,* 191–204.

Dillon, S. M. (2006). *Descriptive decision making: Comparing theory with practice.* Retrieved February 6, 2006, from www.esc.auckland.ac.nz/organisations/orsnz/conf33/papers/p61.pdf

Estler, S. (1988). Decision-making. In N. J. Boyan (Ed.), *Handbook of research in educational administration* (pp. 305–319). White Plains, NY: Longman.

Giesecke, J. (1993). Recognizing multiple decision-making models: A guide for managers. *College & Research Libraries, 54*(2), 103–114.

Grandori, A. (1984). A prescriptive contingency view of organizational decision making: *Administrative Science Quarterly, 29,* 192–208.

Griffiths, D. E. (1959). *Administrative theory.* New York: Appleton-Century-Crofts.

Hanson, E. M. (1996). *Educational administration and organizational behavior* (4th ed.). Boston: Allyn and Bacon.

Hanson, E. M. (2003). *Educational administration and organizational behavior* (5th ed.). Boston: Allyn and Bacon.

Hellreigel, D., & Slocum, J. W. (1996). *Management* (7th ed.) Cincinnati, OH: South-Western College Publishing.

Hitt, W. D. (1990). *Ethics and leadership: Putting theory into practice.* Columbus, OH: Battelle Press.

Howlett, P. (1991). How you can stay on the straight and narrow. *Executive Educator, 13*(2), 9–21, 35.

Hoy, W. A., & Miskel, C. G. (2005). *Educational administration: Theory, research, and practice* (7th ed.). Boston: McGraw-Hill.

Hoy, W. K., & Tartar, C. J. (1995). *Administrators solving the problems of practice: Decision making concepts, cases, and consequences:* Boston: Allyn and Bacon.

Kolb, D. A. (1984). *Experiential learning: Experience as the source of learning and development.* Englewood Cliffs, NJ: Prentice Hall.

Kowalski, T. J. (2003). *Contemporary school administration: An introduction.* Boston: Allyn and Bacon.

Kowalski, T. J. (2005). Evolution of the school superintendent as communicator. *Communication Education, 54*(2), 101–117.

Kowalski, T. J. (2006). *The school superintendent: Theory, practice, and cases* (2nd ed.). Thousand Oaks, CA: Sage.

Lindblom, C. E. (1993). *The science of muddling through.* New York: Irvington.

March, J. G. (1978). Bounded rationality, ambiguity, and the engineering of choice. *Bell Journal of Economics, 9,* 587–608.

March, J. G., & Simon, H. (1958). *Organizations.* New York: John Wiley.

March, J. G., & Simon, H. (1993). *Organizations* (2nd ed.). Cambridge, MA: Blackwell Publications.

McNeil, B., Pauker, S., & Tversky, A. (1988). On the framing of medical decisions. In D. Bell, H. Raiffa, & A. Tversky (Eds.), *Decision making: Descriptive, normative, and prescriptive interactions* (pp. 562–569). New York: Cambridge University Press.

Mitchell, D. E., & Tucker, S. (1992). Leadership as a way of thinking. *Educational Leadership, 49*(5), 30–35.

Osterman, K. F., & Kottkampt, R. B. (1993). *Reflective practice for educators: Improving schooling through professional development.* Newbury Park, CA: Corwin Press.

Owens, R. G. (2001). *Organizational behavior in education* (6th ed.). Boston: Allyn and Bacon.

Razik, T. A., & Swanson, A. D. (2002). *Fundamental concepts of educational leadership* (2nd ed.). Boston: Allyn & Bacon.

Schön, D. A. (1983). *The reflective practitioner.* New York: Basic Books.

Schön, D. A. (1990). *Educating the reflective practitioner.* San Francisco: Jossey-Bass.

Schmid, H., Dodd, P., & Tropman, J. E. (1987). Board decision making in human service organizations. *Human Systems Management, 7*(2), 155–161.

Sergiovanni, T. J. (2001). *The principalship: A reflective practice perspective* (4th ed.). Boston: Allyn and Bacon.

Sergiovanni, T. J., & Carver, F. D. (1980). *The new school executive: A theory of administration* (2nd ed.). New York: Harper & Row.

Simon, H. A. (1960). *The new science of management decisions.* New York: Harper & Row.

Simon, H. A. (1976). *Administrative behavior: A study of decision making processes in administrative organizations.* (3rd ed.). New York: Free Press.

Simon, H. A. (1993). Decision making: Rational, nonrational, and irrational. *Educational Administration Quarterly, 29,* 392–411.

Simon, H. A. (1997). *Administrative behavior: A study of decision-making processes in administrative organizations* (4th ed.). New York: Simon & Schuster.

Slater, R. O., & Boyd, W. L. (1999). Schools as polities. In J. Murphy & K. Seashore Louis (Eds.). *Handbook of research on educational administration* (2nd ed., pp. 323–336). San Franciso: Jossey-Bass.

Slovic, P., & Tversky, A. (1974). Who accepts Savage's axiom? *Behavioral Science, 19,* 368–373.

Stanovich, K. E., & West, R. F. (1999). Discrepancies between normative and descriptive models of decision making and the understanding/acceptance principle. *Cognitive Psychology, 38*(3), 349–385.

Starratt, R. J. (1991). Building an ethical school: A theory for practice in educational administration. *Educational Administration Quarterly, 27*(2), 185–202.

Starratt, R. J. (2003). *Centering educational administration: Cultivating meaning, community, responsibility.* Mahwah, NJ: Lawrence Erlbaum Associates.

Tanner, C. K., & Williams, E. J. (1981). *Educational planning and decision making: A view through the organizational process.* Lexington, MA: D. C. Heath and Company.

Tarter, C. J., & Hoy, W. K. (1998). Toward a contingency theory of decision making. *Journal of Educational Administration, 36*(3–4), 212–228.

Tversky, A., & Kahneman, D. (1988). Rational choice and the framing of decisions. In D. Bell, H. Raiffa, & A. Tversky (Eds.), *Decision making: Descriptive, normative, and prescriptive interactions* (pp. 167–192). New York: Cambridge University Press.

Weick, K. E. (1976). Educational organizations as loosely coupled systems. *Administrative Science Quarterly, 21*(1), 1–19.

Wirt, F., & Kirst, M. (2001). *The political dynamics of American Education.* Berkeley, CA: McCutchan.

Zeichner, K. M. (1991). Contradictions and tensions in the professionalization of teaching and the democratization of schools. *Teachers College Record, 92*(3), 363–379.

Zey, M. (1992). *Decision making: Alternatives to rational choice models.* Newbury Park, CA: Sage.

4 Group Decision Making

Chapter Focus

Intense criticism of elementary and secondary education over the past few decades has increased our awareness that most educators, and especially teachers, practice in relative isolation and are excluded from participating in decisions that affect school climate and effectiveness. Historically, this exclusion was disparaged on philosophical grounds; that is, it is antithetical to democratic principles. More recently, it has been condemned because it stifles professionalism and prevents schools from becoming learning organizations (Kowalski, Petersen, & Fusarelli, 2007). Group decision making has now become a normative standard for schools, and consequently your understanding of decision making is incomplete if you do not comprehend the purposes, benefits, and potential pitfalls of this process.

The purposes of this chapter are to provide a balanced description of group decision making and to illuminate how this process can be deployed in schools to benefit students and the community. Groups are described from a social perspective, and group decision making is defined. Focused attention is given to social and political circumstances that often attenuate the effectiveness of shared authority in making important choices. After reading the chapter, you should be able to address the following queries:

1. How can groups effectively make decisions, including data-based decisions, in schools?
2. How important is leadership to group effectiveness?
3. What alternatives are available for structuring groups?
4. What common problems occur with group decision making?
5. What procedures are available for group decision making?

CASE STUDY

Harrison Elementary School had become a major problem for the school board and superintendent in the West Richland County Schools. Nearly half of the 435 students failed to receive an acceptable score on the state achievement test, and the poor performance was affecting the district's reputation and jeopardizing its standing with the state education department. Convinced that the current principal was unwilling to produce needed changes, the board replaced him. Dr. William Basich, the new principal, was younger and less experienced than his predecessor; however, he believed that improvement was possible, and he was willing to take risks in order to produce positive changes.

Soon after settling into his new position, Principal Basich concluded that the Harrison School Council (HSC) was pivotal to improving the school's performance. The HSC consisted of the following members serving staggered three-year terms:

- Five school employees (three elected by the school's staff and two appointed by the principal)
- Four parents (three elected by the Parent Teacher Association and one appointed by the principal)
- The principal (ex officio)

All five school employees on the committee were teachers, and one of them, Mrs. Deloris Shipman (elected by the school's staff), had been reelected chairperson by the other members since its inception four years ago.

As a first step in pursuing change, Dr. Basich met with Mrs. Shipman and shared his expectation that the HSC would become the driving force behind school reform. Her response was not encouraging. She bluntly told the principal that the council focused largely on noninstructional issues ranging from improving the cafeteria to planning special events. She added that she was opposed to the HSC making important instructional policy decisions since nearly half of its members were not education professionals. Though the principal attempted to disabuse her of this opinion, he failed. Dr. Basich then stated his expectation to the other HSC members during a council meeting.

Mrs. Shipman was not intimidated by the principal's aggressiveness. She countered his comments directly stressing the following points:

- The HSC had become a cohesive group that functioned smoothly. Intruding into the domain of teachers, she argued, would only produce conflict and frustration.
- Blaming teachers or instructional programs for poor student performance on the state achievement test was unfair.
- Nearly all of the 48 percent of the students who failed the state test were eligible for free or reduced lunches—a fact that demonstrated that poor academic performance was linked to economics and family social conditions and not to curriculum and instruction.

Dr. Basich responded by arguing that the academic performance of the students could be improved and that the HSC members had a moral obligation to help these students. In light of the heated debate, the principal was astonished by the members' reactions. Only two others chose to speak, and both supported Mrs. Shipman's views.

After the meeting, Dr. Basich met with Pete Eagan, a fifth-grade teacher and the HSC member who had been appointed by the previous principal. At first, he was reluctant to be candid but after the principal assured him of confidentiality, he communicated more openly. He told the principal that Mrs. Shipman was considered powerful by the other members primarily for three reasons: She was a popular, long-term employee at the school; she was vice president of the district's teacher union; and her brother-in-law was a school board member. He also explained that children attending Harrison lived in two very different communities, one consisting primarily of middle-class families and the other consisting primarily of families living in poverty. None of HSC, including the parents, represented the latter community and, equally notable, none of HSC parent members' children had failed the state exam.

Principal Basich decided that the facts were on his side. He gave the HSC members considerable data about the school's performance and about similar schools that had been able to improve academic performance. His expectation was that the members would evaluate this information objectively and then act rationally. Instead, one of the parents made a motion that the HSC not become directly involved in pursuing curricular or instructional changes; the results of a secret ballot were 8 in favor, 1 opposed, and 1 abstention.

Decision Behavior in Groups

The dilemma facing the new principal in the case study demonstrates two political realities of making inclusive decisions for school improvement.

1. *The public expects education leaders to be both professional and democratic.* Described in the previous chapter, this problem involves the inevitable conflict between expectations that educators simultaneously provide direction and respect the public's political penchants. Accordingly, consequential decisions rarely have been made by one individual. Instead, they have usually been shaped by an acceptable democratic procedure, such as consensus, voting, or compromise (Kowalski, 2006).
2. *Group members usually focus on self-interests.* Predilections expressed by the participants in shared decision making are commonly at odds with each other. Studying how these preferences are conveyed in schools, Malen and Ogawa (1992) reported that decision group members seldom elected to address issues crucial to teaching and learning. Reacting to this proclivity, Mohr and Dichter (2001) noted that the most important task for superintendents and principals is not determining when group decision making works and does not work. Rather it is getting the process to a level of maturity that promotes rigor in teaching and learning. They describe group maturity as a point at which members function as a learning community, proactive and setting their own agendas rather than reacting to those of others.

In the realm of organizational studies, the nature and productivity of group decision making often have been described sarcastically. As an example, a committee has been described as "the unwilling, chosen from the unfit, to do the unnecessary" and a camel has been depicted as "a horse that was designed by a committee." Such negative characterizations arguably are rooted in classical theory—a normative perspective based on the primacy of rationality and technical efficiency (Hanson, 2003; Hoy & Miskel, 2005). Criticisms of group decision making, however, are broader than just organizational design for at least two reasons. First, social and political forces rather than evidence often affect the behavior of committee members and the choices they make collectively (Patton & Downs, 2003; Reitz, 1987). Second, when compared to choices made by experts working independently, group decisions are frequently considered inferior (Conway, 1984; Dachler & Wilpert, 1979).

Social Nature of Groups

Districts and schools are simultaneously educational, political, legal, and social entities (Kowalski, 2006). As social systems, they are composed of individuals and groups interacting in both intended and unintended ways. In an organizational context, groups are classified as either formal (i.e., developed or sanctioned by the formal organization) or informal (i.e., neither developed nor sanctioned by the formal organization) and temporary or permanent (see Figure 4.1). Given the nature

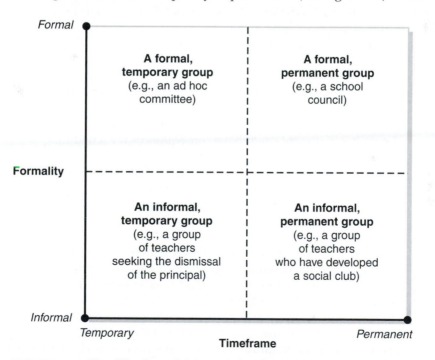

FIGURE 4.1 Classification of Organizational Groups

of this book, the focus here is primarily on decision making in formal groups. However, data-driven decision making also can occur informally, such as four teachers working collectively to make revisions to curriculum or instructional paradigms based on achievement test results.

Schein (1980) defined a group as any number of people who interact with one another, are psychologically aware of one another, and perceive themselves to be a group. However, Wilson (2005) defines a group as "three or more people who perceive themselves as a unit, who are mutually interdependent, and who interact about some common goal" (p. 371). Wilson dismisses the possibility of two-person groups contending that mutual influence is not possible with just two people. That is, minimal conditions for forming a coalition and exerting influence are possible only when a group has at least three members (e.g., two members could unite against the third member). In an organizational context, formal groups almost always are given responsibility for making some types of decisions.

Decision groups are commonly referred to as committees. In organizations, committees are broadly divided into two categories: *standing* or *ad hoc*. A standing committee has a broad purpose and continues to deal with multiple issues under its jurisdiction for a specified period. An example is a discipline committee in a middle school. Such a committee deals with various types of discipline issues, and typically the committee remains intact for the school year. An ad hoc committee has a single purpose, and it discontinues operating after it reaches its objective or after the person who formed it determines its continued operation is unnecessary or undesirable. An example would be a special committee formed to name a new school.

Our understanding of decision groups as social entities is guided by systems theory. Conrad (1994) explains that this theory is erected on three key concepts:

1. *Wholeness.* Schools are composed of smaller interdependent subsystems that act in ways that influence every other subsystem. In a high school, for example, academic departments are subsystems. A change in requirements in the English department could have consequences for scheduling and enrollment in all other departments. A committee that makes decisions and recommendations also is a subsystem.
2. *Boundaries.* A boundary is a system limitation. In the case of a decision group, this concept defines the extent to which the group maintains open dialogue with other school subsystems and with the school's external publics (e.g., parents).
3. *Process.* This concept entails ways in which group members analyze and adapt to information and changing conditions. In highly closed groups (those with rigid boundaries), little or no effort is made to respond to changing school or societal conditions.

Systems theory, as explained by Katz and Kahn (1978), views organizational operations as a linear chain of activities categorized as *inputs, throughputs,* and *outputs.* The following information provides examples of the theory applied to a decision group:

- *Inputs.* This activity entails extracting human and material resources from the district, school, and external environment. Committee members, data, funds to support the committee, and consultants are examples of system inputs.
- *Throughputs.* This activity entails processing inputs; that is, it specifies what the committee does with its resources. Data analysis, critiques, debates, interpretations, and the identification and evaluation of decision options are examples of how system inputs may be processed.
- *Outputs.* This activity entails releasing products (in this case, a decision or recommendation) back into the district, school, and community. Graduation rates, student test scores, and the percentage of students enrolling in higher education are examples of system outputs.

Systems theory holds that subsystems are never totally independent, and the organization's overall effectiveness is rarely attributable to a single cause (Hanson, 2003). Thus, outputs produced by a decision committee may affect the entire school, district, and even external publics. Consider the example of a high school in an urban district that adopted block scheduling. The decision was made by a committee of teachers and administrators from this school. After the concept was adopted, unanticipated consequences surfaced: specifically, teachers in the district's other high schools began demanding that block scheduling be adopted in their schools, some middle school teachers complained that block scheduling was diminishing student interest in elective courses, and a group of parents formally complained to the superintendent that block scheduling was restricting the number of courses their children could complete.

Group Behavior and Data-Based Instructional Decisions

Despite prevalent concerns about group decision making, the process is commonly used in schools. In part, deployment reflects the fact that education institutions, and especially those that are public, are political entities. That is, power is dispersed among formal and informal groups, and as a result, acceptance of a decision is often equally or more important than its quality (Kowalski, 2006). Moreover, changing contexts have created immense pressures for school administrators to engage in democratic decision making (Ogawa, Crowson, & Goldring, 1999). However, the fact that this approach can be highly advantageous, especially when applied by professional practitioners, is less recognized. For instance, consultation among physicians and attorneys concerning practice-based problems characterized by uncertainty and risk is normative. In education, group decision making is now generally accepted as a positive process resulting in distributed intelligence, shared leadership, and communal learning (McBeath, 2001).

Some question exists whether group decision making is appropriate for data-based instructional issues, such as adjusting lessons and assignments based on achievement test scores, intelligence assessments, grades, and so forth. At the school level, requirements for developing individual education programs (IEPs) for students with special needs are grounded in the belief that appropriate programming should be prescribed collectively by professionals having differing expertise and perspectives.

At the school and district levels, most, if not all, academic decisions involve multiple concentric constituencies, such as faculty instructional interests, administrative constraints, student learning outcomes, and community relationships (Petress, 2002). Unfortunately, teachers and even many administrators have not been prepared to make decisions collaboratively or to be an active member of a school learning community (Meadows & Saltzman, 2002). Not surprisingly, research on the possible nexus between group decision making and student learning (e.g., Smylie, Brownlee-Conyers, & Lazarus, 1996) reveals the former can have either a positive or a negative effect on the latter. Other research (e.g., Somech, 2002) reveals that effectiveness is influenced by an intricate mix of decision domain (i.e., the nature of the decision), rationale (i.e., reason or purpose in making a decision), and participant objectives (i.e., what is anticipated as a benefit for the participants). In general, however, group decision making has been found to be beneficial when applied appropriately and executed correctly.

Purported Advantages and Disadvantages of Groups

Both legal requirements to make data-driven decisions and the trend toward establishing learning communities suggest that many important decisions affecting schools and students will be made by groups. Therefore, educators should recognize the potential motives for deploying this process. Somech (2002) identifies three of them.

1. Improving the quality of the decision by focusing on the choices that need to be made
2. Improving the quality of teaching by focusing on learning that occurs among the participants
3. Facilitating administrative work by focusing on the delegation of authority and responsibility

Most commonly, however, group decision making is intended to improve school effectiveness. This approach has both advantages and disadvantages when used in organizations such as schools.

Advantages

The benefits of group decision making are more extensive than most educators realize. The following are examples of how this process can make schooling more effective.

- *Multiple viewpoints.* Groups usually provide a spectrum of viewpoints to be expressed in relation to a problem (Razik & Swanson, 2002). Given the fact that most communities and schools are becoming increasingly diverse, this benefit is quite important.

- *Political acceptance.* It is widely believed that group decisions are more likely to be accepted by a school's various publics, especially if group members are representative of those publics (Ubben, Hughes, & Norris, 2004).
- *Increased information, knowledge, and skills.* A group's collective knowledge in relation to a problem is often greater than the superintendent's or a principal's knowledge (Kowalski, 2003). Though the pooling of these inputs is perhaps the most compelling rationale for group decision making, studies of group behavior reveal that less than anticipated levels of pooling actually occur. This is because discussions tend to focus on shared rather than unique inputs (i.e., information, knowledge, or skills held by only one or two group members) (Beach, 1997).
- *Philosophical congruity with democracy.* Group decision making is compatible with the principles of governance in a democratic society (Sergiovanni, 2006).
- *Professional growth.* Members of decision groups are given an opportunity to grow professionally as a result of being exposed to information and collaborative problem solving (Kowalski, 2003).
- *Employee motivation/morale.* Members of decision groups are typically motivated by opportunities to be creative and responsible (Owens, 2004), and they respond positively to being involved (Kowalski, 2003).

Disadvantages

Unfortunately, group decision making can fail and even spawn more serious problems than those being addressed. The following are examples of possible difficulties:

- *Inefficiency.*[1] Decisions made by groups almost always require more time and greater material resources than decisions made by one person (Clark, Clark, & Irvin, 1997; Luthans, 1985).
- *Social influence.* Often group members care more about social acceptance than about quality decisions. Group dynamics involve coalition building and mutual influence, and these factors may reduce rationality (Reitz, 1987). This issue, commonly referred to as groupthink, is discussed later in this chapter.
- *Mediocre choices.* In the context of groups, mediocre decisions often are made because individual members are able to use the committee as a shield against individual accountability (Luthans, 1985).
- *Political manipulation.* The distribution of power and knowledge among group members is unequal, and therefore the most influential members often are able to intimidate the least influential members. As a result, the group does not function as intended in that the decision reflects the preferences of one or two influential members not the true collective preferences of all members (Janis, 1982).

[1]Many administrators in the past have been socialized to have a negative attitude toward group decision making. This belief is nested in classical theory (bureaucracy), a normative paradigm that stresses technical efficiency and discourages employee participation in the exercise of authority.

■ *Bias and errors.* Group members are prone to express biases and to make errors, just as are individual decision makers; however, the probability of bias and error can be greater if activities are not closely coordinated (Carroll & Johnson, 1990).

■ *Lack of confidentiality.* Ensuring confidentiality is more difficult in group decision making than it is in individual decision making.

Rationale for Using Groups

The realization that organizational learning is critical to school improvement and requirements to make scientifically based decisions (e.g., NCLB) have raised the importance of group decision making. In the case of the latter, collaboration among professionals is essential; in the case of the former, shared knowledge about accessing and using information and data is essential. Three additional factors help make this process normative:

1. *Philosophy.* Many citizens believe that teacher and citizen involvement is appropriate and productive in relation to school improvement (Barber, 1995; Bauman, 1996).
2. *Professionalism.* Participative decision making is in agreement with the professional knowledge base, especially with concepts such as teacher professionalism and collegiality (Fullan, 2001).
3. *Political context.* Collaborative processes can narrow divisions between administrators and teachers that were created by unionism and collective bargaining (Pound & Ewing, 1994), and at the same time, they empower teachers to influence curriculum and instruction decisions (Hallinger, Murphy, & Hausman, 1992).

Leading Groups

Perspectives on the relationship between leadership and decision-making processes have evolved over the past five decades. By and large, the progression can be summarized in three distinct stages:

1. Process based on leadership style
2. Process based on a combination of style and situational variables
3. Process based on professionalism

The three perspectives are illustrated in Figure 4.2.

Describing how leadership style shapes decision making, Tannenbaum and Schmidt (1973) developed a continuum describing variations of autocratic and democratic behavior. Their analysis was predicated on the belief that a manager's leadership style determined how he or she made decisions. Applied to school administration, the continuum of leadership styles helps us to understand why prin-

FIGURE 4.2   **Evolving Perspectives of Leadership and Group Decision Making**

Perspective 1: Dominance of Leadership Style

Example: Democratic or quasi-democratic principals often initiate
group decision making, whereas other principals do not.

Perspective 2: Integration of Leadership Style and Context

Example: Autocratic principals will initiate group decision making, and
democratic principals will avoid group decision making in situations
where contextual variables are highly incongruent with their leadership styles.

Perspective 3: Dominance of Professional Values

Example: Group decision making is accepted as the norm for all matters pertaining to
curriculum and instruction. Autocratic behavior is not tolerated, and principals act
unilaterally only in managerial matters or in emergency situations.

cipals in the same district almost always exhibit contrasting decision-making behavior, even when they are dealing with an identical problem. To demonstrate this
point, consider an example of administrative behavior in a small school district.
The school board adopted a policy requiring principals to promulgate a regulation
stipulating a minimum amount of student homework. The district's four principals
complied but in different ways. The high school principal acted without consulting
teachers or other staff. He distributed a memorandum communicating two points
of information: the school's minimum homework requirement would be one hour
per day, and teachers who violated the regulation would receive a written reprimand. The middle school principal discussed the board's policy at a faculty meeting and then asked teachers to provide input. At the end of that week, she decided
that the school's minimum homework requirement would be 45 minutes per
school day but did not stipulate a penalty for violations. One elementary school
principal relegated the task to the school's advisory council. The members decided
to require a minimum of 3 hours of homework per week. The principal, who also
was the council chair, influenced the decision. The other elementary school principal appointed an ad hoc committee consisting of three teachers and two parents.
She did not exert influence and guaranteed the committee members that their decision about homework would be honored.

In this example, each principal made a different decision in relation to the
board policy. Given that they work for the same employer in the same community,

the variance in their behavior is most likely explained by differences in their leadership styles.

In the 1960s and 1970s, the concept of contingency leadership, personified by Fiedler's theory,[2] became popular (Bedeian & Gleuck, 1983). Generally, contingency leadership is predicated on the belief that effectiveness is determined by a combination of style and situational variables (the context in which the style is applied). Used in relation to decision making, this means that administrators should consider contextual variables (e.g., school culture, past practices, key participants) and personal preferences when selecting a decision-making format. The Maier Model (Maier & Verser, 1982) exemplifies this perspective. The paradigm deploys two variables: *decision acceptance* and *decision quality*. The former pertains to commitment from those who have to enforce or are affected by the decision; the latter pertains to the importance of the decision to the organization's welfare and effectiveness. Each variable is rated as being high or low; interfacing the two possible acceptance outcomes with the two possible quality outcomes produces four decision categories, each prescribing a preferred decision-making format:

- *High acceptance and low quality.* Decisions in this frame are considered appropriate for groups composed of stakeholder representatives because the group members give credibility to the outcome. Since the importance of decision quality is low, the political stature of group members is more important, whereas their knowledge or skills in relation to the problem are not.
- *High acceptance and high quality.* Decisions in this frame also are appropriate for groups provided that the members have political influence with the groups they represent and that they have knowledge or skills relevant to the problem.
- *Low acceptance and low quality.* Decisions in this frame are thought to be inconsequential, and therefore it does not matter who makes them.
- *Low acceptance and high quality.* Decisions in this frame should be made by persons with considerable knowledge and skills related to the problem, and preferably, they should act independently to prevent social or political influences diminishing decision quality.

If followed, decision making with the Maier model is determined by the nature of the decision and not by the administrator's leadership style.

A third perspective on the decision process is rooted in professionalism. It suggests that decisions should be made collegially—a perspective that encourages principals to participate in, but not control, curriculum and instruction decisions (Hoerr, 1996). This approach is exemplified by the concept of the learning community espoused by Senge (1990, 1998) and promoted by numerous authors writing about education (e.g., Mohr & Dichter, 2001). Within this perspective, decision making is viewed as a creative activity and a learning opportunity—for both ad-

[2]See the *Contingency Theory of Leadership Effectiveness,* developed by Fred E. Fiedler.

ministrators and teachers. Collectively, they question, investigate, and resolve problems (Kleine-Kracht, 1993). Sergiovanni (1994) argues that the sources of authority for principals in a learning community should be embedded in shared ideas and not in the legitimate power of their position. In this third perspective, group decision making is the normative approach.

Structuring Groups

As previously noted, groups differ with respect to their objective and duration. Group effectiveness—that is, the extent to which the group achieves its objectives—needs to be considered in light of these two factors. For example, making a politically popular decision is substantially different from making a high-quality decision in relation to school improvement. In determining whether to rely on groups to make decisions, you should know the variables that determine effectiveness and criteria for member selection.

Effectiveness Variables

Defining a group's effectiveness in relation to its decisions is neither a clear nor an easy assignment. Various criteria have been used, such as efficiency, ability to reach consensus, and member satisfaction. In the context of professions, however, effectiveness should be measured by the extent to which a prescribed task is accomplished (Orasanu & Salas, 1993). Social psychologists contend that structural and contextual factors (inputs) shape process (an intermediate variable), which then affects the quality of group decisions (Innami, 1994). In many respects, the most important group decision is determining how the group will make decisions (Owens, 2004). Yukl (2006) identifies seven inputs that determine the quality of process.

1. *Size.* Though larger groups often have the advantage of a broader knowledge base and range of political perspectives, they often incur communication problems. Thus, size should be determined by balancing the need for knowledge, the need for opposing political perspectives, and the importance of intragroup communication.
2. *Members' status.* When there is considerable variation in member status, high-status members tend to dominate low-status members. This is a common problem in schools when nonprofessional staff and parents are on committees with teachers and administrators.
3. *Cohesiveness.* Cohesiveness refers to the extent to which group members share philosophical convictions and goals. Typically, cohesive groups are more effective; however, this factor needs to be weighed in relation to the importance of diversity.
4. *Diversity.* This characteristic pertains to the extent to which group members differ demographically (e.g., age, race, gender). High levels of diversity can

impede cohesiveness and communication and result in frequent conflict. Even so, most school administrators, and especially those in public schools, believe that diversity is essential. Properly led, diverse groups can be highly effective because of the broad perspectives that are expressed in relation to a problem or specific decision.

5. *Emotional maturity.* Working collaboratively with others requires emotional maturity. Group members who lack this quality often are disruptive and aggressive.

6. *Physical environment.* The environment in which a group meets can influence behavior and eventually decisions. For example, location and seating arrangements can transmit symbolic messages about formality, authority, and power. Generally, informal meetings in which participants sit around a conference table in a neutral location are more effective than other options.

7. *Communication technology.* The work of committees is now affected by the degree that technology supports the process. As examples, providing preliminary communication (e.g., agendas and support material) by e-mail, maintaining an electronic bulletin board for group members, and providing access to pertinent data via computers can positively affect the group's productivity.

Other authors have identified additional factors that directly or indirectly influence group effectiveness:

- *Roles.* Groups function more effectively when members have designated roles because conflict over authority and responsibilities is diminished (Kimball, 1995; Patton & Downs, 2003) and work assignments are likely to be distributed evenly (Nutt, 1989).

- *Ownership.* Groups function more effectively when members have a sense of collective ownership and less effectively when members believe that the leader owns the group (Garmston, 2002).

- *Clear and acceptable objectives.* Groups function more effectively when members know the group's purposes and they accept them as being valid and important to the organization's welfare (Nutt, 1989; Patton & Downs, 2003).

- *Leadership.* Groups function more effectively when they have leaders who define goals, provide resources, interact with members, provide rewards (Patton & Downs, 2003), and encourage creativity (Redmond, Mumford, & Teach, 1993). In addition, groups are usually more effective when leaders are transformational rather than transactional (Jung, 2000–2001) and when they advise, trust, teach, facilitate, and coordinate rather than dictate, manage, and dominate (Schmuck, 1972; Yukl, 2006).

- *Members' ability.* Groups function more effectively when they have members who possess pertinent knowledge and process skills (Innami, 1994). In addition, the highest performing members often shape group decisions (Bonner,

Baumann, & Dalal, 2002), and therefore a nexus among member ability, member performance, and group effectiveness is highly probable.

- *Institutional culture.* Groups function more effectively in cultures that value organizational learning, democratic participation, and professionalism (Owens, 2004).
- *Rationality.* Groups function more effectively when discussions are knowledge-based and logical (Innami, 1994), a factor especially relevant to data-driven decision making.
- *Synergy.* Synergy refers to the whole being more than the sum of its parts. In groups, synergistic relationships pertain to outcomes in which the collective product is greater than the sum of individual contributions. According to Lick (2000), members of a synergistic group "inspire and energize each other" (p. 146).

Though we know a great deal about variables that can contribute to group effectiveness, a clear nexus between process and group effectiveness has not been established (Orasanu & Salas, 1993). Decades of studies on shared decision making in education have not provided clear evidence that the approach consistently improves the problem-solving process or the quality of instruction in schools (Malen, 1999). In large measure, this is because the degree to which politics and emotion affect decisions is difficult to predict and to control.

Member Selection

One influential variable determining decisions is group composition. Group members bring values, beliefs, needs, and biases to the process, and to varying degrees these factors influence their behavior. Recognizing this fact, scholars have made efforts to inject rationality into group member selection. Indicative of such efforts, Bridges (1967) recommends using two criteria: *relevance* (i.e., Do group members have a personal stake in the outcomes of the decision?) and *expertise* (i.e., Do group members have knowledge, skills, and experiences that will contribute to the quality of the decision?) Two other criteria have been proposed more recently: *jurisdiction* (Owens, 2004) (i.e., Do group members have claim to legitimate influence over the problems and decisions they will be addressing?) and *trust* (Hoy & Miskel, 2005) (i.e., Does a person trust others and is he or she trusted by others? Can the person be trusted to act in the best interests of the school?).

The latter two criteria can be controversial. The test of jurisdiction, for example, raises questions about the involvement of teachers in traditional schools where they often have little or no influence on matters outside their classrooms. The test of trust may be challenged by critics who believe that loyalty to the organization is basically a guise for selecting members who are known to be submissive to administrative authority. Both concerns are lessened, however, if you believe that schools should be learning communities. In this perspective, teachers should influence major decisions, which are made in the context of open, candid discourse in which participants treat each other as colleagues.

Groups can serve both social and task purposes. From a social perspective, the group provides stature for its members, and therefore participation fulfills a social need. From a task perspective, the group provides a medium for taking action (e.g., solving a problem or making a decision). Filley, House, and Kerr (1976) noted that group members can be identified as being either social-oriented or task-oriented (see Figure 4.3). Group members in the former category see participation as the desired end because membership provides stature and social interaction. Group members in the latter category see action as the desired end because decisions address personal or organizational needs. For example, a task-oriented teacher often seeks to control outcomes by influencing other committee members or by dictating choices. Mixing the two types of individuals on a committee usually spawns group conflict (Nutt, 1989) because some members enjoy meetings and want them to be pleasant, whereas others often are impatient and contentious in promoting a preferred decision.

The selection of juries in criminal and civil cases provides the quintessential example of why member selection is important. Swap (1984), for example, explained how authoritarianism affected punishment decisions. He defined authoritarianism as "the tendency to idealize powerful authority figures, to reject members of outgroups, to adopt conventional lifestyles, and to value discipline and tough-mindedness" (p. 48). Potential jurors who are high authoritarians are much more likely to favor death penalties in capital crimes or long prison sentences for lesser crimes than are low authoritarians.

As the judicial system demonstrates, however, member proclivities are but one factor that shape group decisions. During the trial, predispositions often are altered by rational (evidence), emotional, or political factors that may be generated by any person involved with the trial, including other jurors. The concept of jury nullification offers a clear example. Nullification occurs when guilt is established on the basis of fact but the jury acquits on its own sense of fairness, propriety, prejudice, or any other sentiment or concern (Kennedy, 1998). In essence, the jurors nullify the intent of a law by acquitting a defendant when evidence indicates guilt. This relatively common malfunction in our legal system is replicated in education

Group members differ in orientation.
Each falls somewhere on the continuum below.

Social-oriented   **Task-oriented**
members   **members**

Focus is on stature,   Focus is on the
interaction with others,   group's objective
and meeting personal needs   (i.e., making a decision)

FIGURE 4.3   **Social- versus Task-Oriented Group Members**

when data and other facts are ignored by administrators and teachers for emotional or political reasons (Kowalski, 2004).

Common Problems with Groups

Groups, the same as individuals, differ in their ability to be effective and consistent. Dysfunctions can occur for many reasons, and though some are never completely eradicated, they can be managed. Problem control is most likely to occur in groups in which both leaders and participants recognize the common pitfalls and have the ability to deal with them.

Groupthink

Groupthink is a phenomenon involving goal displacement; it occurs when cohesion becomes more important than an effective decision. Janis (1982) described it as "a mode of thinking that people engage in when they are deeply involved in a cohesive in-group, when the members' strivings for unanimity override their motivation to realistically appraise alternative courses of action" (p. 9). Rationality is diminished and members disregard both options and evidence that do not comply with their beliefs and biases (Janis & Mann, 1977).

Janis (1982) identified four conditions that spawn groupthink:

1. *Preexisting cohesion.* Though cohesion is often identified as a positive factor because it contributes to collaboration and unity, it also can be a detriment. If members already have moderately high or very high levels of cohesion when the group is formed, it is likely that they will act to protect that cohesion. This is often a problem in schools with strong cultures because all or most professional staff members adhere to the same fundamental beliefs.
2. *Isolation.* When groups are isolated from other segments of the organization and from expert opinions, they are insulated from dissenting opinions. Under this condition, a group is unlikely to engage in critical analysis or objective evaluation.
3. *Directive leadership.* If an organization does not have a history or expectation of leadership impartiality, group leaders are more likely to use their authority and power to promote their own ideas. When groups have directive leaders, members focus on pleasing the leader and avoiding open inquiries and critiques that could cause conflict.
4. *Inappropriate or nonexistent norms.* If an organization does not have traditions or rules for group decision making, norms will be determined independently by each group. Often groups will adopt counterproductive norms that discourage dissent, creative thinking, and rational debate.

As groupthink evolves, the social nature of the group serves to control behavior. Members convince each other that they are functioning appropriately even though they are not acting rationally or engaging in critical thinking. If a member challenges the group's intellectual or moral standing, sanctions are imposed to protect cohesion. Social pressures to conform are arguably the most serious obstacle to effective group decisions (Swap, 1984).

Wilson (2005) offers the following suggestions with respect to avoiding groupthink:

- Avoid having members state their preferences and expectations at the beginning of the decision process.
- Members should be allowed to discuss the group's activities with trusted nonmembers and then report the content of such discussions at group meetings.
- Have a consultant or nonmember expert meet with the group periodically to challenge both process and substance.
- One group member should be assigned the role of devil's advocate.

Absence of Trust

Trust entails the degree of confidence group members have in each other. If it is not present, members usually do not communicate openly and do not make commitments. Equally important, they become defensive (Wilson, 2005). The absence of trust can be especially debilitating to ad hoc decision groups, especially if the members are not well acquainted at the time they are appointed or elected to the group. These groups often do not exist long enough for members to build trusting relationships.

When trust is lacking, group members may hide their weaknesses, refrain from open two-way communication, refrain from collaborating with other members, and develop negative feelings about the group. Conversely, when trust is present, members are candid, seek help when needed, ask and answer questions, seek additional information, and develop positive feelings about the group (Lencioni, 2002).

Not Managing Dysfunctional Conflict

Group development theory reveals that there is an inevitable conflict stage but that this phase is essential to a group's health (or long-term effectiveness) (Mohr & Dichter, 2001). Many administrators, however, have been socialized to view conflict as being consistently counterproductive (Hanson, 2003). Groups respond to conflict with one of three behaviors:

1. *Avoidance style:* unassertive and uncooperative behaviors intended to eliminate conflict as quickly as possible (e.g., ignoring the conflict or quickly changing the subject)
2. *Distributive style:* confrontive behavior intended to produce winners and losers (e.g., one party is forced politically to concede)

3. *Integrative style:* cooperative behavior intended to produce mutually acceptable outcomes (e.g., the group reaches consensus on resolving the matter)

Research on decision groups (e.g., Kuhn & Poole, 2000) indicates that those using integrative styles to manage conflict usually make the most effective decisions.

Unfortunately, fearing conflict often leads group members to adopt avoidance styles, and this behavior almost always exacerbates conflict (Wilson, 2005). Symptoms of avoidance behavior include boring meetings, ad hominem attacks, a proclivity to sidestep controversial topics and disagreements, and a failure to maximize the range of knowledge and opinions members bring to the process. Lencioni (2002) notes that a failure to debate and disagree openly about important ideas prompts members to rely on back channels and personal attacks that end up being nastier and more harmful than open debates. Eventually, dysfunctional conflict management results in two problems in relation to the group's well-being: it prevents the group from establishing norms that are essential to its health, and it establishes norms that are destructive to its health.

Poor Communication

Communication problems are rather common in groups. Typically they are associated with elements of institutional climate that range from a lack of material resources to social behavior, to organizational design, to shared values and beliefs (Hanson, 2003). The following are the most prevalent examples.

- *Defensiveness.* Individuals who are not experienced with working in groups or teams may engage in defensive communication. Gibb (1961) listed the following attributes of this counterproductive behavior: (a) evaluating other members negatively, (b) attempting to control or manipulate other members, (c) treating others as though they do not matter, and (d) treating one's own opinions or options as consistently superior.
- *Poor listening skills.* Some group members are unable to capture the deeper meanings in messages (e.g., by observing nonverbal behavior or by reading between the lines); their comprehension and memory skills are poor, and they fail to ask clarifying questions (Spaulding & O'Hair, 2004).
- *Poor language skills.* Some members may have difficulties with grammar, vocabulary, or linguistics that result in encoding and decoding problems. As a result, they misinterpret messages, an error that obstructs decision making (Quirke, 1996).
- *Lack of credibility.* Some members may lack or lose credibility, resulting in communication problems. The most common offense in this regard is lying, and when detected by other group members, the punishment is usually a loss of respect and future mistrust (Howard & Mathews, 1994).
- *Communication oversights.* Some group members, and especially the group leader, may fail to provide necessary information to other group members. If

this occurs, members are likely to form informal communication channels that bypass the official procedures used by the group (Kowalski, 2003).

- *Inaccessibility.* Typically, groups communicate outside of official meetings. Some members, including the group leader, may be inaccessible to other members except during scheduled meetings. This situation diminishes the quality of communication and detracts from the group's effectiveness (Kowalski, 2003).

- *Elitism.* Group members focusing on status power often communicate selectively. That is, they only exchange information with other members who have equal or greater status or who are viewed as power elites (members who have great influence in the group) (Kowalski, 2006).

- *Inadequate attention to effect.* Group members may fail to determine if communication is producing its intended effect. The potential for this problem is highest in groups that have autocratic leaders who avoid two-way communication; for example, they send information via memoranda or e-mail and do not invite responses. Messages delivered in this fashion often are not decoded as intended resulting in a discrepancy between the sent message and the received message (Lysaught, 1984).

- *Information overload.* Group effectiveness also can be diminished by too much information. When members are overwhelmed with data, e-mails, and reports, they may not process the information, may delay reading the information, skim through the information, or may ignore the information altogether (Miller, 2003).

Low Commitment

A group's effectiveness is usually greater when member commitment and involvement are reasonably equal. Therefore, efficacy diminishes when some members are indifferent toward the group and its purposes. Common symptoms of this problem include a lack of direction and priorities, a fear of failure, an unwillingness to take risks, repetitive discussions, second guessing, and constant demands for additional information (Lencioni, 2002).

If differences in member commitment are extreme, the likelihood of a dominant leader or dominant faction controlling the group becomes likely. And as this occurs, the noncommitted members often become fearful, resentful, and envious of those in power—even though their own behavior has contributed to the dominance. After decisions are made, the noncommitted also have a tendency to absolve themselves from responsibility (Gastil, 1997).

Accountability Avoidance

In traditional organizations, managers are often leery of group decision making because they believe that accountability for outcomes is transferred to them. This same belief was prevalent in public education in relation to the adoption of school councils (Kowalski, 1994). Common symptoms of this problem include acceptance of mediocrity, a tendency to procrastinate, and dependency on the group leader. After a decision is made public, some members will distance themselves from the group; for example, they will claim that their input was ignored or that the decision was controlled by the group leader or a faction in the group. Such outcomes are detrimental not only to the future activities of the group in question but also to other formal groups functioning in the organization.

Dysfunctional Members

Groups may suffer simply because they have one or more dysfunctional members. Wilson (2005) listed five types of individuals who fall into this category:

- *Nonparticipant.* This is a member who is uninterested in the group's activities. He or she usually looks bored at meetings, doodles, or contributes very little to discussions.
- *Irresponsible member.* This type of person is late for meetings or misses meetings entirely. He or she rarely completes assignments or reads minutes or other communication provided by the group leader.
- *Side-tracker.* This is a member who consistently tries to divert the group from its task by telling jokes or stories, taking offense at comments made by others, or changing the subject.
- *Dominator.* This is a member who attempts to control the agenda and discussions. He or she often interrupts others, speaks loudly, and exhibits intolerance for other viewpoints.
- *Despicable member.* This type of person exhibits unethical behavior. He or she may make sexist or bigoted comments, lie, belittle others, or betray confidences.

Dealing with dysfunctional members requires strong group leadership and member support. If interventions are not successful, the group may need to act to replace the member(s) who are attenuating effectiveness.

Group Processes

The process a group selects to make a decision can be very instrumental in resolving or managing dysfunctional conditions. Though the appropriateness of any given procedure depends on group size, available time, and leadership expertise, several approaches are considered to be highly effective for decision-making groups.

Nominal Technique

The nominal group approach is primarily intended to overcome common problems that may occur when groups immediately engage in verbal interaction

(Delbecq, Van de Ven, & Gustafson, 1975). Examples of such problems include (a) differences in member status and authority, (b) member feelings of inferiority, and (c) shyness among some members. Before discussion occurs, the problem or issue requiring a decision is explained; members then write down possible options for addressing the issue. All identified options are then shared with the entire group. Discussion commences, and after it concludes members rank the options. The results are tabulated and the decision is determined by the highest score. The approach is thought to provide a more supportive environment, and it diminishes the likelihood of members forming or acting in coalitions (Clemen, 1996).

Delphi Technique

The *Delphi technique* is similar to the nominal approach. Group members, however, do not meet face to face. The process begins by having members identify preferred options, which are collected and shared with all members. Unlike the nominal approach, however, no discussion occurs. Instead, members have an opportunity to reconsider their preferred options after seeing all other options. The process continues until consensus is reached. The Delphi technique has often been deployed by organization executives who wanted to convene a panel of experts to make or recommend a decision. Since it is not necessary for members to be in the same location, the geographic location of the experts is unimportant. Instead of discussion after options are identified, members are given an opportunity to reconsider their preferred options. The process is continued until consensus is achieved. In the past, it was conducted by postal mail but today it is usually deployed using e-mail (Clemen, 1996).

Brainstorming

Groups also can use brainstorming to identify decision options. This approach typically is conducted face to face. Participants state their ideas, which are then recorded without discussion. However, members are encouraged to present modified versions of other member ideas through a process referred to as "hitchhiking" (Clemen, 1996); that is, members refine or augment ideas presented by other members. Once the group reaches a point where no new or modified ideas are suggested, the posted items are critiqued. The process is intended to (a) reduce intimidation (by deferring discussion), (b) promote unconventional ideas (by asking members to "think outside the box"), and (c) promote a large number of ideas (Stein, 1975).

Deferring discussion on ideas is nested in the distinction between the judicial and creative mind. In the former, one relies on analysis and comparisons to make a choice; the latter involves forecasts to visualize new ideas. Nutt (1989) argues that free association and judgments are not compatible, and unless judgment is reserved, members will be reluctant to verbalize ideas, fearing that they will be deemed unacceptable or unimportant.

Brainwriting

Brainwriting is similar to brainstorming. In this process, however, members sit around a table on which the leader has placed sheets containing several written cues for pertinent themes (e.g., criteria for a decision, people affected by a decision, stakeholder demands for a decision, and limitations). Members select a sheet, and after reading it, they add their ideas. At the point that a member has no additional ideas, he or she exchanges the sheet for another one in the center of the table. After reading the cues on that sheet, the member again lists ideas. This process is repeated until members conclude that they have nothing more to offer. The goal is to develop synthesis around themes that are deemed to be cogent to the decision that needs to be made (Nutt, 1989).

Brainwriting works well when members are reluctant to voice their ideas because the process allows them to enter the ideas anonymously. Moreover, it is an effective way to overcome power and status differences among group members and to deal with dominant members or factions. The process effectively eliminates competition in putting forward ideas.

SUMMARY

Despite the fact that teachers and principals make many important decisions alone, they also make choices in groups. And since the trend is toward higher levels of group decision making, you should (a) understand the professional, philosophical aspects, (b) comprehend the political rationale underlying this process, and (c) readily recognize the conditions that make it successful.

The intricacies of group decision making arguably become more complex when their choices must be data-driven. Groups are social entities, and as such they too are affected by politics and emotion, factors that prevent or diminish rationality. Engaging in groupthink, a lack of mutual trust among group members, and having one or more dysfunctional members are primary examples of dysfunctional behavior. Though bias, prejudice, obstructionism, and error are never totally eradicated from either individual or group decisions, these factors can be managed. Techniques described in this chapter can be instrumental in achieving this objective.

In conclusion, two points of information are especially important. First, group decision making has become a normative standard, and the process will become increasingly common in elementary and secondary schools. Second, group decision making is effective when educators understand the process and accept it as a professional norm. Equally important, effectiveness depends on collegiality, individual responsibility, and accountability.

QUESTIONS AND SUGGESTED ACTIVITIES

Case Study Questions

1. Do you consider the Harrison Elementary School council dysfunctional? Why or why not?

2. To what extent is this council a victim of groupthink?

3. The principal could elect to pursue improvement initiatives alone, thus bypassing the council. Do you consider this to be a prudent option? Why or why not?

4. The school council has restricted its jurisdiction to noninstructional issues. What are some possible reasons for this decision?

5. Do you believe that the school council is truly a democratic group? Why or why not?

Chapter Questions

6. Why is it important to identify groups as social and political entities?

7. If you were a principal, what criteria would you use to appoint members to a school council? What criteria would you use to appoint members to an ad hoc committee on setting homework standards?

8. Discuss the ways in which diversity can be an asset and a liability in group decision making.

9. Advocates of shared decision making argue that groups provide a broader knowledge base and greater variety of viewpoints. Are these two purported advantages always realized? Why or why not?

10. The issue of trust was discussed in relation to the organization and in relation to group member relationships. What is the difference between these two perspectives?

11. In what ways are the nominal technique and Delphi technique similar? In what ways are they different?

12. How can communication be a detriment to a decision-making group?

13. Why is accountability avoidance considered a liability for group decision making by many school administrators?

14. What measures can be taken to avoid groupthink?

REFERENCES

Barber, B. R. (1995, April 19). Workshops of our democracy. *Education Week, 14,* 34.

Bauman, P. C. (1996). *Governing education: Public sector reform or privatization.* Boston: Allyn and Bacon.

Beach, L. R. (1997). *The psychology of decision making: People in organizations.* Thousand Oaks, CA: Sage.

Bedeian, A. G., & Gleuck, W. F. (1983). *Management* (3rd ed.). Chicago: Dryden Press.

Bonner, B. L., Baumann, M. R., & Dalal, R. S. (2002). The effects of member expertise on group decision-making and performance. *Organizational Behavior and Human Decision Processes, 88*(2), 719–736.

Bridges, E. M. (1967). A model for shared decision making in the school principalship. *Educational Administration Quarterly, 3,* 49–61.

Carroll, J. S., & Johnson, E. J. (1990). *Decision research: A field guide.* Newbury Park, CA: Sage.

Clark, S. N., Clark, D. C., & Irvin, J. L. (1997). Collaborative decision making. *Middle School Journal, 28*(5), 54–56.

Clemen, R. T. (1996). *Making hard decisions: An introduction to decision analysis* (2nd ed.). Belmont, CA: Duxbury Press.

Conrad, C. (1994). *Strategic organizational communication: Toward the twenty-first century* (3rd ed.). Fort Worth, TX: Harcourt Brace College Publishers.

Conway, J. (1984). The myth, mystery and mastery of participative decision making in education. *Educational Administration Quarterly, 20*(3), 11–40.

Dachler, H. P., & Wilpert, B. (1979). Conceptual dimensions and boundaries of participation in organizations: A critical evaluation. *Administrative Science Quarterly, 23*, 1–39.

Delbecq, A. L., Van de Ven, A. H., & Gustafson, D. H. (1975). *Group techniques for program planning.* Glenview, IL: Scott, Foresman.

Filley, A., House, R., & Kerr, S. (1976). *Managerial process and organizational behavior* (2nd ed.). Glenview, IL: Scott, Foresman.

Fullan, M. (2001). *Leading in a culture of change.* San Francisco: Jossey-Bass.

Garmston, R. J. (2002). It's always the group's group. *Journal of Staff Development, 23*(4), 76–77.

Gastil, J. (1997). *Common problems in small group decision making.* Retrieved February 22, 2006, from www.fao.org/sd/ppdirect/ppan0009.htm

Gibb, J. R. (1961). Defensive communication. *Journal of Communication, 11*, 142–148.

Hallinger, P., Murphy, J., & Hausman, C. (1992). Restructuring schools: Principal's perceptions of fundamental educational reform. *Educational Administration Quarterly, 29*(1), 330–349.

Hanson, E. M. (2003). *Educational administration and organizational behavior* (5th ed.). Boston: Allyn and Bacon.

Hoerr, T. R. (1996). Collegiality: A new way to define instructional leadership. *Phi Delta Kappan, 77*(5), 380–381.

Howard, C. M., & Mathews, W. K. (1994). *On deadline: Managing media relations* (2nd ed.). Prospect Heights, IL: Waveland Press.

Hoy, W., & Miskel, C. (2005). *Educational administration: Theory, research and practice* (7th ed.). New York: McGraw-Hill.

Innami, I. L. (1994). The quality of group decisions, group verbal behavior, and intervention. *Organizational Behavior and Human Decision Processes, 60*(3), 409–430.

Janis, I. L. (1982). *Groupthink* (2nd ed.). Boston: Houghton Mifflin.

Janis, I. L., & Mann, L. (1977). *Decision making: A psychological analysis of conflict, choice, and commitment.* New York: Free Press.

Jung, D. I. (2000–2001). Transformational and transactional leadership and their effects on creativity in groups. *Creativity Research Journal, 13*(2), 185–195.

Katz, D., & Kahn, R. L. (1978). *The social psychology of organizations* (2nd ed.). New York: Wiley.

Kennedy, R. (1998). *Race, crime, and the law.* New York: Vintage Books.

Kimball, L. (1995). Ten ways to make online learning groups work. *Educational Leadership, 53*(10), 54–56.

Kleine-Kracht, P. A. (1993). The principal in a community of learning. *Journal of School Leadership, 3*(4), 391–399.

Kowalski, T. J. (1994). Site-based management, teacher empowerment, and unionism: Beliefs of suburban school principals. *Contemporary Education, 60*(4), 200–206.

Kowalski, T. J. (2003). *Contemporary school administration: An introduction* (2nd ed.). Boston: Allyn and Bacon.

Kowalski, T. J. (2004). The ongoing war for the soul of school administration. In T. J. Lasley (Ed.), *Better leaders for America's schools: Perspectives on the Manifesto* (pp. 92–114). Columbia, MO: University Council for Educational Administration.

Kowalski, T. J. (2006). *The school superintendent: Theory, practice, and cases* (2nd ed.). Thousand Oaks, CA: Sage.

Kowalski, T. J., Petersen, G. J., & Fusarelli, L. D. (2007). *Effective communication for school administrators: An imperative in an information age.* Lanham, MD: Rowman & Littlefield Education.

Kuhn, T., & Poole, M. S. (2000). Do conflict management styles affect group decision making? *Human Communication Research, 26*(4), 558–590.

Lencioni, P. (2002). *The five dysfunctions of a team.* San Francisco: Jossey-Bass.

Lick, D. (2000). Whole-faculty study groups: Facilitating mentoring for school-wide change. *Theory into Practice, 39*(1), 43–49.

Luthans, F. (1985). *Organizational behavior* (4th ed.). New York: McGraw-Hill.

Lysaught, J. P. (1984). Toward a comprehensive theory of communications: A review of selected contributions. *Educational Administration Quarterly, 20*(3), 101–127.

Maier, N. R., & Verser, G. C. (1982). *Psychology in industrial organizations* (5th ed.). Boston: Houghton Mifflin.

Malen, B. (1999). The promises and perils of participation on site-based councils. *Theory into Practice, 38*(4), 209–216.

Malen, B., & Ogawa, R. T. (1992). Site-based management: Disconcerting policy issues, critical policy choices. In J. J. Lane & E. G. Epps (Eds.), *Restructuring the schools: Problems and prospects* (pp. 185–206) Berkeley, CA: McCutchan.

McBeath, J. (2001, December 14). Too many heads improve the broth. *The Times Educational Supplement* (4459), 26.

Meadows, B. J., & Saltzman, M. (2002). Shared decision making: An uneasy collaboration. *Principal, 81*(4), 41–48.

Miller, K. (2003). *Organizational communication: Approaches and processes* (3rd ed.). New York: Wadsworth.

Mohr, N., & Dichter, A. (2001). Building a learning organization. *Phi Delta Kappan, 82*(10), 744–747.

Nutt, P. C. (1989). *Making tough decisions: Tactics for improving managerial decision making.* San Francisco: Jossey-Bass.

Ogawa, R. T., Crowson, R. L., & Goldring, E. B. (1999). Enduring dilemmas of school organization. In J. Murphy & K. S. Louis (Eds.), *Handbook of research on educational administration* (2nd ed., pp. 277–295). San Francisco: Jossey-Bass.

Orasanu, J., & Salas, E. (1993). Team decision making in complex environments. In G. Klein, J. Oransanu, R. Calderwood, & C. Zsambok (Eds.), *Decision making in action: Methods and models* (pp. 327–345). Norwood, NJ: Ablex Publishing.

Owens, R. G. (2004). *Organizational behavior in education* (8th ed.). Boston: Allyn and Bacon.

Patton, B. R., & Downs, T. M. (2003). *Decision-making group interaction* (4th ed.). Boston: Allyn and Bacon.

Petress, K. (2002). An alternative model for decision making. *Journal of Instructional Psychology, 29*(3), 189–191.

Pound, G. A., & Ewing, E. A. (1994). Adversarial bargaining offers poor match with new pedagogies. *School Administrator, 51*(12), 29–30.

Quirke, B. (1996). *Communicating corporate change.* New York: McGraw-Hill.

Razik, T. A., & Swanson, A. D. (2002). *Fundamental concepts of educational leadership* (2nd ed.). Boston: Allyn and Bacon.

Redmond, M. R., Mumford, M. D., & Teach, R. (1993). Putting creativity to work: Effects of leader behavior on subordinate creativity. *Organizational Behavior and Decision Processes, 55,* 120–151.

Reitz, H. J. (1987). *Behavior in organizations* (3rd ed.). Homewood, IL: Irwin.

Schein, E. H. (1980). *Organizational psychology* (3rd ed.). Englewood Cliffs, NJ: Prentice Hall.

Schmuck, R. A. (1972). Developing collaborative decision making: The importance of trusting, strong and skillful leaders. *Educational Technology, 12*(10), 43–47.

Senge, P. M. (1990). *The fifth discipline: The art and practice of the learning organization.* New York: Doubleday.

Senge, P. M. (1998). Leading learning organizations. In W. E. Rosenbach & R. L. Taylor (Eds.), *Contemporary issues in leadership* (4th ed., pp. 174–178). Boulder, CO: Westview Press.

Sergiovanni, T. J. (1994). Organizations or communities? Changing the metaphor changes the theory. *Educational Administration Quarterly, 30*(2), 214–226.

Sergiovanni, T. J. (2006). *The principalship: A reflective practice perspective* (5th ed.). Boston: Allyn and Bacon.

Smylie, M. A., Brownlee-Conyers, J., & Lazarus, V. (1996). Instructional outcomes of school-based participative decision making. *Educational Evaluation and Policy Analysis, 18,* 181–198.

Somech, A. (2002). Explicating the complexity of participative management: An investigation of multiple dimensions. *Educational Administration Quarterly, 38*(3), 341–371.

Spaulding, A. M., & O'Hair, M. J. (2004). Public relations in a communication context: Listening, nonverbal, and conflict-resolution skills. In T. J. Kowalski (Ed.), *Public relations in schools* (3rd ed., pp. 96–122). Upper Saddle River, NJ: Merrill, Prentice Hall.

Stein, M. I. (1975). *Stimulating creativity: Group procedures.* New York: Academic Press.

Swap, W. C. (1984). How groups make decisions: A social psychological perspective. In W. C. Swap (Ed.), *Group decision making* (pp. 45–68). Beverly Hills, CA: Sage.

Tannenbaum, R., & Schmidt, W. H. (1973). How to choose a leadership pattern. *Harvard Business Review, 51,* 162–164.

Ubben, G., Hughes, L., & Norris, C. (2004). *The principal: Creative leadership for effective schools* (5th ed.). Boston: Allyn and Bacon.

Wilson, G. L. (2005). *Groups in context: Leadership and participation in small groups* (7th ed.). Boston: McGraw-Hill.

Yukl, G. (2006). *Leadership in organizations* (6th ed.). Upper Saddle River, NJ: Pearson, Prentice Hall.

PART TWO

Data-Based Decisions

5 Understanding Data-Driven Decision Making

Chapter Focus

Data-based decision making is a disposition and a skill. Educators who use data to make decisions begin to systematically develop purposeful questions that assist them in thinking about how to explore the multiple problems they confront each day at school and in the classroom. They also understand that there are a variety of different types of data that can be accessed, collected, and then used to better inform the practices that occur within a school.

This chapter explores the process of asking the right questions and then collecting appropriate data to answer those questions. Specifically:

1. How can educational decision makers move from nice-to-know to need-to-know questions?
2. What are the different types of data that emerge as a result of the questioning process?
3. How can data be used more effectively by administrators and teachers to ensure that important problems are being addressed?
4. How can the questioning and data collection process be used to enhance school improvement?

CASE STUDY

For several years, Mark Grimko has been analyzing the test scores of his middle-grade teachers. He works hard to make certain that his staff members understand what the test scores mean and how they might be used to influence student achievement.

One big problem he confronts relates to his teachers' knowledge about data usage. Many of the teachers review the data and then appear to ignore them. Some suggest that the use of such data is simply not appropriate and places too much emphasis on testing and student performance and will lead to "teaching to the test." Others just appear apprehensive with regard to the process of matching teachers to students—it seems, somehow, "intrusive" to the educational process.

As a result, Mr. Grimko decides to find a way to "encourage" his professional staff to be more "data engaged." After exploring several different ideas, he finally decides to have a professional development retreat in August, just prior to the start of school. He outlines several key steps:

Step 1: *Create* a teacher data leadership team.
Step 2: *Identify* the ways the district is currently *collecting* data for teacher use.
Step 3: *Pose* questions that help teachers make *connections* between what they know and what they do.
Step 4: *Create* goals for school improvement and determine how those goals will be measured.
Step 5: *Evaluate* or monitor the progress toward defined goals.

He feels ready, but also conflicted. Should he share only the school-wide data? He has access to individual teacher performance data. Should he "protect" teacher identities but publicly share teacher-level performance results? He knows that some states are moving toward the use of teacher identifier systems and that those states have an ability to match teachers to students. His state does not have such capacity, but he can "make the match" because he has access to the students' test results and he knows which teachers "match" the students. Should he make public what he knows so that parents and others have better information or will such sharing compromise the trust that he has developed with his colleagues and prevent him from achieving the program excellence that he desires for the students?

What Is Data-Based Decision Making?

Accessing and revealing data represent a necessary first step in the school improvement process. But, unless data are accompanied by understanding, application, changing practice, reapplication, and "building its use" routinely into the daily life of schools, it is not likely to matter much or make a difference. Indeed, it can create negative consequences and represent yet another example of confusing activity for accomplishment.

Recently when a group of teachers was discussing data-based decision making with one of the authors, a teacher quipped, "Oh, yeah, we did that [data analysis] last year." For this teacher, data analysis is a serendipity, not a habit. To be effective, data-based decision making cannot be seen as a fad that is here today and gone tomorrow; it needs to be routinely adopted as a pedagogical way of life in the school's culture.

It is impossible to read through the literature on data-based decision making and not find a litany of articles titled something like, "Five Steps to Using Data," "Seven Ways to Understand Data," or "Four Steps for Data-Based Decision Making." The simplicity of the titles is not reflective of the complexity of the evidence-based decision-making process for teachers and administrators. Indeed, nearly all such articles evidence a variation on a common theme: data-based decision making is the process of compiling, reviewing, sharing, and using data to assist in improving schools and, particularly, enhancing student achievement. The process is not static. Instead, data-based decision making is dynamic and necessarily avoids a practice educators have adopted for a long time: simply sharing uninformed (or inadequately grounded) opinions. As Blake (2004) suggests, most teachers, when asked how students are doing academically, rely on "cardiac assessment." They rely on intuition and what they feel, not real data, to determine whether students are learning. That "cardiac" method no longer suffices in an "academically flat world" where student achievement data are becoming more widely and readily available for analysis.

Levitt and Dubner (2005) note that if you learn how to look at data in the right way, you can explain riddles that otherwise might seem impossible to understand—there is nothing like the sheer power of numbers to scrub away layers of confusion and contradiction. The numbers surrounding education are essential for better understanding its current status and its real challenges, especially in an environment where sanctions are possible for schools not meeting AYP.

For our purposes and discussion in this chapter, data-based decision making includes four active phases that come after you decide what you want to know and determine why knowing that information is so important in the first place: *collecting, connecting, creating,* and *confirming.* These four phases can take different forms, as you will note in other sections of this book (see, for example, Chapter 11 and the eight steps to school improvement).

These four phases are aimed at helping decision makers arrive at better solutions, use resources more efficiently, and deliver instruction more effectively. They are not quick, simple steps but rather a framework to help bring clarity to the important processes necessary to move data to school improvement.

Why Is Data-Based Decision Making Important?

Data are important. However, having data and not being able to understand or apply their uses parallels having a car with no gasoline. Data without context or analysis simply will not take you anywhere. Collins, author of *Good to Great* (2001), makes a very compelling case for the role of data in his work comparing high-performing companies to low ones. He offers specific differences, through selected principles (e.g., the hedgehog concept), that enable certain companies to become great while others simply fail to achieve their potential. That is, what makes some companies great, while others are only good? The next question asked was whether these corporate "principles" had applicability to the social sectors such as hospitals or educational institutions such as schools. It turns out they did. Collins argues that the principles of greatness apply equally well to the social sectors as they do to the business sectors. While some differences exist between schools and businesses, particularly around the issues that motivate those in the social sectors, one of his principles of greatness is that calibrating success with business metrics is critical. It is not about finding the perfect indicator, but rather, about "settling upon a consistent and intelligent method of assessing your output results, and then tracking your trajectory with rigor" (Collins, 2005, p. 8).

Put another way: "What gets measured and gets monitored gets improved." Improving upon a goal you do not measure in some way is difficult. Measuring can occur in simple ways but it is often influenced by complex social dynamics. For example, ask a group of students to individually go outside and jump from a starting point (with both feet together) and mark where they land. Now, after each person has taken that jump, take the entire class out and have individuals rejump, only this time with the entire class watching. Do it every day for a week. You would be hard pressed not to see a significant improvement in individual jumping performance because the progress is being measured and monitored (and observed by peers!).

Today's context of achieving in a standards-based world offers us the opportunity to mine large data sets that heretofore have not been available. No Child Left Behind (NCLB) requires student achievement testing in grades 3–8 in math and reading. At the high school level, at least one test must be administered to assess student performance. In most districts, much more than a single exit exam exists in multiple subjects.

Some school districts now administer exit exams in selected states (Tennessee, North Carolina) in core subjects. The exit exams used are of three different types: minimum competency exams (MCE), standards-based exams (SBE), and end of course (EOC) exams. Currently, three states administer MCEs, fifteen administer SBEs, and four require EOCs. The MCEs focus on skills below the high school level; the SBEs are aligned with state standards and are targeted to the high school level; and the EOCs assess student mastery in a particular content area at the high school level (see Center on Education Policy, 2006). There is clearly a move away from MCEs to SBEs (ten states required MCEs in 2002, but only two will require them in 2012) and as states move toward the use of standards-based instruments and as more states (twenty-two in 2006) implement mandatory exit exams (as a graduation requirement), teachers and administrators will increase pressure to use data to make better decisions about how best to educate young people; such data should also mitigate confusion about the actual performance of students and help clarify the differential impact of exit exams on diverse student populations.

Such confusion is especially problematic for school boards that are attempting to make public how their schools are performing. Dahlkemper (2002) writes, "Without data, boards have no way of ascertaining whether they are making progress . . . or whether the system is working as a whole" (p. 1). In a time of high accountability everyone associated with schools needs to know what progress is being made by students.

Without data, policymaking is based on hunches or anecdotes instead of accurate information. Data enable board members to make decisions with far greater precision and certainty. The importance of collecting and using data is affirmed from the principals' standpoints. For example, the National Association of Elementary School Principals (2001) indicates that standards for what principals should know and be able to do are to include multiple sources of data as a means of fostering instructional improvement. Clearly administrators are facing more demands regarding data usage, but so too are all others associated with P–12 education who want different types of data as a means of more fully understanding the school environment.

In essence, the data sought are focused on more than student achievement. Increasingly, school personnel are being asked to collect a wide variety of attitudinal data, district achievement data, and standardized test data so that critical questions about student and school performance can be answered. Comprehensive databases are needed. The Data Quality Campaign report (Achieve, 2005) argues for the creation of longitudinal data systems in all fifty states. The authors of the report assert that states need to have in place data collection and data management systems so that practitioners and policymakers can make better programmatic decisions. The sample questions the report proffers suggest the reason why understanding data-driven decision making is an imperative for educators. Examples of critical questions include: How many students drop out after completing the eighth grade? Which schools are able to produce the strongest academic achievement? What percentage of those pursuing postsecondary work have to complete remedial coursework?

Indeed, Data Quality Campaign (published in partnership with Achieve) proffers a series of essential elements for any statewide data system:

1. A unique statewide student identifier
2. Student-level enrollment, demographic, and program participation information
3. The ability to match individual students' test records from year to year to measure academic growth
4. Information on untested students
5. A teacher identifier system with the ability to match teachers to students
6. Student-level transcript information, including information on courses completed and grades earned
7. Student-level college readiness test scores
8. Student-level graduation and dropout data
9. The ability to match student records between the pre-K–12 and postsecondary systems
10. A state data audit system assessing data quality, validity, and reliability) (See Achieve, 2005, p. 1)

Finally, the Institute for Educational Leadership (2000) declares the importance of "instructional leadership that focuses on strengthening teacher and student learning, professional development, data-driven decision making and accountability" (p. 1). All of these components, of course, are consistent with the Interstate School Leaders Licensure Consortium (ISLLC) Standards for School Leaders in which their six standards provide a framework for practicing school leaders and effective school leadership.

How to Get Started: Asking the Right Questions

Years ago, an advisor to a young doctoral student suggested a conceptual filter for doing a dissertation: "What do you want to know? And, if you knew that information, so what?" It has often been said that we are a society that is data rich and information poor. Lots of data are collected; far too little are used to shape the decisions about desired practices.

To get right to the heart of an issue, you must be clear about the question you want to answer before you begin collecting data. Not only do you need to decide what you want to know, but you must also determine the data available to help you answer the question.

The time it takes to clarify questions up front and the data needed to do so save time in the long run. What would you say or do if you had data regarding a particular topic? If the answer is simply, "That would be interesting," then the data probably do not contribute much to data-based decision making. Nice to know information is, simply, nice to know. The question is, what do you *need* to know? And, what happens after you acquire that "need to know" information?

For example, someone could collect data at any school regarding the students who buy lunch, who bring their lunch, or who go home for lunch, assuming the school offers the varied options. Let's say it is a 60–30–10 percent ratio for each option, respectively, over the course of a year. So what? That data could be interesting, but certainly not relevant to student academic performance at the school. However, this information might be relevant to the cafeteria managers who are basing their budgets and profitability margin on the number of students who purchase a lunch. They might combine those data with other data to provide the information with which to make better purchasing decisions.

Aside from asking the right questions, you must choose and collect the correct data that will lead to the answers you want and need. The data must be valid. If you weigh yourself every day on a scale, and consistently weigh 120 pounds, you could say that the scale was a reliable, consistent weight assessment tool. However, if your question centers on how tall you are, the scale would not be a valid measure for height. Although on the surface this appears to be a ludicrous example, we sometimes do something similar with data: That is, we collect information that may not be valid for the purposes of what we need to know. Think of how many decisions are made based on perceptual data alone. And consider the discrepancy at times between the perceived and the real.

How does one move beyond perceptions? Such "movement" occurs after you have your data set (or another set) and you ask the right questions. For example, suppose you have value-added data for individual students at a school. You might ask, given these students' growth or academic progress, what will it take for these students to get to where they need to be academically (e.g., grade level proficiency)? That question, generally, is a better one to ask than simply asking, "What is a particular student's level of academic achievement?" There are times when the latter is important to know, but the former requires critical thought about comprehensive actions to be taken; the latter fosters reflection on what has already occurred (i.e., how a particular student performed).

So, as you start, begin framing questions, but like an investigator who now has data, make sure you have the right questions for that data set. Without those questions (a clear focus), it is impossible to foster the overall improvement that you want for students. Also, familiarize yourself with the data systems available locally and at the state level.

Our point is that you need to be focused on collecting the right data in order to help you answer the questions you posed to initiate any school improvement process. At the heart of collecting data, analyzing them, and posing and testing hypotheses must be a set of critical questions. Once you know the questions, you can begin to assemble the data necessary to help answer them, assuming, of course, the data systems to provide answers are in place.

Types of Data

In Chapter 9 we will discuss the different types of research. But just as there are different ways to collect data, there are also very different data products from varied data collection process. Dahlkemper (2002) notes:

> Data are divided into two categories, quantitative and qualitative. Quantitative data include hard numbers, such as graduation rates, test scores, enrollment figures, employment rates of high school graduates and drop out rates. Qualitative data are based on information gathered from focus groups, surveys with open ended questions, and interviews. Neither kind of data should be mistaken for anecdotes which are nothing more than somebody's perception of an event. (p. 2)

Collins (2005) argues that all indicators are flawed: "Test scores are flawed, mammograms are flawed, crime data are flawed, customer service data are flawed, patient-outcome data are flawed" (p. 8). What matters is not finding the perfect indicator, but insisting upon assembling a body of evidence, quantitative or qualitative, to help you track progress and then having confidence in the data you possess. Understand that data can be quantitative and clear but still not useful, especially if the right questions are not asked.

If data are qualitative, Collins asserts, think of yourself as an attorney combining a body of evidence to argue a case. If they are quantitative, think of yourself as a lab assistant assembling data for subsequent analysis.

Bernhardt (2000) suggests that school process, demographic, perceptual, and student learning data are the four types of most commonly used information:

- School process data include school programs and processes.
- Demographic data include ethnicity, gender, attendance, and grade level.
- Perceptual data provide perceptual views, attitudes, values, and observations of various groups. Perceptual data include data about how people feel.

This information may come from surveying parents, teachers, or students. Or data may evolve through editorials or calls on a call-in radio show about education.

- Student learning and performance data indicate what students have learned or not learned. Such data help educators focus on the most important part of their work: helping students progress academically.

Finally, student learning data are performance based and provide us with results from various standardized tests and other teacher-made assessments, including teacher observations of student behavior. Bernhardt (2000) argues that in the intersection of two or more of these measures of data, observers can discover even richer information. For example, combining demographic data with perceptual data can tell us how student groups experience school differently. Or school process data combined with student learning results tell us which intervention programs are making a difference.

The bottom line is that multiple measures of data can be very useful to help discover patterns, practices, and relationships that can be maintained or improved. Remember that the questions we want answered need appropriate data collected to help answer them. What do data tell us? Why do we use data? The most common answers are that data help you:

- Make informed decisions that lead to improved student achievement.
- Gain an objective picture of what needs to be improved.
- Focus on the right things.
- Discover what is working and what is not.
- Monitor and celebrate movement toward goals and strategies for improvement.

You need not be a statistician to use data effectively. However, we know from experience that many of today's teachers have taken few, if any, data-based application courses. In essence, a knowledge gap exists for most practicing educators between what they learned in preservice programs and what they are now required to know to foster academic student success. They were educated in programs that treated teacher preparation as a craft (where intuition dominates) as opposed to a profession (where a specialized knowledge is required). Using data to make decisions is a specialized skill set. We might add that this data knowledge void on the part of preservice teachers is now actively being addressed by some states. Recent legislation in Ohio, for example, requires that all preservice teacher education programs align their curricula with state academic standards *and* with value-added progress elements defined by the state (see *www.ohiorc.value-added/*). Specific modules on how to access and use knowledge gained from assessments and analyses of assessment results have been developed by the state of Ohio to ensure that new teachers can effectively function in an accountability environment.

The entire standards-based movement has necessitated the robust collection of data. However, not nearly enough attention has been given to providing the professional development necessary to help educators understand, analyze, and apply results. Consider this story described by Bernhardt (2004), which illustrates how a defined problem led to systematic data collection:

> Each year, for several years, a community watched 80% of their [sic] graduates go off to college in the fall, 40% return to the community by Christmas, and almost 95% of those who went off to college return by the end of spring—for good. This recurring problem was discussed widely among teachers and the community. Their hypothesis was that their students lacked experience and social skills. Their students simply did not have the social skills to function in other environments. Everyone "knew" that these students did not interact positively with people they knew, so they could not possibly know how to interact positively with strangers.
>
> Based on this "knowledge," the school district began an extensive restructuring effort centered on working with K–12 students to develop their social and communications skills.
>
> At the request of a consultant, who was brought in to "make this vision a shared community vision," the teachers reluctantly conducted a telephone survey of their graduates to ask them why they had dropped out of college. Almost without exception, graduates said the following: "They made me write. I can't write!" Based on this fact-finding survey, the focus of the restructuring effort changed immediately, and the school district began using data on an ongoing basis to provide a challenging curriculum that kept students engaged in learning, enjoying school and writing! (Bernhardt, 2004, p. 4)

Consider another example. An Ohio school district failed to pass an important operating levy. The common view of the board and administration was that Ohio's poor economy at the time was causing the failure of the levy. People just did not want to pay more taxes. However, when focus groups were convened to talk about a different type and size of another levy request, unanticipated answers came, which provided another theory as to the levy's failure. Specifically, rural community members were concerned that the four elementary buildings might be consolidated into one larger school, effectively ending local community support. When the board passed a resolution indicating support for small community schools and indicated that they had no intention of consolidating the elementary schools, the operating levy passed. That knowledge, based upon data collected through focus groups, led to changes in perception, strategy, focus, and results.

Using Data Effectively

An important part of using data effectively is to make sure not only to ask the right questions, but also to proffer questions to the right people.

In Bernhardt's (2004) example (offered above) the administrators were asking teachers and community members, but not students. In the second example, board members were asking themselves and administrators about the levy failure, but not asking enough community members to identify the root causes of public discontent.

A colleague recently conducted a study of a school district to determine the reasons behind some negative school situations. The researcher's objective was to use students to interview students, teachers to interview teachers, and community members to interview community members so that each group could better determine the actual situation. By asking the right people to ask the right questions, they discovered that identified problems, such as low achievement, high dropout rates, and so forth, were symptomatic of other issues, such as poverty, low expectations, and lack of funding.

Perhaps one of the best uses of perceptual data is found in the use of a wide-scale, stratified, random sample telephone survey administered to residents in a rural school district in southeastern Ohio. Until 1988, the district administered a telephone survey of registered voters once every three years. The district then expanded the process to include significant parent input as well. Some of the questions are the same each time, providing the district with a longitudinal view of the various issues confronting administrators and teachers. For example, respondents are told that students are often given grades of A, B, C, D, and F; the respondents are then asked what grade they would give the school system, which provides the district with a "rough" and longitudinal assessment of how it is doing. The district uses this device to ascertain parent perceptions in various additional areas of interest. In its 2002 version, they asked parent respondents how often they visited the district website, a resource not even available in 1988.

How does the district use all these data? In 1988, they found that most residents, if they had children, learned about school through their children. Not surprising, but because of the respondent data analysis, new efforts went into what was communicated (especially in writing) from the school. No more faded copier sheets that could not be read by parents! The district is currently served by three newspapers with the two largest being on the east and west end of the district, about twenty miles apart. These are important sources of information for residents, but one newspaper rarely provided much news about the district. The editor at the time, after reviewing the survey data, took a different approach toward reporting the news of the district. He began regular features highlighting district events and activities, which proved attractive for parents and residents who wanted more information about what was occurring, and for the newspaper, which wanted to sell more papers.

This story is yet another example of using different kinds of data (perceptual and achievement) to shape what happens in schools. Incidentally, the perceptual data collected by the above "case" school also caused the district to create focus groups to "dig deeper" into issues of expressed "concerns," and by digging deeper, the educational practices of the school were improved and made more responsive to students' educational needs.

Connecting Data to School Improvement

One major purpose of data-based decision making is to make systemic school improvements that have larger, more significant impact on the students being served. For purposes of school improvement, think of processing data in these phases: *collecting, connecting, creating,* and *confirming.*

Collecting Data

Collecting is the compilation of important data. It is putting data into a reportable, easy-to-understand format. The recent report by Achieve (2005), titled *Measuring What Matters,* asserts: "Only a handful of states have data systems with most of the 10 essential elements [described earlier in this chapter] and no state had all 10 elements as of 2005" (p. 14).

Achieve focuses on what states should do, but we would assert that all educators who focus on excellence need to emphasize the collection of good data. Consider one of the most high-performing secondary schools in the United States: University Park Campus School (UPCS) in Worcester, Massachusetts. This school serves a population of students not frequently acknowledged as high performing (i.e., 78 percent come from non–English speaking homes, 72 percent receive free lunches, and 64 percent are minority). Yet in 2002, 2003, and 2004 their passage rates on the Massachusetts Comprehensive Assessment System (MCAS) exams were extraordinary, with no failing students, and in most instances the UPCS students received proficient or advanced scores on the MCAS exams. What is the UPCS secret? One answer is: No decisions are made without data. Indeed, as soon as the UPCS staff knows who its students will be, teachers are working through the scores to determine how best to provide effective instruction.

Collecting good data includes not just the actual data elements, but also determining how to store the data and how to set up the data to show correlations to other databases, and so forth. Collecting data requires anticipating the questions you hope to answer and making sure you have appropriate databases that are flexible and easily accessible to get at the question.

Italian economist Vilfredo Pareto observed in 1906 that 80 percent of the land in Italy was owned by 20 percent of the people. This same ratio was soon applied to various other notable concepts, becoming quickly known as the 80/20 rule or the Pareto principle. The notion is that a small number of people (or events) often produce (or foster) the majority of results. For example, a small handful of salespeople may sell the majority of a particular product, or the most grievances in an organization may come from a small number of employees.

The concept certainly has traction in education. Ask any principal about the handful of troublemakers who create the majority of discipline problems. Or consider the relevance of teaching power standards that influence the majority of important content to enable student success.

Here is another example of the Pareto principle in data analysis. A colleague was analyzing a school district's performance on Ohio's tenth-grade graduation test (in reading). One of the critical questions asked in the analysis was, "What were the most prevalent characteristics of the most difficult items for your subject?" As it turns out, at least in reading, the most difficult 20 percent of the questions (thirteen items) were related to the "information text strand," which is nonfiction information to gain knowledge about a particular topic and then being able to answer questions connected to those topics. These were questions that the vast majority (70 percent) of students did not answer correctly. So what? Let us consider the information text strand. In the easiest thirteen questions, only one question dealt with the concept, while in the most difficult items the concept occurred in seven of them as evidenced by particular phrases such as detail statements and metaphors. Increasing students' proficiency in this area (e.g., understanding metaphors) greatly enhances their chances of success on the most difficult areas of the test.

This process is not about "gaming" the test. It is about analyzing student performance through yet another lens to determine what they have learned or not learned that might impact what they could learn. The Pareto principle provides additional important insights as you pose other questions in determining what data to collect and then identifying how to use that data to more appropriately focus the learning process.

Connecting the Data

The second phase is *connecting the data.* That connection means analyzing the data from different perspectives or combining it with other data. This connecting process is often complex as the following two examples illustrate. But, without the connectedness, the full utility of the data is never realized.

Connecting data to other data sources as well as interpreting them from different perspectives makes it more revealing to users. For example, the Teacher Quality Partnership (TQP) in Ohio (see Case Study in Chapter 7), supported by all of Ohio's teacher preparation institutions, wants to discover not only how beginning teachers are educated, but also the context in which they begin their teaching careers. TQP also wants to explore the students' progress as measured by value-added assessment and to match students to teachers to the programs that prepared these teachers. This study is rich in variables and is being set up to explore how different teacher attributes relate to student progress. The implications are significant. Results will be shared with policymakers who will look at the data from their connecting parts: context and student progress. Schools of education and professors will review these data to look at their "connecting piece" of preservice instruction. Various hypotheses will emerge from this data set that require more study and analysis, but the power of the process is the effort to connect variables and outcomes.

Another example can be seen in Louisiana where Jeannie Burns, Associate Commissioner for Teacher Education Institutions, and George Noell, a Louisiana State University researcher, are developing a comprehensive teacher quality data system. In essence, using value-added measures, researchers are endeavoring to ascertain the relative effectiveness of the state's teacher preparation programs to increase student achievement. Berry and Fuller (2006) observe:

> Using his VAM model, Noell found in his 2003–04 analyses that students of some teachers from some universities systemically demonstrated greater academic achievement, as measured by state standardized tests in English/language arts, than other universities. His preliminary analyses also identified one teacher preparation program whose new graduates taught students whose growth in learning in mathematics surpassed the growth of learning in mathematics of children taught by experienced teachers. Additional analyses in 2004–05 replicated the initial findings. Based upon results of this study, the state decided to explore further the use of a Value-Added Teacher Preparation Program Assessment Model in Louisiana and funded a study to examine the technical qualities and adequacy of the model when using data across all of the state's 68 school districts. We believe strongly with the idea that VAM models help focus attention on TQ and teacher education where it belongs: on increasing student learning. (p. 1)

Clearly, these two examples illustrate statewide comprehensive efforts to connect data, but they occur at the school district and school level as well. Teachers at schools such as those at University Park Campus School use data to create curricula and identify instructional approaches. They connect what they know to create a direction for what they should do to help students learn.

As you can see, some states are systematically collecting data to assess their teacher education programs. Similarly, some school districts have established defined data collection plans in order to make connections. The process addresses assessment questions such as the following (see Depka, 2006):

- On what dates will the assessment be administered?
- Which students will be taking the assessment?
- In what format will the results be collected?
- Who will collect and compile the results for the entire district?
- How will results be reported?
- How will results be shared?
- How will results be used to influence [or shape] instruction? (p. 53)

Creating: Doing Something with the Data

The first two phases are necessary precursors to the third step: *creating*. Creating is doing. It is taking action on what you find, what you suspect, what you think will make a difference. Administrators who collect good data and then appropriately connect the data bases are in a better position to create educational programs that work.

Creating is planning and taking action on the data. If a gap exists between where your students are and where you want them to be, creating means developing goals and strategies to address that gap and then closing it in ways to foster student success.

Suppose your data reveal that parents do not feel part of the school community, or that your low-achieving students are not making suitable gains in math. Then the data-driven decision maker addresses those areas by systematically exploring the reasons for low-achieving students' performance. These strategies are ways of connecting action with data. Creating is not merely planning or strategizing about what to do. It is an active, systemic process of deciding how to use what you know to shape what you will do.

The "creating" process includes (see, in particular, Bernhardt, 2004), but is not limited to:

1. *Defining the problem:* What gains are low-achieving students evidencing in math and how have they performed during the past two to four years?
2. *Articulating hunches regarding the reasons for student performance in mathematics:* What strategies might be tried to enhance student engagement and performance?
3. *Determining if the hunches have validity by examining data relevant to the specific identified hunches:* How are the students performing?
4. *Involving all the relevant "players" and examining multiple data sources.*
5. *Exploring why current practices are manifest:* What forces serve to drive or restrain enhanced math performance for students?
6. *Outlining and implementing a plan of action.*

We use the concept of "creating" because much of what educators have to do once they have good data is to explore what data mean and how to use data in ways to effectively ameliorate problems or address issues revealed by the data. Once educators do this, they are then ready to confirm the findings and consider next steps.

Confirming the Findings

The last step is *confirming.* Did the program or practice make a difference? If not, then why not? And what can be done to improve on what was initiated or implemented?

In this stage, you are evaluating your efforts, learning from feedback, and starting the cycle again. You compiled data. You analyzed it and communicated it to others, developed goals, and identified strategies to make a difference. In the confirming stage, you are reflecting on whether your efforts made the difference you hoped for.

For example, one school's staff decided to make "word walls" to help students develop greater literacy skills and comprehension. When they collected students' data both formatively and summatively, the results were encouraging. The strategy appeared to be successful. Student achievement in reading improved, and at least some data were available to confirm that enhanced exposure to new words engendered enhanced student achievement.

Confirming means answering such questions about whether programs work, considering the feedback, and starting again if programs or practices fall short of expectations. As part of the confirming process, two different types of analyses often occur: formative and summative. The former is an ongoing process and examines "what is": What is occurring in a program? Is the intervention having the desired impact on student learning? The latter (the summative) is a culminating endeavor: Did the program work? Are students performing at a higher level at the end of an intervention (or the end of a school year)?

All four phases—collecting, connecting, creating, and confirming—are part of a dynamic process to obtain the desired results to answer the questions you have posed. As you consider the four phases, reflect on the following school in one midwestern city.

The principal came to the school in 2000. At least 90 percent of the students came from two-parent, high-socioeconomic-status families. The majority of the community members owned their homes. The school housed grades K–5 and had 700 ethnically homogeneous students. Prior to the principal's arrival, only 55 percent of the students were performing at or above the standard in math and 65 percent in reading. At the time, the school was a "data-poor" culture, and any thoughtful needs analysis (that outlined the differences between the actual performance of the students and the desired performance level for them) would suggest the school was "ineffective."

To determine the cause of the "underachieving" problem, the principal asked the teachers two questions. First, "Are your students learning?" And second, "How do you know whether they are academically successful?" In essence, he wanted them to "define the problem" that appeared to be causing the students' weak performance.

Teachers usually base their answers (their hunches) to such questions solely on the students' grades. However, the principal realized that grades are subjective measures. A well-behaved student who works hard can receive good grades and still not be making adequate progress. Indeed, it is common in many affluent school districts for students to be achieving (scoring high on standardized tests) but not growing (evidencing sufficient academic growth from one year to the next).

To incorporate data use, the principal restructured the school day to allow for all teachers, including those in special education, to spend one hour a day of common planning time together. He involved all the relevant players. During this time, teachers worked on their newly assigned spreadsheets that included each of their students' names. The spreadsheets were organized by grade level and contained reading, writing, math, and, in the higher grades, science and social studies.

Throughout each quarter, students were given four to five different assessments and their grades were recorded on the spreadsheets. Some assessments were teacher created and others were provided by the school district. Results were color-coded based on each student's level. (Red was below average, green was at the average, and blue was above average.)

Teachers also were assigned responsibility for creating performance graphs. While the spreadsheets displayed individual student performance, graphs showed all students' performance by subject and grade level. The graphs would show the percentage of students performing below the average, at the average, or above the average, and special education students' progress.

At the end of each quarter, spreadsheets and graphs were formally due and discussed during the school day. This constituted a type of formative assessment. The principal asked the teachers what type of resources they needed and what other changes needed to be made to increase student learning. The teachers were now developing a plan of action.

One of their "plans" was the addition of guided reading groups in the first grade. Instead of staying with one teacher for the entire school day, students who needed more attention in reading, as shown by the spreadsheets, were combined from different first-grade classrooms into one; they then performed guided reading exercises together.

The result of the data collecting, connecting, and creating process was an increase in student performance and learning. During the most recent academic year, 95 percent of students were performing at or above average in math, which is up from 55 percent in 2000. Reading performance also increased from 65 percent in 2000 to the mid-90s in 2004.

The principal learned three lessons from this experience:

- First, a systemic, structured method and procedure must be implemented to assess student learning.
- Second, all teachers in a building must take a collective responsibility for student learning. The principal made it a point to meet with teams of teachers instead of individual teachers to avoid competition and stress. By meeting and working in teams, teachers built this sense of collective responsibility and collaboration.
- Third, data need to be visible in a nonthreatening environment. Without the data being shared openly and frequently, changes cannot be implemented to increase student learning and growth.

The principal's lessons confirm what the literature on evidence-based decision making suggests (see, for example, Bernhardt, 2004). Specifically, good use of evidence entails being systemic in one's approach to data collection. And, being systematic requires thoughtful reflection and clearly defined actions. That reflection requires, suggests Depka (2006), addressing questions such as:

- What do I notice about test results? (What problems appear to be evident? And what do the data suggest about student performance?)
- What needs to be done to promote student achievement and learning? (What are the current practices and what practices appear appropriate to address the problem?)

■ Who needs to be involved in any curriculum development or instructional enhancement work? (Who needs to be involved in implementing a plan of action?)

When these questions are asked and answered, the results can be outstanding, as was evidenced at the midwestern elementary school described above. The principal started data collection practices with teachers and ensured there was shared time to connect the data. The collaboration time that he provided was critical because it allowed everyone to meet and talk about the results. He made sure that all teachers were part of the conversation and that all student performance results from any given grade level were shared collectively.

The teams created plans as a result of this collaboration and then would confirm if things were working. Over a relatively short period of time, the principal created a "data-rich" culture that was aimed at supporting students and not at blaming teachers. It was a planned culture that focused on student learning. More importantly, the data-decision-driven process became institutionalized. Even after the principal left in 2005, the processes he established were sustained and the good student results continued. Evidence-based decision making was now part of the school's culture.

Consider yet another case where a thoughtful principal decided to become more evidence based. The principal has been principal of an elementary school located in a rural area. The building is a K–6 with 150 students with large numbers in special education (40 percent) and large numbers of students (70 percent) on free and reduced lunch. It was recently named "School of Promise" for its 2004–05 test scores. The principal of this school cited several school improvement strategies from the time she began ten years ago when only 10 percent of the fourth graders were proficient in writing, 15 percent in reading, and 5 percent in math. Today, those numbers are dramatically different: 100 percent of fourth-grade students are proficient in writing, 75 percent in reading, and 94 percent in math. Chief among her strategies included significantly enhanced teacher participation and district-wide grade-level meetings twice a month where problems were identified, ideas explored, and data shared openly and thoughtfully. Her sense was that this process created a critical dialogue, but also a sense of competition because teachers wanted their school to be successful. The principal asserts that these "data-rich" meetings also increased a sense of urgency to make necessary changes to ensure that children were not being left behind.

All of these efforts were part of the new school district superintendent's increased data use and concomitant commitment to build a data-rich district culture. The principal believes that defining the problems, collecting the data, connecting the data, sharing the data among teachers, and creatively outlining possible solutions, along with an increased sense of urgency in terms of effective teaching practices, were key catalysts toward improving student performance. This transformation occurred while virtually keeping the same staff over ten years. Success was largely an effort of refocusing the staff's energy and using team cohesiveness to collect, connect, and use data to better serve students.

The School Leader's Role

All educators play a critical role in using data to accelerate student achievement. Arguably though, the principal is the most critical player.

Richard Riley, former governor of North Carolina and Secretary of Education in the Clinton administration, noted at a United States Department of Education Town Meeting in June 1999 that

> the principalship is a position that is absolutely critical to educational change and improvement. A good principal can create a climate that can foster excellence in teaching and learning, while an ineffective one can quickly thwart the progress of the most dedicated reformers. (as cited in Furger, 2000, p. 1)

Frankly, the principal most often sets the climate, creates the focus, and contributes significantly to the culture of the building by what he or she does or fails to do. Some administrators expect little and are appropriately "rewarded"; others demand much and see that teachers and students respond, especially when the demands occur in a climate of respect. In a *New York Times* article Herszenhorn and Saulny (2005) announced that fifth-grade test scores in New York City had gone up by a wide margin (20 percentage points in reading). Principals, teachers, parents, and others offered the explanation for the enhanced performance as hard work. By hard work, they meant a relentless focus on reading literacy and math and a "ceaseless scrutinizing of tests, quizzes and writing samples to understand what students didn't know" (p. 1). They did not report a single pedagogical practice or program, but rather they focused on a concerted effort to use data to shape educational programs.

Concerted efforts do not just happen: They are led, and most often by the principal. In fact, Joyce, Wolfe, and Calhoun (1993) concluded from a literature review on achievement that student learning most often occurs when student learning is the central goal of instruction and, we would assert, when teachers and administrators know how to collect data connected to that goal.

Clear goals (and a plan of action) regarding student learning give teamwork meaning. Too often, we judge whether an innovation has been implemented rather than whether students have learned as a result of an instructional intervention or innovation. While data inform purpose, school leaders must champion not just data use, but also their use as a means to another end; namely, student learning. School leaders can champion data use by:

- *Insisting upon encouraging questioning and problem definition.* This step means posing questions and ensuring that data collection takes place. If the leader gives attention to the data, so will others. Leaders must foster building a culture that encourages questioning, analyzing, critiquing, and facing challenges, especially in the light of less than stellar performance data. School leaders, especially principals, must also provide support for these expectations. That means finding time for teachers to meet, learn, and discuss data.

It is promoting real sharing without a fear of failure. One superintendent who has built a considerable data-rich culture in the district uses this mantra with principals: "No blame, no shame, and no excuses." It is about getting better, and that often means confronting the elephants in the room.

- *Building a data-rich culture, where leaders acknowledge success.* The purpose in using data is not to prove, but to improve. Many teachers, while not motivated by data, are clearly committed to helping students grow and learn. The leader's task is to connect data to doing, showing how analysis can be used as a tool to improving student learning.

  Not all data have to show a deficit or weakness. Leaders can help build the needed culture by celebrating positive trends or patterns in improvement.

  When positive trends are discovered in the data, studying the processes that led to that trend can be examined to look for what led to the success. By peeling back the "data onion," those processes may be able to be applied to less successful trends. For example, if data revealed positive growth in eighth-grade math scores and analysis uncovered that the amount of time spent on the teaching of math had a direct correlation to the improvement, then perhaps that same strategy (increased academic learning time) could be applied to science instruction. Often, the answers to problems can be found within the organization or system. Not all solutions are external, esoteric, or costly; some relate to capacities already evidenced within the system.

- *Encouraging everyone to interpret and analyze and use data.* Administrators must model the use of data for decision making so that staff can begin to understand that it is a priority and part of the expectations of the school culture. Being supportive of teachers as they are learning the basics of data is also an important role.

Most importantly, administrators need to know how to communicate the results of the data interpretation and use process. To this end, they might have a regular newsletter distributed to parents or hold special meetings to discuss data and how they are being used. Many schools have websites for communicating data, and one administrator the author knows sends out an e-mail to all staff every school morning that highlights "data points" that all staff need to consider as they provide instruction for the upcoming day.

The Teacher's Role

Teachers are an integral part of data-based decision making. Of course, in the school improvement effort, classroom goals must align to the school and district overarching goals. These goals are based on a data-based needs assessment.

However, teachers must take another step. They must look at individual student data to make the necessary decisions and adjustments needed to differentiate instruction for students. This may require scaffolding the curriculum to meet the needs of particular students. Without data to support where individual student needs are, teachers may never hit their learning targets. Teachers often get data by being purposeful about data collection. They may create highlighting methods in their grade books (with different grades receiving different colors). Depka (2006) notes that the *highlighting* "creates a visual of those in need of occasional support and identifies students who are experiencing repeated difficulties" (p. 69). Or they may do item *analyses* (see Chapter 11) or use specialized *rubrics* that help provide greater detail about student progress (see www.insightassessment.com).

Teachers can also display anonymous class data showing progress and achievement of the class as a whole that will elicit goal setting. Although teachers can do this in isolation, a collaborative effort will bring stronger results. Getting involved in professional learning communities will break down that isolation and open the doors to collaboration that lead to action. One approach that has been used successfully in getting teachers to work together is the professional learning community approach.

The term *professional learning community* has certainly gained traction in the educational literature. It is about bringing team members together regularly to dialogue on ways to improve learning for all students. Data help inform that discussion. Teachers can collectively disaggregate the data to look for patterns and trends in various subgroups.

The Students' Role

Let us not leave students out of the equation. Students of all ages can collect and record personal data as well as set goals based on these data. With some guidance from teachers, students can create data notebooks that contain charts, graphs, and tables that monitor their own progress and achievements. Students engaged in data-based decision making in creating their own goals tend to take more responsibility for their own learning. In one "data-rich" school, students (K–12) keep their own "data notebooks." These notebooks vary by grade level, but each student sets individual goals for achievement as well as behavior (i.e., attendance, homework).

Students keep track of test scores, reading levels, and periodically write or "depict" how they are doing in relation to their goals and the goals of their class. They use charts, graphs, and organizers to record and represent data. One enlightening moment came when a third grader went through his grade 3 academic journal and discussed and analyzed his progress using his own data. That student felt a sense of empowerment, and school suddenly had meaning because the student possessed a level of ownership in terms of the expected and real outcomes.

S U M M A R Y

In the end, data analysis is a tool; a means to an end. It is an active process that, when coupled with sound professional judgment, can lead to better decisions for children. A sage once said, "We spend too much time building ships, when we need to have more people yearning for the sea." We need both.

Understanding the data-based decision-making process means that educators understand the nexus between collecting data and making use of that data to inform what happens at a school and in a classroom. Unfortunately, too many educators are afraid of data. They are afraid of what they might reveal, what they might not understand, or, worse yet, what they might mean once they have a better knowledge of what exists. Confidence in adults and students is created in an old-fashioned way: through knowledge. And that knowledge or competence is engendered through becoming actively engaged in the use of data and discovering that it can help shape and improve student learning. And when data are not available, do not permit that void to mitigate the quest for excellence. In Collins' (2005) words: "It doesn't really matter whether you can quantify your results. What matters is that you vigorously assemble evidence—quantitations and qualitations—to track your progress" (p. 7).

Data-based decision making is aimed at creating competence in educators so they will have the knowledge, skills, and tools to enhance what they do best: Help children learn. When that occurs, schools begin the transition to greatness.

QUESTIONS AND SUGGESTED ACTIVITIES

Case Study Questions

1. Mark Grimko seeks to create a teacher data leadership team. Which teachers should be selected to participate on such a team? Only veterans? Only those who are committed to using data? Why?

2. What types of goals for school improvement should be created? That is, should administrators focus primarily on academic goals? Explain how you would structure such goals.

3. What are the reasons for the apprehension concerning sharing individual teacher student performance data? Why are many educators (and especially those in teachers' unions) apprehensive about "drilling down" to the classroom level?

4. Why might the process of matching teachers to students (by classroom and subject) be problematic if not offensive to some teachers?

Chapter Questions and Activities

5. Plan an action research study using two or three different types of data to answer a "burning" classroom question. What data might you need? How will you collect them? What might you do with the results?

6. Value-added modeling (VAM) is becoming popular (see, for example, what is occurring to assess teacher preparation programs in Ohio and Louisiana). Why might some schools and teachers oppose VAM's use for assessing their effectiveness?

7. We identify a four-step process for using data: collecting, connecting, creating, confirming. Which of these steps is, in your opinion, most complex? Why? Which is the easiest to implement? Why?

8. We describe University Park Campus School in this chapter. The school as of 2005 had few dropouts and a 97 percent attendance rate. That school has identified certain design principles, such as "No decisions without data." What are the design principles for the school in which you work? Is data-based decision making one of the design principles? Why or why not?

9. Using data to make decisions is a key to school improvement. What are ways in which principals can incorporate time during the day for such discussion?

REFERENCES

Achieve, Inc. (2005). *Measuring what matters: Creating a longitudinal data system to improve student achievement.* Washington, DC: Author.

Bernhardt, V. L. (2000). *Designing and using databases for school improvement.* Larchmont, NY: Eye on Education.

Bernhardt, V. L. (2004). *Data analysis for continuous school improvement.* Larchmont, NY: Eye on Education.

Berry, B., & Fuller, E. (2006). *The value of value-added methods in identifying effective teachers.* Retrieved October 1, 2006, from www.teachingdata.org/pdfs/vam_bberry.pdf#search='The%20value%20of%20valueadded%20methods%20in%20identifying%20effective%20teachers%20and%20Berry'

Blake, V. (2004). *Contemporary school leadership course.* ASCD Professional Development. Retrieved October 20, 2006, from http://shop.ascd.org/productdisplay.cfm?productID=pdo40c38

Center on Education Policy. (2006). State high school exit exams: A challenging year. Washington, DC: Author.

Collins, J. (2001). *Good to great: Why some companies make the leap and others don't.* New York: HarperBusiness.

Collins, J. (2005). *Good to great and the social sectors. Why business thinking is not the answer.* Boulder, CO: Author.

Dahlkemper, L. (2002). School board leadership: Using data for school improvement. *NSBA Policy Research Brief, 27*(1), 1–4.

Depka, E. (2006). *The data guidebook for teachers and leaders.* Thousand Oaks, CA: Corwin Press.

Furger, R. (2000, October 1). *New help for school administrators.* Retrieved October 1, 2006, from www.edutopia.org/php/article.php?id=art_168

Herszenhorn, D., & Saulny, S. (2005, June 12). What lifted fifth grade test scores? *The New York Times,* 1.

Institute for Educational Leadership. (2000). *Leadership for student learning: Reinventing the principalship.* Retrieved October 20, 2006, from www.iel.org/programs/21st/reports/principal.pdf

Joyce, B. R., Wolfe, J., & Calhoun, E. (1993). *The self-renewing school.* Alexandria, VA: Association for Supervision and Curriculum Development.

Levitt, S., & Dubner, S. (2005). *Freakonomics: A rogue economist explores the hidden side of everything.* New York: HarperCollins Publishers.

National Association of Elementary School Principals. (2001). *Leading learning communities: NAESP standards for what principals should know and be able to do.* Alexandria, VA: Author.

6

Research to Drive Education Decision Making

Chapter Focus

The No Child Left Behind law placed a premium on the use of scientifically based research to ground classroom practices, especially in reading. Unfortunately, what "passes" as strong research is often heavily debated by both practitioners and researchers.

This chapter examines the different types of research available to and used by educators. The authors explore how the research that is available can be used to inform school and classroom practices. Particular attention focuses on the following questions:

1. What is the role of research in school improvement?
2. Why is it important to research practices that are prevalent in classrooms?
3. What types of research are common in educational settings? And is one type preferable to another type?
4. How can and should the different types of research be used to improve educational decision making?

CASE STUDY

Jonas Mikas serves as superintendent for a large school district in the southeastern part of the United States. For the past several years he has repeatedly read stories about the achievement gap that separates black and white students. Although parents in his community have not put pressure on him to deal with the problem, he feels a personal responsibility to respond because he knows what the research says and what the reality is for students in his school district who come to school from different racial, ethnic, and socioeconomic backgrounds.

Jonas considers some basic facts as he looks at the achievement gap problem. He knows that the black-white achievement gap is a well established educational fact. The documented black-white gap on the National Assessment of Educational Progress (NAEP) and other state-level achievement tests continues to be a major concern to classroom educators and educational leaders and policymakers. Although scores for all racial groups have gone up, wide gaps in test scores remain between different racial and income groups. The question plaguing concerned stakeholders is not who is to blame but what needs to be done to correct the "gap" problem.

The blame approach is complex, problematic, and, at times, ideological. Some clearly blame P–12 schools, or at least place heavy responsibility for the problem on school practices. Large numbers of students of color in the United States live in urban contexts and attend urban schools—these are schools not known for academic effectiveness or excellence. The "schools are the problem" adherents suggest solutions specifically related to school practices: Ensure a highly qualified teacher in every classroom, reduce class sizes (especially in the early grades), develop sound and equitable grouping practices, create more comprehensive tutoring programs that individualize the attention provided to students, and make school choice a reality.

Others, such as Richard Rothstein, believe that the achievement gap problem is more social than educational. That is, social class as reflected in differential health care, child nutrition practices in urban environments, and exposure to environmental toxins such as lead are the keys to why some succeed and others fail. Rothstein asserts, "Closing the gaps between lower class and middle class children doesn't just require better schools. It requires social and economic reform that would give children more equal chances to succeed in schools" (Economic Policy Institute 2007).

So, what is it? The schools? The environment? Jonas is not sure how he should respond given the mixed messages that he receives from the research. The "message" he determines to be appropriate will dictate the practices and approaches he attempts to put into place. That is, how should educators such as Jonas Mikas respond when acknowledged experts cannot agree on the salient causes of a serious educational problem such as the black-white achievement gap?

Role of Research in School Improvement

The overall quality of research in education remains arguably weak. Part of the reason for the lack of clear results relates to the absence of good experimental (gold standard) research in education. Such research is often quite expensive to conduct and frequently conceptually inaccessible to practicing teachers and administrators. Indeed, far too many educators totally ignore research findings in the process of making decisions about the instructional practices that they use in the classroom. Some do so because they simply teach the way they were taught. Others contend that the research being conducted is irrelevant to the demands and complexity of their classroom lives (Bransford, Brown, & Cocking, 2000). The real issue for school administrators is to know what type of questions need to be asked to foster school improvement and then to find ways to explore those questions through open dialogue and critical inquiry. That is, school administrators can enhance programs if they understand how to look critically at the programs for which they have responsibility. They can do this by focusing on several dynamics (see Bransford, Brown, & Cocking, 2000; Kimmelman, 2006), three of which are of particular interest to us:

1. Examining existing instructional practices (and collecting data on those different practices)
2. Assessing educational materials, especially those that are new to a program or school (and determining what patterns emerge from assessments)
3. Extending the knowledge base through the development of key research findings (and making a commitment to practices that appear supportable)

Bransford and his colleagues argue that, where possible, teams of disciplinary experts, pedagogical researchers, cognitive scientists, and teachers should be involved in exploring critical pedagogical questions. Ideally, this model of practice would be an educational reality. Practically, it is a logistical impossibility, at least for most schools and school districts. That does not mean, however, educators cannot either undertake some research and data collection (which we will describe in more detail in Chapter 7) or become critical consumers of published research (the primary focus of this chapter). Indeed, Kimmelman (2006) argues for administrators to create "data retreats" where teachers consider and reflect on data relevant to school-based practices.

Examining Current Practices

The key element associated with examining current practices is to ensure alignment between what is occurring in a school or classroom and the established principles of learning proffered by those who offer "prescriptions" for the educational process, whether researchers, pedagogical experts, or professional associations such as the National Council of Teachers of Mathematics. For example: Does a school's curriculum emphasize depth over breadth? Does the curriculum provide students with opportunities to explore preconceptions? Are the appropriate formative assessments (see Chapter 7) built into the instructional process? And is there an appropriate emphasis on depth of concept understandings as well as memory of basic facts?

These questions can be asked, explored, and even answered to a certain degree, regardless of whether experts are available to assist with a critical review of curricular practices. That is, teachers can make decisions about content depth even if the experts fail to agree on how much depth is required. More fundamentally, as Bransford and colleagues (2000) note, those curricular practices that appear efficacious need to be studied in depth in order to determine if they truly are effective: Are they resulting in enhanced student learning and achievement?

In essence, much of what occurs through examining current practices is an active questioning regarding whether a logical alignment exists between the defined curriculum and the use of established principles of learning that must be in place for enhanced student learning to occur.

Assessing New Materials

Not all aspects of the curriculum are as strong or as clearly defined as they should be. Ask most teachers what content is clear, cogent, and adequately covered and they can usually identify units of study (or sections of those units) that are structured to maximize student learning. Other sections are perceived to be (or in fact are) weak.

Teachers and administrators need to actively develop and enhance those curriculum materials that are weak to better ensure that they reflect "key principles of learning" (i.e., are structured to support student learning for understanding) and to ensure that what is taught can be presented clearly, thoughtfully, and with sufficient depth to ensure student learning. Bransford and colleagues suggest that this means creating curriculum designs that "engage students' initial understanding, promote construction of a foundation of factual knowledge . . . and encourage the development of metacognitive skills" (p. 256).

The authors also focus on several salient questions or issues around the use of formative assessments. As we will discuss in the next chapter and as researchers have now clearly documented, good formative assessment (e.g., providing corrective feedback) leads to enhanced student learning. Good data-based decision making requires that teachers possess data about students in order to shape the instructional decisions they make to enhance learning. Critical to that process is using formative assessments in ways that inform instruction rather than define student performance. Two practices appear critical: (a) providing feedback that is specific and suggestive of how to improve performance, and (b) providing tests and homework that relate directly to defined learning goals (Kimmelman, 2006).

Extending the Knowledge Base

Bransford and his colleagues (2000) view extending the knowledge base from a couple of different perspectives, but one, in particular, seems relevant to administrators who use data to make decisions. Specifically, what preconceptions dominate a subject area of study? Those preconceptions influence how content is both taught and learned by students, and they dictate the depth of understanding required of students to ensure that they understand the content they are exploring. In essence, teachers are not just teaching factual knowledge, they are working to ensure that students can contextualize facts within a discipline and analytically use those facts in more fully utilizing disciplinary knowledge.

So what might this look like or entail? Bransford and colleagues illuminate the notion:

> . . . consider the topic of marine mammals as it might be taught in early elementary school. That unit would be likely to include identification of the various marine mammals, information on the features that distinguish marine mammals from fish, and perhaps more detailed information on the various types and sizes of whales, the relative size of male and female whales, etc. To the marine biologist, this information is the interesting detail in a larger story, which begins with the question:

"Why are there mammals in the sea?" A unit organized around that question would engross students in an evolutionary tale in which the adaptation of sea creatures for life on the land takes a twist: land mammals now adapt to life in the sea. The core biological concepts of adaptation and natural selection would be at the center of the tale. Students would come to understand the puzzle that marine mammals posed for scientists: Could sea creatures evolve to mammals that live on land and then evolve again to mammals that return to the sea? They would come to understand the debate in the scientific community and the discovery of supporting evidence. And they would have cause to challenge the widespread misconception that evolution is a unidirectional process. (p. 260)

Ideally, disciplinary conceptual frameworks are part of a curriculum, and students have opportunities to explore them. Exploring ideas (and preconceptions) is essential if teachers are to ensure that students complete their P–12 experiences with the skills they need to master more complex domains of knowledge in their subsequent academic experiences.

Clearly, in the early grades, a premium will be placed on ensuring that students know certain facts (in subjects such as mathematics) and can read with fluency and evidence appropriate decoding skills in subjects such as reading. But, in the later grades in-depth knowledge is required in order for students to be academically competitive (see Hirsch, 2006). That in-depth knowledge is acquired by helping students think deeply (and critically) about the ideas that are central to each discipline.

Preparing to Research Educational Practices

As we noted in the previous section, research is an important part of evidence-based decision making. Good teachers and administrators are gathering all types of quantitative and qualitative data regarding the educational practices they use to structure practice. They carefully examine extant practices, they thoughtfully assess the curriculum materials being used, and they carefully explore disciplinary concepts and preconceptions. All of these require thoughtful research and in-depth study.

One reason so many schools fall short of excellence is that they do too much pedagogical "practicing" and too little researching about those practices. An example of this predisposition to "practice" before researching adequately an idea is how educators have used multiple intelligence (MI) research. Howard Gardner first proposed the idea of MI in 1983. Educators took the idea and ran with it, creating a whole cottage industry with professional development experts encouraging teachers to MI classrooms. The MI pedagogical globalization even resulted in MI classrooms and MI schools (e.g., the Key School in Indianapolis).

In essence, educators were immediately attracted to the MI concept. Part of the attraction was attributable to the extraordinary explanatory power of MI.

Theories have two types of power: explanatory and generative. The former helps bring order and coherence to something that otherwise appears random; the latter "orients investigators to the future by offering new frameworks for studying unknowns and contributing new knowledge to the field" (Chen, 2004, p. 21). Once educators understood the tenets of MI, many (perhaps most) immediately embraced its apparent logic. It simply made sense to think of students evidencing certain types of intellectual abilities (musical or mathematical or linguistic).

Interestingly, the evidence suggesting that MI really impacts student learning is limited, and where it exists it has been conducted by those who appear to embrace the MI theoretical construct or who provide inadequate documentation as to the real impact of the approach on student learning (see Willingham, 2004). If hope clouds observation (something Frank Herbert, author of the *Dune* trilogy, once noted), then a researcher who is attracted to the MI concept will be hard pressed to study it disinterestedly.

Critics of MI view it as more rhetoric than science. They contend that Gardner developed criteria and then ran "candidate(s) intelligences through them [the criteria and] . . . provides no hard evidence—no test results, for example, that his colleagues [can] evaluate" (Traub, 1998, p. 21).

Our point is not to bash MI but rather to note that good evidence-based decision making requires that teachers and administrators conduct thoughtful research or reviews of research before they advocate a practice. Moving from theory to practice requires both a depth of understanding of the theory and an ongoing search for hard data to support or refute the efficacy of a practice. To some it may represent progressive pedagogy to use MI approaches, but the real question is whether the "new" MI pedagogy enhances student learning.

Though we clearly understand that administrators and teachers cannot be active, scientifically based researchers, they do need to become active consumers of all types of research. In Chapter 7 we will discuss the different ways to collect data about classroom teaching practices and schools, including the use of action research. In the remainder of this chapter we examine the wide variety of experimental (quantitative), qualitative, and descriptive research that occurs for the purpose of determining how and when to use research findings to inform classroom practice.

Types of Research

The No Child Left Behind legislation is significant for many reasons. It set new, rigorous standards for having established achievement goals (i.e., criteria for what constitutes academic success), for ensuring highly qualified teachers in classrooms, and for ensuring that scientifically based teaching practices are used in schools across the country.

The use of research to ground practice is controversial because there is so much variability in both the quality and the type of the research being conducted. Complicating the issue is the way ideology (and the biases and assumptions of the researchers conducting the research) shapes findings. That is, just as those who sold cigarettes and funded research on smoking tended to find smoking "less harmful," so, too, those who argue for or against certain educational practices tend, when conducting research, to find what they are looking for when exploring a research question.

Still, just because problems exist with the conduct of research does not suggest that all research findings should be ignored or dismissed. Instead, it is imperative that administrators and teachers who act as evidence-based decision makers clearly study research findings (the results), examine how those findings were developed (the methods), and identify who conducted the studies (the researchers). In this section we focus primarily on the second of these: the methods. We will also discuss, in general, the types of results that surface and some considerations regarding who conducts the research.

Quantitative (Experimental) Research

As we suggested earlier, the No Child Left Behind legislation places a premium on research and its conduct and use. It explicitly values quantitative (experimental or quasi-experimental) research; that is, it values research that is "empirical, peer-reviewed, and relies on multiple measures and observations" (Lauer, 2006, p. 10). Entire books are written on how to conduct experimental research. For our (your) purposes, however, there are some basics that need to be considered regarding the conduct of quantitative studies.

First, good experimental research begins by trying to answer some type of causal question: Is the new reading program enhancing the performance of the fourth graders in reading? Or will student achievement be increased if teachers systematically vary their instructional approaches? Asking a good research question is not easy, and even when a good question is asked, it can be difficult to design a study that helps a researcher answer the question.

Second, once a question is asked and the study designed (i.e., the treatment is identified and to whom and how it will be administered), then the researcher is able to address the question systematically. That treatment or intervention might be a new math or reading program, an innovative way of dealing with misbehavior, or a specialized type of professional development for teachers that helps them know how and when to use inquiry strategies to teach science.

The gold standard for research is an experimental design; this occurs when subjects receiving (or not receiving) interventions are randomly assigned to a treatment or control group. Lauer (2006) describes a true experiment in which random assignment occurs:

A researcher is studying whether teacher professional development increases student achievement. Prior to the beginning of the school year, half the fourth grade teachers in a school district are randomly assigned to receive professional development in reading (the treatment group), and the other half are randomly assigned to receive no professional development in reading (the control group). To conduct the random assignment, each person on the list of fourth grade teachers in the district is assigned a number via a random number generator. Teachers with even numbers are assigned to the experimental group and those with odd numbers are assigned to the control group. At the end of the school year, the achievement gains in reading by the students of the two groups of teachers are compared. It is assumed that because teachers were randomly assigned to the two groups, teacher characteristics that might influence reading achievement favor neither the treatment group nor the control group. (p. 23)

When random assignment is not possible, then researchers use quasi-experimental methods. Quasi-experimental approaches are often used in education because it is so difficult to randomly assign students to either groups or classrooms. As a result, matched groups are structured, with a researcher identifying similar groups and then providing one group with an intervention, withholding it from another, then studying the differences in performance.

In experimental studies, quantitative data are the result; those data are often related to student achievement, largely because of the increased NCLB emphasis on student achievement.

Once data are available, the fun and trouble begin. The fun is in determining whether an intervention worked (or did not work), though negative findings often are as important as positive results. With positive results readers need to be cautious about leaping too quickly from findings to conclusions and, more importantly, from conclusions to generalizing to all settings based on what researchers found to be true in *one* setting.

Bracey (2006) outlines two specific cautions (among many principles of data interpretation) regarding the use of research findings.

1. *Statistically significant findings may not be practically significant.* The reason is that statistical significance is easier to achieve the larger the group. With very large groups it is possible that small performance differences will yield statistical significance. The issue is whether that small statistical difference suggests any practical or real implications for practice.

2. *Correlation is not the same as causation.* Just because two things are correlated does not mean that one causes the other. Poverty correlates with lots of different variables (including student achievement) but it does not cause all poor students to perform poorly; rather, as Bracey (2006) suggests "as poverty increases, [students'] test scores go down" (p. 74). There is a temptation to see in correlation, causation, but to truly assert causality requires substantial research, typically gold-standard experimental research, which explains in education why we have so few "treatments" that can be used with the confidence that they will impact student achievement.

Figure 6.1 describes the research associated with the use of teacher-centered versus student-centered instructional approaches. Few approaches in education have been studied (and heatedly debated) more fully than teacher- and student-

FIGURE 6.1   **Teacher-Centered versus Student-Centered**

Few issues have drawn more active debate over the past decade than how classrooms should be structured: teacher directed or student centered? Progressive educators argue for a focus on the student and his or her interests. Conservative critics of progressivist practices demand more teacher-centeredness . . . and they point to what they describe as the mountain of evidence that favors the conservative argument.

Chall (2000) wrote an entire book on that "mountain of evidence" in which she synthesizes all of the varied quantitative and descriptive studies. Her conclusions:

1. The teacher-centered approaches appear to be particularly efficacious for low-socioeconomic-status students.
2. The "traditional, teacher-centered approach to education generally results in higher academic achievement than a progressive student-centered approach." (p. 182)
3. The teacher-centered approach appears to be more powerful at both the elementary and secondary levels.

These conclusions appear to suggest that student-centered instruction does not have a place in P–12 contexts. But the complexity of using educational findings is clearly illuminated by one of Chall's final qualifying statements:

> As research evidence becomes available, we may well find that each approach has some advantage for academic achievement at different levels of education and proficiency. We may find that the traditional approach is *more effective* for beginners who first acquire knowledge and skills. Then, as they move beyond the basics, a progressive approach may prove more effective. (p. 183)

The debate over teacher- versus student-centered instruction suggests how important it is for administrators and teachers to be critical consumers of research. Research findings do not *dictate* practices to use, they *suggest* what practices might be used. Being a professional means making judgments, and those judgments need to be based on the best available research.

Source: J. S. Chall (2000). *The academic achievement challenge.* New York: Guilford Press.

centeredness, yet despite all the research no firm conclusions emerge about what constitutes best practice in all settings with all students. Clearly, though, some "directions" for teacher practice do emerge—for example, for teachers working with children who live in poverty (i.e., teacher-centered models appear to be more effective in fostering student achievement).

The nexus complication between correlation and causation is clearly illustrated in the recent spate of reports suggesting Algebra II as a critical gateway to academic success. Specifically, those who link academic rigor with educational success highlight the "Algebra II imperative." Recently, Kentucky, Michigan, Indiana, and other states instituted more rigorous secondary core curricula. Ohio, not to be outdone (especially by Michigan), proposed and then adopted in 2006 the Ohio Core—a set of enhanced academic expectations (particularly in mathematics and science). Ohio policymakers have strongly argued for the importance (almost to the point of causality) of Algebra II's relationship to student academic success (see Figure 6.2) and to the state's future economic possibilities.

Ohio and other states have enhanced the mathematics standards because they have taken correlations (from a variety of research studies) and made causal inferences in the form of policy recommendations. Bracey (2006) offers a caution about making such a leap:

> A few years back, the College Board reported that students who took algebra early (eighth or ninth grade) went on to take a rigorous high school curriculum and were likely to attend four-year colleges. The board labeled algebra a "gateway" course and recommended that schools offer it to more students so that they, too, would take a tough academic regimen in high schools and go on to a four-year college. . . .
>
> I don't have actual data to refute the College Board, but its conclusion represents a causal interpretation of a correlation coefficient. I think it might well be wrong. I would interpret the correlation differently. Schools, whether we like it or not, sort students. They identify talent. Teachers, counselors, and administrators identify the students they think can handle an algebra class or an IB program or whatever. The identification process is certainly not perfect, but I think this is likely what's going on: Kids whom the schools funnel into algebra early are those who the school thinks will go on to take solid geometry and trig and maybe calculus, plus natural sciences, and then head to a four-year institution of higher education. Early taking of algebra doesn't lead to a four-year institution; it reflects the selection process extant in schools. (p. 78)

As you can see, understanding and using quantitative research can be complicated. That complexity should not deter you; rather we encourage you to be critical consumers of the emerging research and to use it to guide the practices you use in the classroom. You do not need to know everything to know some things. Start

---

FIGURE 6.2   **Why Is Algebra II So Important?**

Students who complete Algebra II are **three times** more likely to earn a college degree at a four-year institution than if the highest level mathematics course they took was geometry.

Some people ask, "Why is Algebra II so important? Isn't content from this course used directly in only a handful of occupations?"

That's a fair question. And the answer is yes. Algebra II **content** is directly used primarily in certain technical occupations. But the evidence suggests that the rigor and discipline of Algebra II are valuable in other, less direct ways.

Students who take advanced mathematics courses such as Algebra II develop logic and reasoning skills that can help make them more productive in the workplace. In fact, Algebra II is widely considered to be the best predictor of success in college and high earnings in the world of work.

Source: *The Talent Challenge: What Ohio must do to thrive, not merely survive, in a flat world.* Columbus: Ohio Business Alliance for Higher Education and the Economy.

with what is known and then continue to critically reflect on the more uncertain aspects of practice.

Qualitative Research

During the past several decades, much of the research undertaken in education has been qualitative in nature. There are many explanations for this circumstance; each has some plausibility. Some attribute the qualitative "explosion" to the tendency on the part of educational researchers in general and doctoral students in particular to avoid the perceived statistical rigors of experimental and quasi-experimental designs. That is, on the surface, conducting ethnographic descriptive studies appears easier. In fact, good qualitative research is quite difficult and complex to conduct, but to the novice, especially one fearful of statistics and math aversive, it appears less complicated than an experimental or quasi-experimental design.

One of the problems associated with qualitative studies is the tendency of readers to look for causal connections and generalizable conclusions. Good qualitative research is *not* about establishing causal linkages, and it is certainly not about generalizing for a broader population what was evidenced for a single (or limited) group or individual. Rather, it is focused on describing (through narratives) an educational practice or school reality with sufficient detail that a reader can more fully understand the practice or the culture within which a particular practice is occurring. Some qualitative researchers approach a problem anthropologically (e.g., studying the broader relationships between a school and the community it serves); others explore problems sociologically, and typically a bit more narrowly by studying particular variables within school and community settings (i.e., what is the relationship between educational achievement and student socioeconomic status); still others study schools and schooling biologically by using techniques that parallel those of human ethnologists (i.e., how is space used by children and how does that space impact human interactions) (Lancy, 1993).

Each of these approaches (anthropological, sociological, biological) is grounded on a different set of theoretical assumptions, and the way in which results are represented also will be influenced by the tradition that grounds the researcher's work. Three of the most common ways to represent findings in qualitative research are through field studies, case studies, and personal accounts.

Field studies are used by those with both anthropological and sociological backgrounds. Typically, researchers with anthropological perspectives rely heavily on narrative to describe a phenomenon. Those in the sociological tradition may also use some quantitative (survey instrumentation) data to shape or contextualize their field work descriptions. Sociologists tend to ground their findings within some broader "grand theory"; anthropologists study groups and are less inclined to rely on a broader theory to contextualize findings. Rather, through detailed descriptions of particular cultural settings, they attempt to help readers understand a specific cultural phenomenon for what it represents and means. Unfortunately, many of the traditional research journals have been reluctant, until recently, to publish field studies or ethnographic research. Though there are several reasons for this circumstance, one of the most pronounced, according to Lancy (1993), is that "ethnographers use a wide variety of analytical frameworks from the traditional structural/functional analytical approach . . . to the more recently employed Marxist or critical theory framework . . . thus making it difficult to compare across studies" (p. 55).

Case studies appear similar to, but in fact are quite different from, ethnographies or field studies. Case studies are based on qualitative data (such as descriptive narratives) and rely somewhat less on survey instruments. When and where surveys are used is often to ensure that parallel data are secured across all the individuals (or groups) being studied within a particular context. Unlike ethnographies, where research questions are *not* specified, with case studies research questions are articulated prior to the investigation. Case studies are also typically written for a defined audience. For example, one of the authors is working closely with an innovative early college high school, and researchers (Mike Nakkula and Karen Foster) created a case study of that school and another early college in Los Angeles (see Wolk, 2005). The cases are available for the general public but the specific audience most interested in what the researchers observed are other stakeholders and educators starting early colleges. In particular the researchers were trying to understand the ways in which students in early college settings make meaning out of the early college experience. Figure 6.3 provides an example of how the findings in the early college high school cases are represented. Notice both *how* the data were collected by the researchers (in this instance, a team from Harvard) and *how* the findings are presented within thematic categories (e.g., education identity, continuous support, and caring relationships). Also, note how the researchers use words (data) from the students within the early colleges to highlight and support their findings (or categories).

FIGURE 6.3   Results from Year One Early College Study

In 2005, after following the first class of ninth graders at WAHS and DECA [the two early colleges], the Harvard study, led by senior researchers Karen Foster and Michael J. Nakkula, issued an interim report. Researchers interviewed students, teachers, administrators, and parents from the two schools, along with faculty and other staff of the university partners. In addition, they surveyed all of the DECA and WAHS students, using two standardized measures. With the Across Time Orientation Measure (ATOM) they assessed students' past experiences, present interests, and future hope and worries. They used the Hemingway Measure of Adolescent Connectedness to assess the relative degree of connection adolescents feel to different domains in their lives, including school, family, friends, future prospects, and risk-taking behavior.

With only its first phase completed, the research project's findings are preliminary and much remains to be learned. Still, the findings to date are compatible with previous research on effective schools, and Drs. Foster and Nakkula feel the new schools "are off to a good start, despite the research surfacing the inevitable challenges that new schools experience in starting up."

FIGURE 6.3   *Continued*

An Educational Identity

Early college high school teachers help their students to develop an "educational identity." Students' ultimate success in high school may depend largely on how they perceive their future with regard to higher education. Because early college high school students tend to have had negative and disappointing educational experiences, and as such generally lack the skills and commitment needed to succeed in college, they are unlikely to realistically see themselves as future college students. Early college high school teachers and advisors keep a focus on the future and, without overwhelming their students, project high expectations for them. According to Dr. Foster, teachers and advisors play an important role in "holding" this prospective educational identity for their students until the students gradually come to see the possibility of higher education: "It is as if the teacher periodically lends the student a 'telescope' through which to see a future self succeeding in higher education at a time when the student may be struggling with considerable academic challenges in the present."

One WAHS student explains how a teacher sometimes writes "nothing on the board. And we'll have to write our own notes like in college. Because the professor isn't going to stand up there and write everything on the board. So he's telling us, 'Look, I'm going to do this. I'm preparing you.'"

Continuous Support

WAHS and DECA teachers nourish the development of this educational identity by continuously helping the students meet the demands of a challenging academic curriculum. They also gradually join with students in experiencing educational aspirations that the young people have often not even considered. They strive to convince their students that it is never too late. That counters a message that underperforming students all too often get from adults: that they have squandered their chance ever to go to college.

Caring Relationships

At both schools, the development of each student's educational identity is firmly rooted in caring relationships, new and challenging learning pursuits, and powerful experiences of learning spaces. As research has shown, caring relationships between teachers and students enhance student learning and motivation. Drawing on the strength of these relationships, early college high school students describe learning as "fun" because it is "interactive, cooperative, relevant, and culturally responsive to their lives."

DECA and WAHS students describe their school as "like family," and, write Foster and Nakkula:

> [There is] little doubt that some students experience teachers and advisors as more committed and caring than family. . . . Based on their relationships with key teachers, students refer to their schools as "havens" of care, safety, and support. It is this culture of care that is [fundamental in] helping students cope with learning challenges that in many respects far exceed anything they have experienced previously.

Source: Wolk (2005).

Personal accounts are either self-generated or prepared by what Lancy (1993) describes as a "professional stranger." A number of individuals have created first-person (self-generated) accounts of their first year of teaching. Indeed, some of these make for compelling reading because they capture so much of the raw emotion of the first-year professional experience. Other accounts are generated by professional observers and are more generally descriptive of what it means to be a teacher, principal, or superintendent. The first book (co-authored) by one of the authors of this text provided detailed descriptions of twelve first-year teachers and was titled *Biting the Apple: Accounts of First-Year Teachers.* The first-year teachers' lives were observed and then described by "professional strangers" who carefully documented the reality of the first-year experience by both observing the teachers' interactions with students (see Figure 6.4) and then interviewing them on why they responded to students in particular ways.

There are a wide variety of excellent personal accounts available for educators to read. Many of these accounts are compelling and controversial. Much of Jonathan Kozol's work (*Ordinary Resurrections, Amazing Grace, Savage Inequalities*)

FIGURE 6.4   "Professional Stranger" Description of Classroom

Bill spent a great deal of time during class at his desk. He gave directions, answered questions, and covered lesson material while sitting at the large wooden desk located at the front of the room. Students lined up and waited for his assistance. Class control was difficult because Bill had to help the students standing at his desk, and, at the same time, keep the students at their desks quiet. The difficulty of working with one or two students and keeping the other thirty quiet was particularly noticeable whenever the students worked on independent projects or reports.

One day early in November, for instance, the students were working on sports reports. Bill was helping students at his desk when a loud crash jarred the room. Bill looked up and observed two students, Frank and Dave, standing next to an overturned chair. "Dave, Frank, get back up here. Who told you to go back there?" The students meekly picked up the chair and returned to their seats. Bill looked at the class and said, "All right get out your English books." The students walked around putting some materials away, getting others out. Bill gave them about five minutes for the transition in activities. "Okay, Joan, please read the directions for the assignment on prefixes." The class quieted down. The students discussed the definition of a prefix and gave examples. "For tomorrow I want you to do page 103." The class got louder when Bill stopped talking about the assignment and returned to his desk.

"Don! Amy!" Bill called out the names of two students who were not working on the English assignment. The students started back to work but the rest of the class got louder. Bill stared at the restless students and said, "Mark, you owe me fifty sentences." Mark was leaning back in his chair and staring out the window. There was a pause, the class became a little quieter. "Mike, you owe me fifty sentences." Mike was talking to a neighbor. The class got very quiet. Bill commented, "I guess you folks like to write sentences."

Source: Ryan, K., et al. (1980). *Biting the apple: Accounts of first-year teachers.* New York: Longman.

falls into this category because he is able, through cases, to describe in detail circumstances that, if presented or viewed in any other way, would lose their emotional power. Of course, one of the criticisms often directed at Kozol and others is that they focus too much on a language of emotion, but even the harshest critics would not likely deny the dramatic power of the message when delivered through the personal account lens. (See Figure 6.5 for a partial listing of some of the popular personal account books.)

Descriptive Research

A third broad category of research that educators might access consists of descriptive research studies. Thus far we discussed experimental/quasi-experimental studies and qualitative (ethnographic) research. With experimental studies researchers are exploring causal questions. With qualitative research the emphasis is on context and meaning. With descriptive research the focus is related to describing a phenomenon, often with data taken from a large database and varied sources (Picciano, 2006). That is, researchers are exploring what is occurring and why (see Lauer, 2006). Descriptive research questions are structured to include this "what and why" element. For example:

1. Do low-performing teachers not have academic majors in the content area they are teaching?
2. Do small high schools evidence higher student performance level for the students who are enrolled?

FIGURE 6.5   Personal Accounts (Selected Examples)

Conrack, by Pat Conroy, describes the author's teaching experiences in the middle grades in the Tidewater, South Carolina, area.

36 Children, by Herbert Kohl, presents a candid description of what it is like for a well-educated (Harvard) man to teach urban black children.

Class Dismissed, by Meredith Maran, describes a year in the life of a U.S. comprehensive high school with white, black, and Latino students.

Savage Inequalities, by Jonathan Kozol, describes several school situations and outlines the physical facility inequalities that exist in some of America's poorest urban neighborhoods.

Teachers Talk, by Estelle Fuchs, is one of the classic texts regarding the experiences of first-year teachers. Fuchs draws on the personal journals of classroom neophytes to capture the reality of beginning teaching.

How Children Fail, by John Holt, is a best-seller in educational circles describing how and why so many students fail.

Tales Out of School, by Patrick Welsh. A teacher at a large, diverse public high school describes what happens inside and outside to track some students to success and others to the future.

There are different types of descriptive studies: simple descriptive, comparative descriptive, and correlational (see Lauer, 2006).

Simple descriptive studies focus on describing a group of persons (teachers, students) or programs. There is no effort to randomly assign subjects (experimental) or to study one or two individuals in considerable depth by recording behaviors or events ethnographically; rather, the focus is on the characteristics of a group (or groups) and then using those findings to potentially apply to other groups with similar characteristics.

Comparative descriptive studies simply "describe and compare the characteristics of two or more groups of participants" (Lauer, 2006, p. 27). For example, in the Teacher Quality Partnership research being conducted in Ohio (see case study at the beginning of Chapter 7), the researchers are administering survey instruments to preservice teachers from each of Ohio's fifty teacher education institutions. Each institution will be categorized by type, and the researchers will be able to identify differences in the data by institutional type. The researchers want to know what different prospective teachers have experienced during their undergraduate education studies in an area such as classroom management. The researchers are now reporting those findings, with the dependent variable being the perceived amount and effectiveness of classroom management instruction. No independent variable is evidenced; that is, the researchers are not varying the amount of classroom management instruction that occurs at each institution; they are simply describing what the preservice teachers are reporting. Recently, one of the co-authors of this text was on a statewide task force to study teacher quality for poor and minority students, and much of the research undertaken by the group was ex post facto comparative descriptive: How does teacher experience (number of years taught) relate to student academic achievement? Does national board certification for teachers relate to student academic performance? That is, the researchers were both describing and comparing the characteristics of groups (Lauer, 2006).

One of the studies examined as part of the task force's (noted above) ex post facto comparative descriptive work was Cavalluzzo's (2004) study regarding whether national board certification effectively signaled teacher quality. Cavalluzzo examined approximately 118,000 student records and then assessed teacher professional characteristics vis-à-vis student achievement in mathematics. Specifically, each student performance record was linked to a set of teacher characteristics and school environment. Questions Cavalluzzo explored included

- Whether the teacher is new or experienced.
- Whether the teacher has regular state certification in high school mathematics or middle school mathematics.
- Whether the teacher holds a teaching position in mathematics or has another primary job assignment.
- Whether the teacher has an advanced degree.
- The selectivity of the teacher's undergraduate school.
- Whether the teacher has National Board Certification (NBC), a pending application, or failed or withdrew from the program. (p. 2)

Cavalluzzo found that students with National Board Certified (NBC) teachers made larger achievement gains than those with teachers who either had failed the NBC process or had decided not to pursue the advanced certification.

One final type of descriptive research consists of *correlational studies*. For example, you might want to know the relationship between the amount and type of reading professional development that teachers have experienced and student reading performance. To make such a determination, the researcher might calculate the relationship between the span of data on both variables, number of hours in phonics or phonemic awareness of professional development, and the student achievement scores.

Notice in all these types of studies the researcher is not assigning subjects to groups and administering some type of treatment (i.e., an experimental study) or describing in-depth the experience of one or two teachers (i.e., an ethnographic study).

All three of these types of research are important to educators. Accessing such research at times will be important if good policy or classroom practice decisions are to occur. In the final section of this chapter, we describe how and when different individuals might use the types of research to make better evidence-based decisions.

To help illustrate the possible uses, we will rely on some of the recent work that has been conducted on small schools, particularly small high schools, and also some of the work on teacher quality. Each illustrates how research could or should be used to inform practice.

Illustration I: As noted earlier, one of the co-authors helped create an urban early college high school. Although he did not use research in precisely the manner outlined below, the following description captures both how a new idea might be explored and how research can be used in the exploration process.

Start with an idea and question. *Idea:* Small schools for urban students. *Question:* Can a small high school in an urban environment enhance the performance of students (graduation rates and enrollment in a postsecondary option) from high-poverty backgrounds?

As the co-author began to explore the small-school concept, he (and others) read several ethnographic studies of small schools. One of those (the Met School in Providence, Rhode Island) received a great deal of national publicity, so he read an in-depth study about its development. He also read other qualitative pieces that describe in considerable detail how high schools either reformed or restructured to better meet the needs of adolescents using personalized approaches (see DiMartino, Clarke, & Wolk, 2003).

Once he had a good feel for what he (and his colleagues) wanted programmatically for the school based on the qualitative studies and texts that were read (and school visits that were made), he and his co-developers began to structure the school. Researchers from Harvard (as part of a *Jobs for the Future* study) conducted a very intensive multiyear qualitative study of the program (see, for example, Wolk, 2005), but that provided information on only one aspect of the program. Other types of data were needed to assess program quality.

Ideally, to really test whether the school evidenced the effectiveness that was hoped for (does its program limit dropouts and enhance student performance?), he needed to use some type of experimental design to randomly assign students to the program and other students to a "control" situation. That was not possible. Unfortunately, because of time and cost, he was not able to develop any type of quasi-experimental design—that is, to match students with a comparison group at another school. Hence, what now exists is a reasonably good description of what he and others are doing but not very good data on the early college's comparative effectiveness.

Notice he was thoughtful in deciding on the model he wanted, but not nearly as vigilant in conducting (or working with others to conduct) quasi-experimental research that would help determine the efficacy of the approach. There are reasonable explanations for the "missed opportunity" but because he failed in ways that parallel lots of other innovative educational designs, he is now limited in what he (or others) can claim about the program's effectiveness.

Illustration II: No issue has sparked more controversy in recent years than how to teach reading. The debate about best practice is often very ideological. The reports issued on how teachers should teach young people to read are abundant in number and varied in terms of conclusions (see Manzo, 2006). There are some salient points of agreement, but an ideological divide often exists, and even where ideological disagreements do not surface, differential understandings about what the research means do emerge. One point of absolute agreement among all the different stakeholder groups is that teachers make a difference. And, if teachers make a difference, then one critical element is how they are trained. That is, what types of professional development experiences do they have at the preservice level to prepare them for the classroom?

To answer this question, the National Council on Teacher Quality (NCTQ; a conservative think tank) decided to explore how education schools taught preservice teachers about the reading instruction process. The NCTQ report (2006) starts with a synthesis of what it argues is the accepted science of teaching reading:

- Early identification of children at risk of reading failure
- Daily training in linguistic and oral skills to build awareness of speech sounds, or phonemes
- Explicit instruction in letter sounds, syllables, and words accompanied by explicit instruction in spelling
- Teaching phonics in the sequence that research has found leads to the least amount of confusion, rather than teaching it in a scattered fashion and only when children encounter difficulty
- Practicing skills to the point of "automaticity" so that children do not have to think about sounding out a word when they need to focus on meaning
- Concurrently with all of the above, building comprehension skills and vocabulary knowledge through reading aloud, discussing, and writing about quality children's literature and nonfiction topics

■ Frequent assessment and instructional adjustments to make sure children are making progress. (p. 102)

The authors of the report then randomly selected a sample of 72 elementary education programs from among the 1,271 higher-education institutions in the United States. The NCTQ research represents an example of a *descriptive research* study. That is, the researchers simply describe (based on the sample) the characteristics of the preparation programs. Here are selected NCTQ findings:

■ Almost all of the sampled syllabi received a failing grade in terms of teaching research-based practices.
■ Only 15 percent of the sampled programs taught all components of the science of reading (and 23 percent taught none of the science of reading approaches).
■ Accredited institutions are no more likely to teach the science of reading than nonaccredited programs.
■ Teacher educators appear resistant to teaching the science of reading.

Based on these findings, the NCTQ authors proffered some recommendations for states, membership organizations, textbook publishers, the federal government, and education schools. For example, for states NCTQ (2006) recommends the development of strong reading standards and licensure tests based on those standards. For education schools they recommend, not surprisingly, that faculty expertise in the area of reading be enhanced.

Notice that based on this descriptive research, the NCTQ develops policy recommendations for a wide variety of stakeholder groups. This is not surprising because, in general, the purpose of descriptive research is to inform policy decisions (see Lauer, 2006).

The problem with descriptive research, however, is that readers need to be critical consumers of the research findings and of how those findings were developed. Specifically, who conducted the research, what assumptions are they making, and do they have ideological biases that may influence their findings? We are *not* suggesting that just because a group is ideological (conservative or liberal), its research should be ignored. Indeed, we encourage administrators to be consumers of all types of research reports. However, it is important for readers to know that the biases researchers possess may influence the conclusions they reach.

As an example, the NCTQ is historically hypercritical of education schools. They, like others such as the Fordham Foundation, have argued for alternative teacher licensure systems and an end to the education school licensure monopoly. In conducting their reading study, they drew a sample from across the United States (a random sample) that did not include Ohio, a state that has *very* heavy reading requirements (including mandatory phonics content) for preservice teachers. We are not suggesting they intentionally skewed the "random" sample and excluded Ohio. We are suggesting that if another pro-education school group had conducted the research, it might have ensured through a stratified sample (i.e., stratified by states) that strong-reading-requirement states would be included.

Using the Research

We conclude this chapter by briefly discussing how different groups/individuals might use the different types of research to ensure better evidence-based decision making.

Teachers and administrators will find descriptive research to be interesting but often not especially helpful to the specific classroom problems they confront. On the other hand, it is enormously complicated for teachers to interpret much of the experimental and quasi-experimental research because of the sophistication required to interpret study results. What is not appropriate is for a teacher to reach a conclusion on what to do instructionally based on one research study.

Teachers and administrators who are using research to make data-assisted decisions should consider the following:

1. Access, when possible, qualitative research on the topic that provides thick, rich narrative descriptions of how teachers are using a particular "instructional treatment."
2. Identify research on the "treatment" or approach and determine what, if any, patterns exist in the findings. Further, look for research articles and not just concept papers. If quantitative, the former tests and explores a hypothesis; the latter explains or explores an idea based on the perspectives or views of an author. Both types of articles can be useful but only the research provides an indication as to what impact a particular instructional intervention is making. Concept pieces describe why an intervention is needed or how to use it. The research offers insight into whether an intervention makes a difference.
3. Identify research synthesis manuscripts where experienced researchers have sorted through the research (and assessed its quality) and then identify the patterns and conclusions for practitioners. Slavin (2003) describes this approach:

> In order to judge the research base for a given program, it is not necessary that every teacher, principal, or superintendent carry out his or her own review of the literature. Several reviews applying standards have summarized evidence on various programs.
>
> For comprehensive school reform models, for example, the American Institutes for Research published a review of 24 programs. . . . The Thomas Fordham Foundation. . . . commissioned an evaluation of 10 popular comprehensive school reform models. And [other researchers] . . . carried out a meta-analysis (or quantitative synthesis) of research on 29 comprehensive school reform models. Research reviews facilitate the process of evaluating the evidence behind a broad range of programs, but it's still a good idea to look for a few published studies on a program to get a sense of the nature and

quality of the evidence supporting a given model. Also, we should look at multiple reviews because researchers differ in their review criteria, conclusions, and recommendations. Adopting a program for a single subject, much less for an entire school, requires a great deal of time, money, and work—and can have a profound impact on a school for a long time. Taking time to look at the research evidence with some care before making such an important decision is well worth the effort. Accepting the developer's word for a program's research base is not a responsible strategy. (pp. 15–16)

Some think tanks regularly distribute synthesis pieces (e.g., the Thomas B. Fordham Foundation, Education Trust, the Brookings Institution, and the North Central Regional Educational Laboratory—see www.learningpt.org). Most of the professional associations (e.g., National Science Teachers Association) periodically produce best-practice synthesis papers. Examples are readily available by accessing the websites of any of the professional associations (see Figure 6.6).

Policymakers will find the descriptive research to be especially efficacious, and, indeed, if one carefully examines policymaking around the country, it becomes apparent that legislators are attending closely to the work conducted by groups that specialize in complex descriptive research. One excellent example of this is the work of the Education Trust. The director of the Education Trust, Kati Haycock, is a regular speaker at state-level conferences on topics such as the black-white achievement gap and teacher quality. She uses research findings from descriptive studies to prod policymakers toward practices that will enhance classroom practices and teacher talent. Some examples of her factoids drawn from descriptive studies (see Haycock, 2002–2003) are:

- 30 percent of core academic courses are taught by teachers who lack appropriate certification.
- In low-poverty schools, 17 percent of the teachers lack appropriate certification.

FIGURE 6.6 Professional Associations

Social Studies
From the National Council for the Social Studies: www.ncss.org

Science
From the National Science Teachers Association: www.nsta.org

Mathematics
From the National Council of Teachers of Mathematics: www.nctm.org

English
From the National Council of Teachers of English: www.ncte.org

- In high-minority schools, 28 percent of the teachers lack appropriate core academic certification.
- In low-minority schools, 19 percent lack the certification.

Haycock draws on Sanders and Rivers's (1996) research to show that effective teaching clearly makes a difference, and hence the quality of the teacher is significant. She then illustrates why the No Child Left Behind legislation is an imperative if all students are to be provided with a quality teacher. Haycock proffers the specific provisions for equalization (regardless of socioeconomic or racial status) such as notifying parents when their children are taught by unqualified teachers (the "parents' right to know" requirement) and then "soft" provisions for legislators to consider.

Some of Haycock's "soft" recommendations that are now being considered across the country include

- Bonuses for teachers who teach in high-poverty schools.
- Intensive (and improved) professional development for teachers who work in urban environments.
- Increased assistance for high-poverty students and better support systems and reduced teaching loads for their teachers.

SUMMARY

Using research to inform practice is important. This chapter focused on how the wide variety of educational stakeholders can and should use research to improve what is occurring within schools. And, more and more research is being conducted to inform schooling practices. As an example, the U.S. Department of Education's Institute of Education Sciences has, since 2002, spent almost $41 million on forty-five different (see Viadero, 2006) "cognitive translation projects." Their studies have examined

1. The use of manipulatives in teaching arithmetic skills.
2. The evolution of particular academic skills in young children.
3. The use of "cramming" as a study strategy.

Some of the findings are intriguing and easily applicable. As an example, if you want students to remember material for a long time, what review intervals should be used? The answer: the optimum "ratio for spacing out study sessions: 10 to 20 percent of the interval over which students are expected to recall the information" (Viadero, 2006, p. 13). So, if you want to remember the material well for just one year, then review it about every two to three months.

No one type of research is sufficient to fully understand an educational practice or problem. And fully understanding a problem requires much more than a single research study. All forms of research have some merit, and each type will have utility and power depending on the role or responsibility that a particular individual evidences.

For teachers, administrators, superintendents, and policymakers the one generalization that appears supportable is to read widely and to look for patterns in what a variety of researchers are finding. Truth does not rest with the insights of one researcher; rather truth, where it exists pedagogically, emerges when diverse research strategies begin to yield common findings. One of those common findings that is well documented is that teachers do make a real difference in creating quality learning environments. And, we would argue, teachers who make that difference are individuals who know how to use data (indeed, all types of information) to make informed pedagogical decisions and who are engaged in ongoing professional development that helps them see how to use what they know to inform practice. They are also individuals who through experience know the "feel" of what really works. In Davis's (2007) words: "The findings of published research alone probably won't get you to the promised land . . . trust your gut" (p. 578).

In this chapter we focused on how others collect data and teachers use that data. In the next chapter we focus more specifically on how teachers and administrators collect their own data, often using action research methods, that allow them to determine the value or efficacy of a program they have implemented.

QUESTIONS AND SUGGESTED ACTIVITIES

Case Study Questions

1. The case study that introduces this chapter describes the conflict that occurs when experts disagree about what causes a problem such as the black-white achievement gap. What "next steps" should you take when researchers reach different conclusions about prescriptions for best practice?

2. The conclusions that researchers reach about topics such as the black-white achievement gap are often influenced by the biases they possess prior to conducting the research. How can you better understand what those biases might be?

3. The United States government is now most interested in "gold standard" scientifically based research that includes studies using experimental or quasi-experimental designs. Even assuming the validity of this focus, what are the "limits" for teachers and administrators in doing this type of research with different racial or ethnic groups in public schools?

4. What approach should practicing educators take to make them better consumers of research findings?

Chapter Questions and Activities

5. In this chapter, we draw on the research of Bransford and others to identify program dynamics that need to be considered in any effort to enhance teacher effectiveness and student performance. We identify three dynamics. Identify others that you view as essential, especially for the school context in which you currently work.

6. Educators want students to both know content and to be able to use that content to deal with situated problems. There currently exists a real tension between those who argue for more factual knowledge and those who want enhanced "situated" learning. How would you know if the right balance has been achieved for the students in your school or school district?

7. What are the two different types of theories used in understanding an idea or problem? What theoretical approach do you believe educators favor? Why?

8. Select a problem of practice that you are confronting—something like, for example, how and whether to use inquiry learning in the classroom. Attempt to find both a qualitative (ethnographic-like) and quantitative (experimental) study on inquiry learning. In what ways are the findings of the different studies of use to you? What are the limits to using the findings?

9. Why does NCLB place such a high premium on quantitative research methods?

10. Why are descriptive research findings often of more use to policymakers and of less utility to classroom teachers?

REFERENCES

Bracey, G. W. (2006). *Reading educational research: How to avoid getting statistically snookered.* Portsmouth, NH: Heinemann.

Bransford, J. D., Brown, A. L., & Cocking, R. R. (Eds.). (2000). *How people learn.* Washington, DC: National Academy Press.

Cavalluzzo, L. (2004). *Is national board certification an effective signal of teacher quality?* Alexandria, VA: The CNA Corporation.

Chall, J. S. (2000). *The academic achievement challenge.* New York: Guilford Press.

Chen, J. (2004). Theory of multiple intelligences: Is it a scientific theory? *Teachers College Record, 106*(1), 17–23.

Davis, S. H. (2007). Bridging the gap between research and practice: What's good, what's bad, and how can one be sure. *Phi Delta Kappan, 88*(8), 568–578.

DiMartino, J., Clarke, J., & Wolk, D. (2003). *Personalized learning.* Lanham, MD: Scarecrow Press.

Economic Policy Institute. (2007). *Social class—not school reform—most impacts Black–White achievement gap.* Retrieved March 17, 2007, from www.epinet/newsroom/releases/2004/05/040503 rothsteinPR-final.pdf

Haycock, K. (2002–2003). Toward a fair distribution of teacher talent. *Educational Leadership, 60*(4), 11–15.

Hirsch, E. D., Jr. (2006, April 26). Reading-comprehension skills: What are they really? *Education Week, 25*(33), 52, 42.

Kimmelman, P. L. (2006). *Implementing NCLB.* Thousand Oaks, CA: Corwin Press.

Lancy, D. F. (1993). *Qualitative research in education.* New York: Longman.

Lauer, P. A. (2006). *An education primer.* San Francisco: Jossey Bass.

Manzo, K. K. (2006, January 11). Long-delayed U.S. panel on reading yet to be named. *Education Week, 26*(3), 16–17.

National Council on Teacher Quality. (2006). *What education schools aren't teaching about reading and what elementary teachers aren't learning.* Washington, DC: Author.

Picciano, A. G. (2006). *Data-driven decision making for effective school leadership.* Upper Saddle River, NJ: Pearson Merrill Prentice Hall.

Sanders, W. L., & Rivers, J. C. (1996). *Cumulative and residual effects of teachers on future student academic achievement.* Knoxville: University of Tennessee.

Slavin, R. E. (2003). A reader's guide to scientifically based research. *Educational Leadership, 60*(5), 12–16.

Traub, J. (1998). Multiple intelligence disorder. *The New Republic, 20,* 20–23.

Viadero, D. (2006). Cognition studies offer insights on academic tactics. *Education Week, 26*(1), 12–13.

Willingham, D. (2004). Multiple intelligences: The making of a modern myth. *Education Next, 4*(3), 18–24.

Wolk, R. A. (2005). *It's kind of different: Student experiences in two early college high schools.* Boston: Jobs for the Future.

7 Collecting and Accessing Data

Chapter Focus

Data are now available in the public domain for quite literally every school in the United States. Years ago, parents moving to a new city might inquire of realtors or friends about the quality of the schools in different school districts. That still occurs, but the Internet enables any parent (or any other interested party) to ascertain all types of information about a school or school district through a simple Google search.

This chapter explores all the different data sources that can be accessed and used to collect information about schools. Specific questions to be addressed include:

1. What are the external data sources that are readily available for anyone to access? And what is the difference between direct and nondirect data sources?
2. What internal data collection systems can be used by administrators to better understand how teachers and students are performing?
3. What are the advantages and disadvantages of different direct and indirect teacher and classroom observation systems?
4. What should observers look for as they examine different teacher and student artifacts?
5. When and how should teachers engage in personal action research?

CASE STUDY

All of Ohio's major educational organizations have begun to work together to systematically link teacher performance and student achievement. The initiative, the Teacher Quality Partnership (see www.TQP.org), brings together all fifty Ohio teacher preparation institutions, both major teacher unions (the Ohio Federation of Teachers and the Ohio Education Association), and the Ohio Board of Regents and Ohio Department of Education Association. All are working together to collect data on how teachers are prepared, how they subsequently perform in classrooms, and what impact that preparation has on student progress and achievement.

The Ohio TQP effort is a next-generation research study in education. It represents a new way of thinking systematically about how to assess preparation programs and subsequently restructure those programs in ways that rely more on data and less on ideology. Education has historically been very ideologically driven. Teachers believed in a way of teaching even though they could not necessarily empirically support their approach. Many simply taught the way they were taught. Teacher educators also believed in particular ways of preparing teachers—often with a bias toward student-centered, constructivist approaches. What has been absent have been good data to support what constitutes effective practice.

The TQP effort is oriented toward the systematic collection of data and then the use of that data to inform the way teacher preparation occurs. Ideology will likely always be evidenced in professional practices, but the Ohio model represents an important step toward collecting and distributing real data to guide both how teachers are prepared and how they engage in professional practice once they enter classrooms.

Interestingly, Ohio is not the only state undertaking this type of systematic research. Using a large database for teachers and teacher education institutions, Louisiana researchers were able to identify the fact that certain "selected" teacher preparation institutions did a better job of "abbreviating" the weak learning gains associated with teachers in their first year or two of teaching and were able "to deliver" to Louisiana classrooms teachers who "looked" more like veterans (see Haycock, 2006). Delivering more "experienced" teachers to classrooms is important because of the fact that so many beginning teachers exit teaching by their fifth year (up to 40 percent by some estimates), which means that classrooms are constantly being repopulated with neophytes (a circumstance particularly pronounced in high-poverty schools), and those neophytes are statistically less able to foster the student learning progress engendered by more experienced teachers.

Data Sources: External

There is, at present, no shortage of data about schools. The absent ingredient is often identifying and isolating good data. Within the public domain a wide variety of sources exist that educators can go to if they want to know more about schools and the student achievement at those schools. Unfortunately, public-domain data are also of limited utility. Why? First, the data "out" are only as good as the data "in." That is, unless those entering the data use exactly the same metrics, measures, or procedures, the realities of one school can be quite different from the realities of another, even though the data may look similar. Second, public domain data are often not accessibly user-friendly for educators or parents. Because all 50 states use different tests, measures, and approaches, a real absence of common metrics exists and that void makes it difficult for educators, even psychometrically astute ones, to make good judgments based on published data.

We examine in this chapter how data are acquired and provided through both *direct* and *nondirect* sources. The direct sources are those that are government related and include standard protocols for collecting and organizing data for public consumption. The nondirect entail the involvement of nongovernment 501c3 organizations that operate for the express purpose of disseminating data to parents and other stakeholders about the demographics of schools and the performance of students. That is, some vendors now use public domain data in ways intended to ensure that information about P–12 schools is more accessible to parents and educators. They typically obtain that data from a variety of direct sources.

Direct Sources

Two of the most common and heavily used direct sources are the National Center for Education Statistics and the fifty different state department of education websites.

National Center for Education Statistics (NCES; see www.nces.ed.gov). This federal source is associated with the Institute of Education Sciences (www.ies.ed.gov), United States Department of Education. It offers a wide variety of hardcopy and electronic information about schools. A quick search of the NCES website illustrates the breadth of the data available on P–12 schools (public and private), colleges, universities, and libraries.

The NCES site is easy to use and provides basic information about schools and student performance. For example, one of the authors accessed the site and simply typed in the school name, school district name, and state for the first school he taught in over thirty years ago. In addition to basic information about the school (e.g., mailing address and phone), the NCES site also provided the total number of students, classroom teachers (FTE), and student/teacher ratio. It indicated the school's type (a public school) and whether it was a Title I school. Finally, it provided data on enrollment by grade, ethnicity and gender.

The problem with the NCES data site is that it provides only a superficial view of a school, consisting largely of basic demographic data and the data are often a year or two old, with finance data typically almost three years old (see Education Gadfly, 2006). Still, the data offer a demographic snapshot of what teacher and student populations look like.

Some of the NCES publications also provide thoughtful data analysis. For example, *Education Statistics Quarterly* (an NCES publication) provides not only extensive data but also descriptions of particular educational problems and a synthesis of some of the conclusions that can be drawn from the extant national data. The annual *Conditions of Education* report (COE) provides a statistical portrait of education in the United States. It is especially helpful in understanding issues such as student academic achievement (particularly with international comparisons) and national enrollment and demographic trends.

NCES publications are free (hard copy and electronic) and usually very current (though often based on somewhat dated data). Examples include the *Nation's Report Card* and the *Digest of Education Statistics.*

The *Nation's Report Card* provides a compilation of the results from the National Assessment of Education Progress (NAEP). Though not all students in all states are currently tested, the passage of the No Child Left Behind legislation will eventually require that all states participate in NAEP testing.

The *Digest of Education Statistics* provides a summary of educational data in the United States. It typically covers a wide range of topics vis-à-vis elementary, secondary, and postsecondary education (see Brendon, 2003). Many educational researchers rely on the NCES data and especially the prodigious compilation of data tables they provide covering a wide range of topics relevant to P–12 educational practices.

NCES also issues periodic reports on topics of special interest. On the date this section was written two such reports focused on "Fathers of U.S. Children born in 2001" (which consisted of findings from an early childhood longitudinal study) and "The Postsecondary Experiences of High School Career and Technical Education Concentrators" (which provided examples of the types of schools attended and courses taken by graduates).

State Departments of Education.   Most, if not all, state departments of education have websites with substantial data about schools. A simple Internet search of any state's department of education will indicate how much data are available. Clearly, some states have better (more user-friendly and comprehensive) websites than others, and just as understandably those sites are constantly being restructured. Some are simply more accessible to parents. Two of the stronger sites, at least from the authors' view and on the date when this chapter was written, were Florida and Colorado. (Quite obviously, all states are constantly restructuring their websites.)

The Florida site is organized around data for students, parents, and educators. Hence, a student who is interested in a college degree can readily access information about particular institutions and programs, including current tuition and fees. Or educators who want information on teacher qualifications or adequate yearly progress data can see what is expected (e.g., all schools must demonstrate a 1 percent improvement in the percentage of students proficient in writing, and high schools must also demonstrate a 1 percent improvement in graduation rates). If you access the Florida site you can see for virtually every school the most recent AYP school level report. An example for one school (Alachua, A. L. Mebane Middle School) is provided in Figure 7.1.

The Colorado site is not quite as user-friendly but, like Florida's, contains a myriad of data about both public and private schools, and it also enables users to access some of the nondirect web resources such as Private School Review (described below).

Nondirect Sources

Greatschools.net and the Private School Review are examples of two nonprofits that convert public domain data to a format for parents and other significant stakeholders.

Greatschools.   Greatschools.net has information (using public domain data) on virtually every school in the United States. If you go to the Greatschools.net web-

FIGURE 7.1   2005 Adequate Yearly Progress (AYP) Report—School Level, *Alachua, A. L. Mebane Middle School (0221)*

Did the School Make Adequate Yearly Progress?	Provisional	Percent of Criteria Met: 83%	
Total Writing Proficiency Met:	YES	2005 School Grade:	B
Total Graduation Criterion Met:	NA		
	95% Tested	Reading Proficiency Met	Math Proficiency Met
Total	YES	YES	YES
White	YES	YES	YES
African American	YES	NO	NO
Hispanic	NA	NA	NA
Asian	NA	NA	NA
American Indian	NA	NA	NA
Economically Disadvantaged	YES	NO	YES
Limited English Proficiency	NA	NA	NA
Students with Disabilities	YES	NO	NO

Source: Florida Department of Education, www.web.fldoe.org/nclb/default.cfm?action=report1&school=0221&level=school&district=1

site you can see the comprehensive nature of the available data. For example, on the day this chapter was being written, one of the authors learned that his daughter was moving to Noblesville, Indiana. Going to the Greatschools.net website, he was able to identify basic school information on each of the Noblesville schools, which included test scores, teacher statistics (i.e., students per FTE teacher), student demographics (for the school in comparison to state averages), and principals' and parents' views about the educational programs at the different Noblesville schools.

Not only is Greatschools focused on the dissemination of data electronically, but it also relies on some personal (face-to-face) contacts. In projects underway in both San Francisco and Dayton, Ohio, Greatschools has created hotline approaches that enable parents within urban settings to contact "experts" who can help them make sense of the accumulated school-based data. They also sponsor, in cooperation with local educational vendors, enrollment fairs that assist parents in understanding how different schools are performing.

The nondirect sources are becoming especially important as school choice initiatives become more prevalent. Indeed, Greatschools's mission explicitly states that it is "committed to providing parents with information and tools to choose schools, support their children's education, and improve schools in their communities." Parents are provided with information (electronic and hard copy) that allows them to assess their child's school and then to use that data/information comparatively to determine what other school options might be appropriate to consider.

Education, especially in urban settings, is moving toward enhanced choice. The voucher initiatives now prevalent across the country focus on helping parents use data to make informed decisions about where their children can receive the best educational opportunity. The twentieth-century model of education focused on making P–12 schools available to all children. (A 1925 Supreme Court decision made school attendance compulsory, but students could not be required to attend a public school.) The twenty-first-century schools are not only available but increasingly are being organized to provide parents with a variety of private and public choices. Even parents in remote, rural areas are increasingly able to utilize virtual options if they do not like locally available face-to-face educational offerings. And as parents become better informed and more critical consumers, they will exercise choices in ways that hopefully benefit their children. The complexities of exercising choice are exacerbated by the realities of poor information and misinformation. Teske, Wolf, and Hill (2006) describe the problem of the misinformation often proffered to parents:

> Opponents [of choice] often send the message that "these options are not real, don't trust them," or "they say the options are free, but someday you will have to pay the money back." School districts [and we suggest others] also hide the existence of options required by the federal No Child Left Behind law. Again, grassroots information, from trusted neighborhood sources like other parents and ministers, is necessary to make real choice for low-income families. (p. 44)

The Greatschools site gives parents an opportunity to provide reviews (on a five-star scale) about the school their child attends. They are permitted to provide any comments about a school's educational programming, though all entries are read and evaluated by Greatschools using defined criteria for acceptability. Negative reviews that are inflammatory or that mention a specific teacher are not permitted.

Private School Review.   Privateschoolreview.com provides readers (especially parents) with access to information on private schools throughout the country. Parents who access the site simply enter their zip code and then indicate the distance they are willing to travel to secure a school for their children. They can also identify specific characteristics of the school such as whether they prefer co-ed, all girls, or all boys.

Once a particular school is identified, the site then provides information on school level (grade levels at the school), religious affiliation, total students, student body type, percentage of students of color, and even the number of students at each grade level. The number of teachers as well as the teacher-to-student ratio are offered along with broader demographic information/population of the community (in that zip code) percentage with college degrees, average age of population, average household size and median income, and the median housing unit costs.

Information from Private School Review assists parents as they make choices regarding which schools best meet their child's personal and educational needs. Such information, now readily available with the click of a mouse, illustrates the flat educational world that is emerging. Vast amounts of data are now available for parents to assist them as they make school choices. Administrators even a decade ago did not have to be overly concerned about how their school "looked" because there was limited data transparency and few educational options that parents could exercise if they did not value the programs at a local school. That situation has changed. Through direct and nondirect sources (Private School Review and Greatschools), parents have access to lots of data, and administrators, though they should not be driven by such data, need to be aware of how parents are beginning to use data to make decisions about where to live and how to educate their children.

One other type of nondirect source emerging in some states consists of sites especially established to assist educational leaders. An example of that is the Ohio School Leaders Community of Practice (see www.ohioschoolleaders.org). In addition to information on current research and policy issues (e.g., high school transformation efforts and voucher plans), the site also provides a data tool to assist educational leaders in quickly assessing how their school (or any school in the state) measures up.

By typing in the name of any Ohio school, those conducting a search can first see the "performance designation" given to the school (excellent, effective, continuous improvement, emergency), which provides information on state indicators met and the state's performance index rating. In terms of federal requirements, the site indicates whether adequate yearly progress (AYP) was or was not met, which provides an indication of the achievement levels for all students in a school. Further, it provides more detail on AYP for each school for all students and all student subgroup populations. It also explains in detail the "safe harbor" provisions (i.e., schools that are unable to make AYP but are still able to reduce by 10 percent the number of nonproficient students in any single subgroup during a specific year) (see Kimmelman, 2006).

Most importantly, perhaps, the "tool" provides some suggestions (specifically oriented to each school) for school leaders to explore as they plan for ways to enhance school improvement. Such data and resources assist school leaders as they think critically about both current student performance and future school-based efforts to enhance that performance.

Data Sources: Internal

As you examine the emerging enormous database for schools, it becomes apparent that both qualitative and quantitative data forms are being used to represent the reality of selected school practices. Though most of the direct and nondirect sources described above emphasize quantitative measures and are externally derived (test scores, teacher student ratios), it is also apparent that quantitative and qualitative sources are being developed by administrators and teachers to provide richer descriptions of the pedagogical practices within schools.

During the past decade or so there have been "paradigm battles" over the efficacy of how best to collect data vis-à-vis research problems. Researchers tend to fall into one of two camps: qualitative or quantitative. In actuality, both forms have merit and utility. As Picciano (2006) suggests, "If we accept [that] . . . data-driven decision making [is] . . . using data analysis to inform educators in determining courses of action involving policy and procedures, then it is obvious that data in any form is appropriate for informing decision makers" (p. 42).

Outlined in Figure 7.2 are the different data collection tools, data analysis tools, reporting formats, and research methods associated with both qualitative and quantitative methods. (As administrators and teachers examine the approaches, they need to realize that the process of using data to make decisions is different from the process of collecting data through educational research—see Chapter 6.) In the latter, the focus is on formulating a hypothesis and testing it to draw conclusions. In the former, educators are asking a question and then collecting existing, relevant data that will assist in answering the question (see Picciano, 2006).

Data-driven decision making requires stating a problem or question. It necessitates an understanding of what data sources to use (or create) to answer the question. Earlier we discussed some of the external (federal and state) direct and nondirect data sources that already exist and that could be used to inform educational choices. We now turn to the process of collecting new data *in situ*. How can it be done given the multiple time demands confronting administrators and what

FIGURE 7.2   Qualitative versus Quantitative Methods

	Qualitative	Quantitative
Data collection tools	Direct observation Document analysis	Surveys Testing
Data analysis tools	Review of field notes Discussion among team members	Statistical analysis
Reporting format	Rich textual descriptions	Interpretations of results Frequency distributions Contingency tables Statistical charts and displays
Research methods	Ethnography Case study Action research	Correlation Experimental Action research

Source: Adapted from Picciano (2006), p. 42.

approaches make sense? As noted earlier, administrators (similar to educational researchers) will collect or have access to two different types of data: qualitative and quantitative. Each has value; each has defined limitations. Some of that data, regardless of type, will be about teacher performance and behaviors. Other data relate to student achievement: How much student learning is occurring in a teacher's classroom? In this section we focus on the ways that administrators can collect different types of data about teachers, and in the final section we examine how teachers can collect data on their own about problems of practice that they are confronting. In essence, even though there is a lot of data "out there," a need still exists for administrators to collect data unique to their needs.

Direct Observation and Analysis

Administrators who observe teachers often *look* at classrooms but do not appreciate or recognize what is important. They look but actually do not see. A quick examination of a classroom may yield speculation about a teacher's performance, but in order to confirm or negate such speculation, an administrator must examine classroom practices in detail. Erikson (1986) noted that without deliberative analysis of what is occurring in a classroom, several problems associated with "evidentiary inadequacy" occur. Specifically:

1. The observer simply has too little evidence to draw any meaningful conclusions.
2. The observer draws only one type of evidence and hence may not comprehensively understand either the problem or what was observed.
3. The observer fails to observe long enough to assimilate the "key aspects of the complexity of action . . . in the setting" (p. 140).

That is, if an administrator observes *any* teacher for 5 minutes (the "right" 5 minutes), that teacher can look very good or very bad. Clearly, an administrator who is observing a teacher must strive to collect evidence from different sources, using varied methods, and do so for a sufficient time period to ensure that what was observed represents the reality of what actually occurred. In the words of Berliner (1976), the administrator must know "when and where to observe" (p. 8).

In direct observation, observers use either quantitative or qualitative approaches. With quantitative direct observation the observer is selecting a particular teacher behavior or action (or student behavior) and narrowly examining it. Indeed, many quantitative observation instruments are very low inference (i.e., two persons observing the same action would reach the same conclusion about the observed teacher behaviors). Figure 7.3 provides an example of a low-inference observation form on teacher questioning and student participation. Notice that there is very little inferencing (or guessing) required of the observer. That is, it is reasonably clear as to who is called on, and it is also reasonably clear as to whether the respondent was a volunteer (student raised hand to respond) or nonvolunteer (student did not raise hand).

Observation instruments can be structured in many different ways. Some "sign" instruments simply register whether a behavior occurs in the classroom (i.e., did the teacher call on nonvolunteers or ask higher-level questions). One of the tables that appears later in this chapter on "selected response instruments" would be illustrative of a sign instrument. Figure 7.3 is a sign instrument that also

FIGURE 7.3 Student Rotation Participation Checklist

Which students participate in a discussion conducted by a teacher? To determine the answer, an observer should draw a diagram of the classroom and then create a square for each male and circle to represent each female student in the classroom (see below). Observe the teacher as he or she conducts a recitation and place a checkmark (√) on the desk of each student called on during the lesson. Place a slash through the checkmark (√) if the student called on is a nonvolunteer (i.e., does not raise his or her hand, but is called on by the teacher without volunteering).

At the end of the observation period, the observer will know who is being called on and who is being excluded. What pattern emerges? Can the pattern be explained? What does the research suggest about who is called on? When should nonvolunteers be called on as opposed to volunteers?

Observers can also indicate, at least to some degree, the race of students with W–White, B–Black, A–Asian, H–Hispanic, and O–Other. What patterns emerge in terms of the students called on to participate? Are students of color disproportionately excluded? Included? Does it appear as though seat location is a factor in terms of student race/ethnicity?

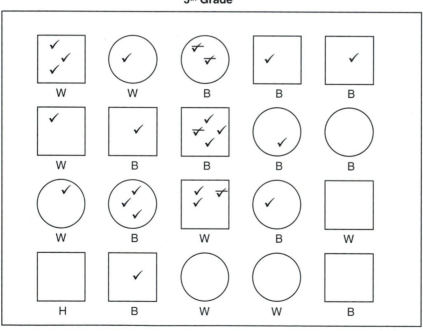

Mrs. Williams's Classroom
5th Grade

registers the frequency of the observed behavior (i.e., How many nonvolunteers were called on? or How many higher-level questions were asked?). Rating instruments enable the observer to assess the degree to which something (a behavior) occurs (e.g., if an observer were to assess a teacher's movement around the classroom, a five-point scale could be established with a "1" of *never moves* to a "5" of *constantly moves*) (see Borich, 1999). Sign and rating instruments are two of the most commonly used to collect more quantifiable data.

With evidence the observer can then analyze what was observed, professionally share the findings with the teacher who has been observed, and compare what has been observed with what extant research has established as Best Practice. For example, research suggests that boys typically have many more interactions with teachers than do girls, and though some of the interactional differences are due to behavior (i.e., boys tend to act out more than girls), it is still clear that the added attention may result in enhanced benefits in areas such as science, especially at the older grade levels (see Streitmatter, 1994).

Provided at the end of this chapter are a couple of suggested resources that include instruments that can be used to conduct direct observations and the available research that can be used to "inform" the data emerging from such observations. Evidence-based decision making requires that administrators both collect data and know how to interpret what those data mean—and the latter requires a better awareness of both established and emerging research findings. For example, a reasonable amount of research exists to support the following pedagogical generalizations about teachers in terms of providing feedback to students in order to enhance academic achievement (see Marzano, Pickering, & Pollock, 2001):

1. Feedback should be corrective in nature (i.e., is specific in terms of what a student is doing that is correct or incorrect).
2. Feedback should be timely (i.e., is provided soon after student performance).
3. Feedback should be specific to a criterion (pp. 96–99).

Using these three generalizations the authors developed a high inference observation form (see Figure 7.4). High inference items require more observer judgment and must, necessarily, be used with more caution when reaching conclusions about a teacher's performance.

The point is that classroom observations should be purposeful and focused. For example, beginning teachers in some states are assessed using the Educational Testing Service (ETS) PRAXIS III observational instrument. Though it is debatable how much research grounds this instrument, it is an example of using an instrument in a focused way to examine specific teacher behaviors (e.g., teacher planning and preparation, classroom environment, instruction, and professional responsibilities).

Whenever possible, the observer should rely on supportable research evidence, not intuitive judgments, to dictate what constitutes good teaching. It is intuitively logical to assume that good teachers are warm and caring. Supporting this with research, especially context appropriate research, is more difficult to

FIGURE 7.4   Teacher Feedback Form

Observe a teacher on at least three occasions as he or she teaches a specific skill to the students such as long division or solving radical equations. Based on those three observations, respond to the following statements.

	Almost never			Almost always	
1. The teacher tells students when they perform a skill/process correctly.	1	2	3	4	5
2. The teacher identifies specific ways in which students are not performing a skill correctly.	1	2	3	4	5
3. The teacher provides prompt feedback regarding student performance.	1	2	3	4	5
4. The teacher ensures that students know specifically what they are supposed to be able to do in terms of using a skill.	1	2	3	4	5
5. The teacher returns student work promptly with corrective feedback.	1	2	3	4	5

accomplish. Davis (2007) articulates what he perceives as issues connected to "context" transfers of research findings:

> Practitioners often presume that because an empirically supported principle of human behavior or learning or an innovative program or practice seems to work in one setting or context, it will apply just as well in different settings. . . . For example, will a reading program that works well for a certain group of inner-city minority students elicit comparative levels of growth for minority students in middle-income suburban settings? Will a successful approach to developing English language skills with immigrant Asian children from developed countries work equally well with immigrant Hispanic children from developing countries . . . ?
>
> The answer to these and many other questions like them is, "Sometimes yes, and sometimes no." However, one thing is certain: just because an empirically supported practice works well in one context doesn't mean that it will work well in other contexts. (p. 576)

Administrators and teachers must become critical consumers of research: Are the findings from research or scholarship that is accessed the result of conceptual exploration regarding pedagogy, or are they the result of rigorous research utilizing experimental designs? Have the research findings emerged from multiple contexts, or are the conclusions idiosyncratic to one setting? Few studies of the experimental type occur in education in multiple settings, and this circumstance limits the number of research findings that necessarily should and do ground and guide comprehensive pedagogical practices.

Qualitative observations can be made using either *anecdotal reports* or *ethnographic records* (see Borich, 1999). With anecdotal reports, the observer describes in particular detail some "critical incident" (e.g., a student refusing to do an assignment) that occurred in the classroom. Using a narrative approach the observer provides as much descriptive detail as possible and attempts to ensure that the facts are outlined and interpretations about those facts are clearly separated. What are the facts? How might those facts be interpreted?

With an ethnographic record, on the other hand, the observer, argues Borich (1999), generates a "report [of] events sequentially, as they occur, without selecting a specific focus or incident" (p. 45). With anecdotal reports there is exclusive focus on one incident, and with the ethnographic approach events are documented as they occur. Ethnographic (qualitative) models enable the observer to better understand an event because the surrounding contextualizing events are described. On the other hand, because the sequence is documented, the observer necessarily pays less attention to all the details, which are available in anecdotal reports.

Direct observation is one method for collecting quantitative or qualitative data about teacher performance, but relying on it exclusively is highly problematic. As a result, many administrators also examine the artifactual materials developed by and for teachers.

Indirect Observation and Analysis

Teacher performance reflects what the teacher is actually doing in a classroom. Much more problematic to ascertain is *why* the teacher is doing what he or she does while teaching. Understanding the *what* requires contemplating the *why* and the why requires that a principal or teacher look beyond the surface teacher behaviors. In the previous section, we discussed focusing on what teachers actually do while teaching: What specific behaviors do they evidence? In this section we explore why they act as they do. Some of those actions require that an observer examine the documents that the teachers rely upon to shape instruction (the curriculum) and the artifacts that result from instruction (student work).

Identifying Learning Targets

We assume that every school district possesses a course of study and curriculum and that it is matched (or aligned) to state academic content standards and testing requirements. This is a problematic assumption, but a sufficient number of districts are or should be structured in this way across all the states to warrant the assumption's validity for future practice. At the time this chapter was written the American Federation of Teachers noted that only eleven states evidence strong academic standards tied to aligned grade-level tests (California, Indiana, Illinois, Nevada, New Mexico, New York, Ohio, Tennessee, Virginia, Washington, and

West Virginia). Such alignment is essential to the ability of students to perform well on state-mandated high-stakes tests.

With such alignment, teachers and administrators can explore the following questions and examine documents to ensure that appropriate answers exist for each question. We rely heavily on the work of Gregory and Kuzmich (2004) to shape the material we present. Specifically, three key questions are suggestive of what you might explore in examining a teacher's instructional practice:

1. Are specific learning targets for each unit of study defined and outlined, and have teachers been selective in identifying those targets?
2. What specific content must students know and be able to demonstrate?
3. Are appropriate assessments created to determine if students learned what they needed to learn?

Learning targets require that teachers do much more than simply know the content standards for their state or the national standards for the discipline they teach (see Figure 7.5). Teachers also make professional decisions about the power standards they want to emphasize during the instructional process. Power standards are those content understandings/skills that require primary *focus*. A review of the academic content standards for any state suggests that there is literally too much content for most students to learn well. Teachers need to make choices, and what administrators need to examine (and critically reflect on) are the learning target choices that teachers make.

Examples of power standards are available online (see www.making standardswork.com). Examples of math power standards are provided on the Center for Performance Assessment website (www.makingstandardswork.com). For example, for sixth-grade mathematics, power standards might include "number of operations with and without a calculator" or "measurement in English and metric units" (see www.makingstandardswork.com/clients/q_and_htm#SECT9). With such power standards the teacher ensures what every student will know and administrators can determine if teachers are being selective about what is taught and if their lesson plans reflect the power standards' points of emphasis. Actually, the National Council of Teachers of Mathematics (NCTM) has now created what it describes as grade-level Curriculum Focal Points (CFPs). These focal points (though somewhat controversial) are intended to specify the mathematical content that students need in order to be successful in dealing with more advanced mathematical topics. They provide state and local leaders with ways to critically examine whether what is emphasized matches with what students really need *and* they are a step toward ensuring that mathematical content depth is assured (see www.NCTM.org).

As teachers define learning targets and power standards (and use approaches such as CFPs), they should consider and make decisions regarding the use of the different categories of targets that exist: knowledge, reasoning, skill, and product (see Chappuis & Chappuis, 2002). The choices the teachers make

FIGURE 7.5   National Standards for Selected Disciplines

Art

From the Consortium of National Arts Education Associations:
www.artsedge.kennedy_center.org/professional_resources/standards/nat_standards/index.html

Social Studies

From the National Council for the Social Studies: www.ncss.org/standards/stitle.html

From the National Center for History in the Schools, UCLA:
www.sscnet.ucla.edu/nchs/standards/

Science

From the National Science Teachers Association:
www.nap.edu/books/0309053269/html/index.html

Mathematics

From the National Council of Teachers of Mathematics:
www.nctm.org/standards/

English

From the National Council of Teachers of English:
www.ncte.org/standards/

Music

From the National Association for Music Education:
www.menc.org/publication/books/standards.htm

Foreign Language

From the American Council on the Teaching of Foreign Languages:
www.actfl.org/public/articles/details.cfm?id=33

about the content to be taught, coupled with the time committed to ensuring students have exposure to requisite content, will influence student achievement.

Knowledge targets are those basic understandings that ground each of the subjects taught in school (i.e., math, science, history). A student, for example, needs to know how to construct a paragraph, spell words properly, and structure a sentence with a subject and verb. Knowledge targets are those basics that every student should know and be able to recall from memory.

Reasoning targets include the ability of students to use what they know to solve the different kinds of problems that they experience and confront. Reasoning targets require that students compare and evaluate information in order to reach logical and thoughtful conclusions. A student does not reason without facts or knowledge. The knowledge targets provide the grounding so that students can use what they know to make appropriate critical applications.

Skill targets require knowledge that enables a student to perform with automaticity. A student who can read with oral fluency or manipulate lab equipment effortlessly is skilled. Chappuis and Chappuis (2002) describe this knowledge-reasoning-skill progression in reading: "In reading students must learn how to read certain words by sight (knowledge), how to generalize from specific instances to a broader context (reasoning), and also how to read aloud with expression (a skill)" (p. 50).

Product targets are the tangible outcomes of the learning process. A student might prepare a written review or create a science project. In math he or she might develop a graph that uses knowledge about precipitation levels to document how global warming is cyclical. Or the student might create an original essay that discusses how globalization and modernity are contributing to and exacerbating the cycles of global warming. In essence, the product targets are what teachers and others read or review as a result of the students' overall learning.

Without clear learning targets it is difficult (if not impossible) to determine where instruction should occur and to assess what students have learned. The learning targets also foreshadow (and should be aligned with) the assessment process. That is, once a teacher knows the content that is being or has been taught, it logically follows how that learning might best be assessed. The teacher is the *key*. The teacher needs to identify both what must be learned and then assess whether it was learned.

Unfortunately, far too many teachers rely on textbooks to dictate the curriculum. This is a mistake. First, textbooks often do not match well with state academic standards. True, textbook publishers are getting better at creating matches, but equally true is the fact that in far too many states a real disconnect exists between approved textbooks and defined academic standards. Further, the textbooks make little or no effort to identify power standards. That is something accomplished on the local level by the teacher (or a group of teachers).

A second problem with textbooks is the significant unevenness that exists in their quality (i.e., in terms of accuracy of information and selection of supporting material). Ravitch (2004) rated a number of different history textbooks and clearly describes how important it is for states (and teachers) to be more directly involved in the process of establishing what academic content will be learned and then assuring that alignment exists in the presentation of that content. She writes:

> The present system of statewide textbook purchasing has warped the writing, editing, and production of textbooks. *It should be abolished.* States like California, Texas, and a score of others should not dictate the content of textbooks through their power to pre-select books en masse for almost all pupils in their state's public schools. This power is too easily compromised by pressure groups and by bureaucratic demands. The states should set their academic standards, align their tests to those standards, and leave teachers free to select the books, anthologies, histories, biographies, software and other materials that will help students meet the standards. (p. 65)

The content students are to learn is defined in the district's written curriculum. That document should clearly define the various learning targets and the available resources to help teachers ensure those targets are met. In essence, what happens in a classroom should match what is defined in the district's curriculum, and that curriculum should, in turn, be aligned with the state's academic content standards. This alignment process is clearly articulated by Chappuis and Chappuis (2002), but it also is important to note, as they do as well, that with alignment comes enhanced student achievement.

> When classroom assessments match the district curriculum, when the district curriculum is aligned to the state content standards, and the large-scale summative assessments used for accountability purposes have been selected or designed to match those same content standards, our schools are testing and reporting progress on what they are teaching. Research repeatedly shows that, when teachers map out their instruction using a well-written curriculum, and then choose teaching materials and lessons that address the specific learning targets, student achievement increases. (p. 56)

With clear learning targets and appropriate content resources, it is now possible to examine the efficacy of the assessments being used by the teacher. Evidenced-based instructional decision making entails using information about what students have learned to then determine *how* instruction should proceed with assigned students.

Creating Learning Assessments

Examining the outcomes of student learning requires an understanding of the structure of the assessment process. Thus far we have discussed how important it is for clear learning targets to be established. Once teachers have those targets in place (the *what* to be learned), they can then identify appropriate assessment methods (the *how* of whether the content was learned). Chappuis and Chappuis (2002) identify four different types of teacher-made assessments: selected response, essay, performance assessment, and personal communication.

Each of these has a different purpose and teachers must decide how much data to collect in order to be confident that students have learned what was taught. Just as good data analysis always begins with a cogent question, so, too, good observation of how teachers are using assessments must begin with a question: *Is the method for collecting information about student learning both most suitable and sufficiently adequate to assess whether students know what has been taught?*

Selected Responses

Selected response tests require that students select an answer from among several defined options. True-false, matching, multiple-choice, and fill-in-the-blank are examples of selected response. These types of assessments appear easy to construct, but there are a variety of ways in which each approach can be compromised if not done correctly, a circumstance that is quite likely given the fact that many practicing teachers have never had any type of assessment course in their teacher preparation program.

Figure 7.6 provides an example of sample questions that an administrator (or teacher) might ask in reviewing the selected response assessments that a teacher uses in classroom student performance. More extensive reviews of teacher-made assessments should occur (and concomitant professional development) if prob-

FIGURE 7.6   Sample Questions to Ask in Assessing Various Selected Response Instruments

	Yes	No
True–False		
1. Is each item clear in meaning and without ambiguity?	___	___
2. Does each item avoid the use of unnecessary clauses that convolute meaning?	___	___
3. Is complex vocabulary avoided?	___	___
4. Does each item avoid the use of double negations?	___	___
Matching		
1. Are the lists of premises and responses homogeneous (composed of similar elements)?	___	___
2. Are more responses than premises provided?	___	___
3. Are the items (premises and responses) logically ordered?	___	___
4. Are the directions for how the items are to be matched clear?	___	___
Multiple Choice		
1. Does the stem have a self-contained question?	___	___
2. Is each distractor/alternative reasonable and plausible?	___	___
3. Are negatively worded stems avoided?	___	___
4. Is the stem written to include essential information?	___	___
Completion		
1. Is there only one correct answer that can be used?	___	___
2. Is the fill-in-the-blank plausible so that a knowledgeable student can respond?	___	___
3. Is only one fill-in provided for each item?	___	___
4. Are the answers for completion items specific (objective) rather than general (subjective)?	___	___

lems are apparent in the tests that a teacher uses (i.e., teachers are having difficulty assessing levels of student academic growth).

Essay Questions

Essay questions are a means of assessing both student knowledge and reasoning abilities (Chappuis & Chappuis, 2002). Teachers need to ensure that essay questions are both clearly defined and appropriately scored. The former requires that a teacher provide sufficient detail regarding an intended response so a student understands what is expected. The latter requires that teachers create rubrics for assessing student responses.

Students may structure their responses in different ways, but each response should share certain identifiable characteristics. Rubrics assist the teacher in ensuring that the required elements are evident. Teachers use either analytical or holistic rubrics in scoring essays. Analytical rubrics require a more explicit scoring guide. Popham (2006a) describes the process:

> In an analytic scoring approach, a student's response is assigned a given number of points on each evaluative criterion separately. For example, suppose in a government class the teacher had created an essay question for which the ideal response focuses on four distinct problems in a current political crisis. The teacher develops a rubric that gives students up to five points for each of these four problems, that is, twenty points for a perfect response. For each of the four problems, the teacher assigns one point if the student's response mentions the problem, one or two additional points if the problem is well described, and one or two more points if the problem's possible solution is described. (p. 226)

Holistic rubrics are simpler to use. A teacher reads a student's response and then provides a single overall assessment. Holistic rubrics are easier to use in terms of time, but they provide far less detailed feedback in terms of the ways in which a student's response may have been deficient.

Performance Assessment

Performance assessments enable students to use reasoning and performance skills to create some type of demonstrable product. A student who gives an oral exhibition regarding some topic or who creates a science fair exhibit is completing a performance assessment.

Teachers will typically grade or evaluate a performance assessment by judging the content the student presents, assessing how that content is organized, evaluating the actual delivery of the information (i.e., does the student have appropriate eye contact with the audience?), and assessing the efficacy of the language the student uses (Chappuis & Chappuis, 2002). Some teachers develop their own rubrics for performance assessments, but electronic rubrics for performance assessment are also available (see http://4teachers.org).

Personal Communication

Personal communication is a fourth way to assess student knowledge. One-on-one discussions between teacher and student constitute an efficient and effective way of directly assessing what a student knows and how well he or she knows it.

Obviously, no observer can make an adequate assessment of a teacher's use of any (or all) of these methods based on just one or two classroom visits. Evidence-based decision making requires that an observer make frequent (and often more in-depth) classroom visits. In making visits/observations it is imperative that the observer be purposeful. That is, focused "looking" is needed if an observer is truly going to "see and understand" what is happening in a classroom. As a consequence, make classroom visits count and pay particular attention to how, for example, a teacher is assessing student learning *and* how the teacher then uses those assessments to guide subsequent instruction. Even "casual," informal visits can be purposeful since classroom "walk-through" data can be obtained using a hand-held palm pilot-type device using proprietary software such as E-Walk (http://media-x.com).

To maximize the effectiveness of more formal administrator observations, let a teacher know what you want to observe, identify specific questions you will try to answer as a result of the observation (e.g., does the assessment approach of the teacher complement the material being taught?), and take time to provide feedback on what was observed (Boudett, City, & Murname, 2005).

Why is this focus on different forms of teacher assessment so important? Quite bluntly, it is significant because formative assessments (teacher-made tests) are incredibly important to enhanced student achievement. A prodigious body of research (conducted in multiple contexts) now exists to document the fact that strengthening what teachers do in terms of formative assessments impacts the learning gains of students. Interestingly, such an emphasis also helped close achievement gap differences between groups of students. Black and others (2003) write, "improved formative assessment [helps] the . . . low attainers more than the rest, and so reduced the spread of attainment [the achievement gap] while also raising it overall" (p. 9).

Notice that we have placed the emphasis here on formative (teacher-made) assessments, not summative (more standardized) assessments. The reason relates to the current NCLB reality. Many (perhaps most) state tests students take are instructionally insensitive. In the words of Popham (2006b):

> they were created using a traditional psychometric strategy that . . . makes students' socioeconomic status the most influential factor in determining which students get high or low scores. . . . Even if a state has created customized, "standards-based" tests in an effort to better measure students' mastering of the state's content standards, or curricular aims, the tests can still turn out to be instructionally insensitive. (p. 32)

Popham goes on to describe how states can work to construct instructionally *sensitive* tests (e.g., limit the number of curricular learning targets), but the average teacher cannot control what a state does and mandates. He or she can control what occurs in his or her own classroom; hence, our point of emphasis is at the school and classroom level (and on formative assessment).

For new teachers (those in their first three years of teaching) feedback on assessment is particularly important. Researchers (see educationtrust.org) have now documented the fact that new teachers tend to be less effective (especially in the first two years of practice) and that it is imperative either to weed out or to provide intensive professional development for those who fail to produce appropriate achievement gains in students. For administrators in states where the effectiveness of individual teachers can be assessed, the process of determining which teachers to assist is somewhat simplified. But for new teachers regardless of geography, too little student achievement data will be available and, as a result, it is imperative that administrators spend time (more time) in their classrooms providing detailed feedback on how the teacher is collecting and using formative data about student performance to inform what he or she does instructionally.

Personal Action Research

Thus far we have been examining the ways in which an observer (typically an administrator) collects and uses data about a teacher. Unfortunately, no observer, regardless of how skilled he or she might be, has the time or ability to collect all the data needed to really enhance student achievement.

Good teachers, just like skilled practitioners in other professions, are always trying to understand (to reflect on) what they are doing and to determine whether it is working. They engage in a form of action research. The action research process has essentially seven steps (Jenkins, 2003):

1. *Reflect*: Start by thinking about your classroom or school. What is working, and what isn't working? Which student is having academic or social problems?
2. *Focus*: Select one of the aspects from your reflection as the focus on your study. Choose something over which you have some control or influence.
3. *Clarify questions*: Develop one to three specific, measurable questions that capture the focus of your action research.
4. *Collect data*: Decide what data you will need and the best way to collect the information. Existing documents such as lesson plans, student work, and standardized test results provide data. . . . Collecting three types of data enables you to look at the situation from multiple perspectives.
5. *Analyze data*: Read notes, journals, and transcriptions of tapes to find patterns and trends that provide answers to your guiding questions.
6. *Take informed action*: What answers to your questions do the data suggest? Think about how these data can help you make decisions about your classroom and school.
7. *Report results*: Because the answers you find relate specifically to your education setting, they aren't necessarily true for other teachers or situations. . . .

Figure out who in your building, district, or state should know about your action research and share the results with them. (pp. 36–37)

Bainer (2003) and White (2005) suggest that there is a clear pattern to the action research process. It starts with a teacher (or teachers) carefully considering some aspect of the classroom environment that emerges as a result of personal observation. Once the observation is made about some pattern in the students' performance that needs to be understood, the teacher then develops a focus, hypothesis, or *question* that needs to be addressed or answered. The teacher then collects data relevant to that question and then analyzes the data in order to inform subsequent instructional action.

For some, action research might actually consist of a research project, with some students in treatment groups and others in control groups. For others, it may emerge as an outgrowth of professional development where one group of teachers is using one set of instructional practices and another group is relying on different approaches. As a result of the different practices, do the data reveal variations in results? Why? What is happening?

An example illustrates the way in which the action research model might operate in a classroom context. Remember, the teacher is trying to understand what some pattern emerging from data means. Is something new occurring that requires verification or clarification (White, 2005)? In this case the teacher is exploring the implications of "buddy reading" and student oral reading fluency, and it is based on a real teacher confronting a real issue.

A third-grade teacher (Anne) wanted to know if pairing her students with students in the seventh grade for 30 minutes of buddy reading twice a week would improve her students' oral reading fluency scores, or word count per minute (wcpm). She also wanted to know if results differed across two groups in her class, students for whom English is a second language (ESL) and students who are not ESL. She gathered oral reading fluency scores at the beginning and end of her action research project, and analyzed the data for improvement. She reported the student performance in quartiles. Based on the analysis of performance, she noted that the performance of her class improved overall, but that non-ESL students improved more than ESL students. In reflecting on the research, Anne noted that she had hoped the ESL students would have improved at least as well as the non-ESL students, but that more time with buddy readers might lead to greater improvements for the ESL students.

Anne also kept a teacher journal throughout the research study. When she analyzed her journal entries, she found that her third-grade students were enthusiastic about reading together. She was a bit surprised to learn from reading her journal that the seventh graders looked forward to the sessions as much as her third graders. She did note, however, that not all seventh graders were as enthusiastic. One commented on the fact that her third-grade buddy read so slowly it was easier to read to her. Another commented that her third-grade partner was a better reader than she was. Anne concluded from the results of her study that she would continue the buddy reading program, with some adjustments (Kinnucan-Welsch, personal communication, 2006).

Notice the way in which the teacher reflected on practice in an effort to understand the efficacy of a particular instructional approach and also was highly focused in terms of the direction of her data collection and in the way in which she fashioned the question for investigation. She then collected and analyzed data and made a decision about whether to continue using buddy reading in the future.

Effective teachers gather and use data in different ways. And effective administrators encourage teachers to use not only the data that are collected by those outside the classroom but also by the teacher who has the most direct and intimate contact with the students on a daily basis. The data collection is important, but it is precipitated by questions: What is or is not working? Why? The questions lead to the collection of data, which leads to evaluating those data and the emergence of "next-step" actions.

SUMMARY

This chapter examined the different ways in which administrators and teachers collect and access external and internal data. At times they can directly access databases at both the federal and state levels. At other times they might find it efficacious to use indirect databases where agencies have synthesized information in a way to make it more readily accessible to a variety of stakeholders and constituents. All of this type of data is collected through public domain and made available on a variety of websites.

Administrators and teachers also have responsibility for directly collecting their own data. Without such instructionally sensitive data collection procedures (i.e., that is, data collected for a specific purpose and at the point of instruction), administrators and teachers will be unable to fully understand the impact of what they are doing relative to the students' performance. There are clear limitations associated with direct data collection procedures, but if the data are used to understand practices and their impact rather than to dictate how teachers should respond, they can be useful and beneficial in efforts to enhance overall instructional practice and student achievement.

Observational Resources for Administrators

In observing more formally and systematically the teacher behaviors in the classroom, two excellent resources (that include a myriad of low- and high-inference observational instruments) are:

Good, T. L., & Brophy, J. *Looking in Classrooms*. New editions of this text are available about every two years, and it is an excellent resource for synthesizing information about teacher effectiveness behaviors. (See Amazon.com for latest edition.)

Borich, G. D. *Observation Skills for Effective Teaching.* Provides examples of observation instruments and also grounds those instruments on the available research. (See Amazon.com for latest edition.)

QUESTIONS AND SUGGESTED ACTIVITIES

Case Study Questions

The opening case focuses on a statewide research agenda exploring the relationship of teacher quality to teacher preparation.

1. What ideas that you acquired in your professional preparation program were clearly grounded on scientifically based research? For one of those ideas, see if you can identify a research study (not a concept piece) that supports the practice you learned. For example, if you were encouraged to use constructivist approaches, to what degree is there research (not conceptual articles) to support its use? (Note: In the 1930s a study titled the "Eight Year Study" investigated traditional versus progressivist or constructivist models; do an Internet search of "Eight Year Study" and see what conclusions were reached.)

2. Teacher education programs are often criticized as being too ideological. What is the difference between a curriculum grounded on ideology and one based on empirical research? Why is it likely that many programs focus more on the former than the latter?

3. Should ideology never be a part of teacher or administrator preparation? That is, should those programs that prepare teachers and administrators only be permitted to proffer practices that are grounded on scientifically based research?

4. The gold standard for scientifically based research is randomized field trials (i.e., having individuals randomly assigned to groups and then utilizing a treatment to some and no treatment to others). Why is such research conducted so infrequently in education?

Chapter Questions and Activities

5. In what ways are direct data sources (such as NCES) superficial in terms of the information they provide for a school?

6. Go to the state department of education website for your state. Is the site easy to navigate? What data are provided for the school in which you teach (or for schools with which you have some familiarity)?

7. What are the advantages of low-inference observation forms? Some argue that low-inference instruments are reductionistic (i.e., they focus too narrowly on specific teacher behaviors such as teacher questioning). What are the limits to using low-inference instruments?

8. Analyze the lesson plans for a teacher over a two- to three-day period. Are the learning targets for his or her lessons clear? What specific knowledge, reasoning, skill, and product targets are apparent?

9. Describe why teacher-made tests are more instructionally sensitive than are the tests mandated by the state.

REFERENCES

Bainer, D. B. (2003). Action research with impact. *Focus: ENC, 10*(1), 35–37.

Berliner, D. (1976). Impediments to the study of teacher effectiveness. *Journal of Teacher Education, 27*(1), 5–13.

Black, P., Harrison, C., Lee, C., Marshall, B., & Wiliam, D. (2003). *Assessment for learning: Putting it into practice.* New York: Open University Press.

Borich, G. D. (1999). *Observation skills for effective teaching* (3rd ed.). Upper Saddle River, NJ: Merrill.

Boudett, K. P., City, E. A., & Murname, R. J. (2005). *Datawise.* Cambridge, MA: Harvard Education Press.

Brendon, L. K. (2003). The National Center for Education Statistics: Our one-stop source of school data. *Focus: ENC, 10*(1), 34–35.

Chappuis, J., & Chappuis, S. (2002). *Understanding school assessment.* Portland, OR: Assessment Training Institute.

Davis, S. H. (2007). Bridging the gap between research and practice: What's good, what's bad, and how can one be sane? *Phi Delta Kappan, 88*(8), 568–578.

Education Gadfly. (2006). Retrieved June 15, 2006, from www.edexcellence.net/foundation/gadfly/issue.cfm?id=246&edition-

Erickson, F. (1986). Quantitative methods in research on teaching. In M. C. Wittrock (Ed.), *Handbook of research on teaching* (4th ed., pp. 119–161). New York: Macmillan.

Gregory, G. H., & Kuzmich, L. (2004). *Data-driven differentiation.* Thousand Oaks, CA: Corwin Press.

Haycock, K. (2006, June 27–28). *Good teaching matters.* Presentation at the NASH/EdTrust CEO Institute, Big Sky, Montana.

Jenkins, D. B. (2003). Action research with impact. *Focus,* 10(1), 35–36.

Kimmelman, P. L. (2006). *Implementing NCLB.* Thousand Oaks, CA: Corwin Press.

Kinnucan-Welsch, K. (2006). *Personal communication.* The illustration is based on the work of a University of Dayton graduate student, Erin Gregory, who used action research to study "buddy reading" procedures.

Marzano, R. J., Pickering, D. J., & Pollock, J. E. (2001). *Classroom instruction that works.* Alexandria, VA: Association of Supervision and Curriculum Development.

Picciano, A. (2006). *Data-driven decision making for effective school leadership.* Upper Saddle River, NJ: Pearson/Merrill, Prentice Hall.

Popham, W. J. (2006a). *Assessment for educational leaders.* Boston: Pearson.

Popham, W. J. (2006b, April 19). Educator cheating on no child left behind tests. *Education Week, 25*(32), 32–33.

Ravitch, D. (2004). *A consumer's guide to high school history textbooks.* Washington, DC: Thomas B. Fordham Institute.

Streitmatter, J. (1994). *Toward gender equity in the classroom: Everyday teachers' beliefs and practices.* New York: State University of New York Press.

Teske, P., Wolf, P., & Hill, P. (2006, April 19). Poor parents can be good choosers. *Education Week, 25*(32), 44.

White, S. H. (2005). *Beyond the numbers.* Englewood, CO: Advanced Learning Press.

Technology and Information Management

Chapter Focus

Technology that stores and facilitates the use of data provides the potential for changing the landscape of decision making in schools (Wayman, Stringfield, & Yakimowski, 2004) but it does not guarantee this transition. In fact, studies have shown that teachers and principals who have been required to use databases often became frustrated by them (Wayman, 2005). Unfortunately, some observers myopically believe that one or two experts should be responsible for technology, and therefore the topic has limited relevance to teachers and principals. Though technology systems should be easy to understand and easy to use (Chen, Heritage, & Lee, 2005; Lachat & Smith, 2005), they will not be used extensively or appropriately by employees who are not information literate.

The purposes of this chapter are to provide an overview of information systems and to explain their utility in relation to data-driven decision making. First, basic terms are defined and then their structure and deployment are discussed. The value of information technology in relation to decision making is nested in database development, access, and management; therefore, databases also are given focused attention. Finally, the relationships among technology, data-driven decision making, and educator competencies are summarized. After reading this chapter, you should be able to address the following questions:

1. What is information technology?
2. What is the difference between being technology literate and information literate?
3. What is a database?
4. What security measures need to be taken to protect data?
5. What are data warehousing and data mining?

CASE STUDY

When Ashley Martinez agreed to be the principal of Roosevelt Middle School a few months ago, she knew the superintendent expected her to provide leadership for implementing data-driven decision making. During the employment interview, the superintendent assured her that the school district had and was continuing to accumulate pertinent information that could be used to improve student performance. He also told her that the school district was investing heavily in computer technology. "What we need next," he told her, "is your enthusiasm and expertise so that teachers will take advantage of these resources."

After beginning her new job, Principal Martinez learned that little had been done at the district level to establish an infrastructure to facilitate data-driven decision making. For example, there were two different student databases being controlled by separate administrators:

1. Those containing test data were maintained by the school district's director of assessment and evaluation.
2. Those containing demographic and academic progress data were controlled by the school district's director of student personnel services.

Although the administrators controlling these databases reported to the associate superintendent for instruction, neither was willing to relinquish control, and the associate superintendent was unwilling to mandate that the information be combined.

Moreover, computer networking was controlled by the technology director, who reported to the associate superintendent for business. The superintendent realized that having separate databases complicated matters for administrators and teachers. He appointed an ad hoc committee to address the issue, but after six months the committee reported that they were hopelessly deadlocked. None of the administrators currently controlling databases was willing to compromise. The superintendent, though personally supportive of a unified framework, decided that he would not mandate that one be created. Consequently, accessing student data remained a difficult and time-consuming task for principals and teachers.

Principal Martinez also learned that district administrators and her predecessor had done little to prepare teachers to engage in data-driven decision making. Two district-wide, one-day workshops were conducted, but they focused almost entirely on basic explanations of the process and the reasons why the process was mandatory under the provisions of federal law and subsequent state policies. Though most Roosevelt teachers said they were computer literate, the principal observed that some teachers rarely used computers in their classrooms. After reviewing personnel files, she also discovered that only six of thirty-seven teachers had completed a graduate-level course in statistics, tests and measurements, or student assessment procedures.

Information Management Concepts

Regrettably, the situation facing Principal Martinez has not been uncommon. Many schools are drowning in data but lacking effective delivery systems and the proficiencies essential for transforming facts into useful information.

Though computers were placed in most classrooms, media centers, and administrative offices after 1980, they were rarely used to facilitate administrative and instructional decisions. Instead, information technology (IT) focused almost exclusively on using computers to enhance classroom instruction (Loveless & Longman, 1998). The passage of the *No Child Left Behind Act* (NCLB) in 2001, however, has literally forced educators to reexamine why and how they deploy technology. Data-driven decision making in particular requires them to have access to pertinent information, from multiple sources, and in multiple time frames (Salpeter, 2004). Equally important, educators must be able to translate data first into pertinent information for making current decisions and then into knowledge that can be applied to future decisions (Carroll & Carroll, 2002).

Currently, the drive to create and use technology to facilitate decision making has become a top-level priority in most school districts. Reaching this objective, however, has proven to be difficult for at least six reasons.

1. Many educators are not information literate and some are not even technology literate (Wenglinsky, 2005).
2. Many school districts have not constructed a user-friendly management information system that educators will use (Carroll & Carroll, 2002).
3. Many educators continue to have an aversion to using statistics and to engaging in data-based assessment (Carroll & Carroll, 2002).
4. The vast majority of administrators and teachers completed professional preparation and entered practice prior to NCLB. Therefore, they were socialized in school climates in which data-driven decision making was not a normative practice (Wayman, 2005).
5. School technology directors often know little about educational assessment data and assessment and evaluation directors often know little about IT (Brooks-Young, 2006). As a result, the two functions frequently operate as parallel but unrelated enterprises.
6. Administrators have played a limited role in pursuing technology policy at the district and school levels (Nance, 2003). Yet leadership provided by administrators has been found to be an important factor in determining technology outcomes (Anderson & Dexter, 2005).

These persisting conditions clearly undermine the success of NCLB in general and data-driven decision making specifically. Consider, for example, one provision of this federal law. NCLB mandates state officials to ensure that student progress is assessed in reading, mathematics, science, and English language proficiency. Data from requisite tests constitute a powerful diagnostic and prescriptive tool for both instruction and future teacher staff development programs (The Education Trust, 2004). Accessing state test data, test pattern data files, and other student data and then applying them to decisions in a timely manner is improbable in schools that lack effective technology infrastructures or in schools where teachers and principals are unable to use the technology infrastructure appropriately.

Technology and Information Literacy

Constructs such as computer literacy, technology literacy, and information literacy may appear nebulous, but in fact they are critical bridges between ideology and action (Petrina, 2000). *Technology literacy* is basically framed by two conditions:

1. Acquiring basic knowledge and skills about computers.
2. Being able to apply that knowledge and those skills in practice.

More exacting definitions of technology literacy, however, have been dynamic, reflecting the continuous development and application of computer science (McMillan, 1996). In the case of contemporary education, a technology-literate principal or teacher at least knows how to

- Use the Internet.
- Modify a Web page.
- Construct a personal database (e.g., spreadsheet).
- Access/use organization databases.

Information literacy, by comparison, involves knowledge and skills essential for engaging in data-driven decision making. Lenox and Walker (1993) defined this concept:

> Implicit in a full understanding of information literacy is the realization that several conditions must be simultaneously present. First, someone must desire to know, use analytic skills to formulate questions, identify research methodologies, and utilize critical skills to evaluate experimental (and experiential) results. Second, the person must possess the skills to search for answers to those questions in increasingly diverse and complex ways. Third, once a person has identified what is sought, he or she must be able to access it. (p. 314)

An information-literate person, therefore, is one who understands connections between accurate information and intelligent decision making. According to Doyle (1992), such a person is able to

- Formulate questions based on information needs.
- Identify potential sources of information.
- Access sources of information through computers.
- Evaluate information.
- Organize information for practical application.
- Integrate new information into an existing database.
- Use information in critical thinking and problem solving.

Educators, however, have commonly struggled with two pertinent tasks. The first is framing questions so that data can be aggregated or disaggregated to facilitate solutions. The second is selecting and using appropriate statistical data and techniques (Carroll & Carroll, 2002).

Information Technology

In its most basic form, IT is described as a computer-based tool used for storing and processing data, typically in an organizational context (Haag, Cummings, & McCubbrey, 2005). This apparatus is divided into two categories: hardware and software. The former includes

- Input devices such as a mouse and a keyboard.
- Storage devices such as disks (e.g., CDs, DVDs, flash drives).
- Output devices such as printers and monitors.
- Connecting devices such as cables and ports.
- Operating devices such as central processing units (CPUs) and random access memory (RAM).
- Telecommunication devices such as a modem and network connection.

The software category includes

- Operating systems such as Mac OS or Windows.
- Utility systems such as popup blockers and antivirus programs.
- Application programs such as Word, PowerPoint, and Excel.

According to Sarmiento (2006), the following three characteristics are the most promising aspects of IT.

1. The ability to construct real-time data representations in multiple formats (e.g., numeric and graphic).
2. The ability to engage and empower a learning community by providing distributed access to appropriate data and analytical tools.
3. The provision of automated guidance that mediates analysis and adds significant value to the mechanical process of data processing.

Although extensive financial support for acquiring IT in public schools has been common, skeptics have challenged the wisdom and efficiency of this investment. Specifically, they have argued that computers in classrooms either have not been used appropriately or they have not made a significant difference in student learning. Though numerous studies have examined facets of these allegations, findings have been inconclusive (Owston & Wideman, 2001; Schacter, 1999). In the absence of compelling evidence about the value of computers in relation to student learning, critics of NCLB have argued that additional investments in IT are unwarranted. The detractors, however, have neglected to point out that IT provisions in NCLB go well beyond putting computers in classrooms. The law's intent is to have districts and schools develop technology infrastructures that will facilitate decisions about instruction. Obviously, using technology to deliver instruction and using technology to facilitate critical decisions about instruction are substantially different processes.

Management Information System

A management information system (MIS) focuses on three aspects of IT: planning, development, and use. Duffy (2000) noted information management should identify an organization's additional information needs and then develop structure for using IT to create, capture, and use information to meet the organization's goals. The development of an MIS can be qualitative or quantitative; experts on this topic (e.g., Jarke, Jeusfeld, Quix, & Vassiliadis, 1999) recommend the former. The effectiveness of an MIS, regardless of its capacity, is attenuated if it (a) cannot be used properly by employees, (b) contains the wrong types of information, or (c) contains the right types of information in the wrong form. Moreover, development of any part of a school's ecology should be guided by the principle that "form follows function" (Kowalski, 2002). Performance specifications (or educational specifications) detail what administrators and teachers need and want to do with information; these requirements then guide the development of the MIS.

According to Telem (1996), the development of an MIS can be visualized across four stages:

1. Defining the system
2. Constructing the system
3. Implementing the system
4. Operating and maintaining the system

Explanations of these stages are provided in Figure 8.1.

In a district or school, a well-constructed MIS provides educators with a means for

- Acquiring new data.
- Accessing volumes of stored data.
- Selectively organizing data to facilitate decision making and problem solving.

Applications can be categorized broadly in the following operational areas.

- Student management (e.g., student records, scheduling, health services)
- Curriculum, instruction, and assessment (e.g., standards, lesson plans, student progress records, standardized test scores, and grades)
- Human resources management (e.g., employee records, payroll, staff development)
- Financial and support services (e.g., budgets, accounting, facility records, transportation records, food services records, inventories) (Sarmiento, 2006)

Defining
Describing the system's intended
purposes and structure

Constructing
Designing the system based on
intended purposes and structure

Implementing
Acquiring the necessary
human and material resources

Operating & Maintaining
Controlling and sustaining
the system once it is operational

FIGURE 8.1   Development Stages for an MIS

There is no universal design for an MIS. Features and value to users vary across institutions. Nevertheless, Haag, Cummings, and McCubbrey (2005) identified four characteristics that commonly determine if a system is effective.

1. *The system is timely.* Data are made available when they are needed and they are continuously updated to ensure they remain relevant. The speed of a user's computer can attenuate timeliness; for instance, a teacher may not be able to download a report in a reasonable amount of time.
2. *The system is accessible.* Data lose value if users are unable to access them. As an example, a teacher may not be able to access the MIS because of security measures.
3. *The system is usable.* Data provided are valid, accurate, and presented in a form that is understood by intended users. In addition, users should be able to save data in preferred software (e.g., Excel spreadsheet).
4. *The system is multidirectional.* Data are able to move downward, upward, and horizontally in a school and from the school outward to community and vice versa.

Though schools always have acquired and maintained considerable data, the information was usually unorganized and inaccessible, at least to most teachers. This partly explains why accumulated data were rarely used to inform important decisions. Lamenting this fact, Carroll and Carroll (2002) noted that at best, decision making in schools prior to NCLB was based on raw data from a single source (e.g., from a test administered by a teacher) and at worst on hunches and untested hypotheses. Unmistakably, NCLB was designed to change this condition. First, the law requires schools to have an MIS. Second, it requires educators to use it to convert data into information and then transform information into knowledge (Petrides & Guiney, 2002).

Building and Using Databases

An MIS for databases is called *database management information systems* (DMIS). It provides a process for entering data and accessing information using IT; it is a tool intended to make the content of a database more practical for users (Picciano, 2006). The relationship among a DMIS, IT, a database, and users is shown in Figure 8.2.

Broadly, two types of evidence can inform the practice of educators. The first kind is generic and is provided by research and theories. These data are commonly

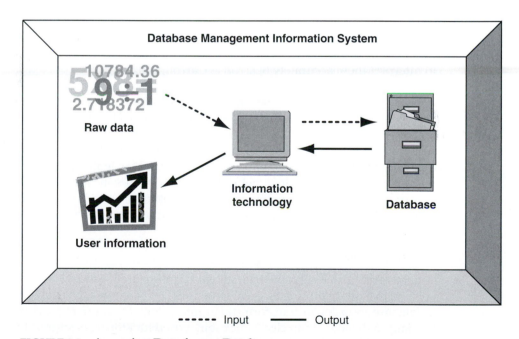

FIGURE 8.2   **Accessing Data from a Database**

made available in professional books and journals. Research findings and conclusions about the short- and long-term effects of retaining students in first grade are examples. Though educators are commonly required to study theory and research in professional education courses, many practitioners fail to use and extend this knowledge after entering practice. In his studies of public schools that spanned more than two decades, Sarason (1996) concluded that both administrators and teachers rarely read contemporary literature on pedagogy and organizational behavior. A persistent indifference toward research-based evidence largely explains why educators have been susceptible to education fads and why they often have passionately advocated curricular programs based solely on personal ideologies (Kimmelman, 2006).

The second category of evidence consists of facts specific to the educator's practice. Included are data about (a) students (e.g., individual test scores, grades), (b) the community (e.g., demographic profiles), (c) the school (e.g., policy, aggregate student data), and (d) government (e.g., federal or state mandates, legal requirements). Both generic and specific evidence are critically important to making effective decisions in scientific professions. Physicians, for example, are expected to remain current on research in their profession (generic knowledge) and to maintain current data on their patients (specific knowledge). The integration of the two types of knowledge substantially increases the probability that the practitioners will make effective decisions in serving their patients. We should expect no less of teachers and administrators.

Schools have often been described as "data rich but information poor." Stated differently, school officials have maintained vast amounts of student-related facts, such as standardized test scores, grades, and attendance records, but they have not organized these data in a fashion that allows teachers to retrieve them quickly or to interpret them accurately (Carroll & Carroll, 2002).

At the district level, administrators have customarily maintained extensive operational data, such as financial records, personnel facts, and facility information. Although they were used periodically to make isolated managerial decisions, managerial data sets typically were not integrated, nor were they connected to student data. At the time NCLB was enacted, only a handful of school districts had developed a data warehouse and an MIS that could facilitate data-driven decisions made by instructional personnel (Jametz, 2001). Thus in most school districts, a lack of resources necessary for accessing, manipulating, and interpreting data has been a primary obstacle to data-driven decision making (Wayman, 2005).

Database Basics

A database is a collection of facts, statistics, and related information organized according to a predetermined logical structure. Data are raw facts; they are placed in a database in order to transform them into information (or processed facts). Essentially, a database is an electronic cabinet used for storing electronic folders (Rob & Semaan, 2004). The cabinet also includes metadata (or data about data) stored in a *data dictionary*, a compilation of data components, their names, and their characteristics. A database is managed by the DMIS.

A database is usually relational; that is, it is constructed using a series of two-dimensional tables (or files), allowing it to be reorganized and accessed in different ways (Haag et al., 2005). Relational databases are typically structured around the following three characteristics:

1. *Entities:* a person, event, object, or related item
2. *Entity sets:* a named collection of entities
3. *Attributes:* an entity characteristic

Entities are stored in a matrix of intersecting rows and columns (i.e., a table) (Rob & Semaan, 2004). Consider a school database containing employee data. A single employee is an entity, all employees are an entity set, and data entries (e.g., degree level, years of experience, salary) for each employee are attributes. An example is provided in Figure 8.3.

To be useful to teachers, a database should have the capacity to provide *purposeful data disaggregation.* Lachat, Williams, and Smith (2006) described this quality as "being able to connect information about students who have particular characteristics to the programs and practices to which they have been exposed and the knowledge and skills that they have acquired" (p. 19).

FIGURE 8.3   **Database Table: Eleven School Employee Entities and Selected Attributes**

Primary keys	Entities		Attributes			
Employee ID number	Name, last	Name, first	Position	Degree	Years of employment	Room
32101	Anderson	Paul	Teacher	M.S.	32 years	109
32104	McTavish	Sarah	Teacher	B.A.	29 years	104
32107	Smithson	Angela	Teacher	M.A	27 years	105
32111	Petersen	George	Custodian	N/A	24 years	127
32131	Krubalski	Mildred	Librarian	M.L.S.	15 years	120
32132	Eagan	David	Teacher	B.S.	15 years	107
32139	Constantine	Andria	Principal	Ed.S.	13 years	101
32148	Hoseva	Maria	Teacher	M.Ed.	8 years	103
32149	Keedy	Jonathan	Teacher	M.S.	7 years	111
32157	Wadala	Bonnie	Cook	N/A	3 years	125
32159	Yulivich	Janice	Secretary	N/A	2 years	100

According to Haag and colleagues (2005), an effectively constructed database should include three features:

1. *Appropriate data views:* a feature allowing users to see the contents of a database in a preferred manner (e.g., alphabetically or chronologically)
2. A *data manipulation subsystem:* a feature allowing designated school personnel to add, alter, or delete information
3. A *report generator:* a feature allowing users to select data for inclusion in a specific report (e.g., a report to the school board on the performance of fourth-grade students on the state competency examination)

Gray and Watson (1998) advise that information stored in a database should be subject oriented and nonvolatile. The former attribute means that data are stored by subject areas across a district or school. The latter attribute means that "read only" data are stored, preventing users from altering stored information. In a district or school, warehoused data could pertain to fiscal management, personnel, school facilities, transportation programs, student demographics, student assessment data, and student academic achievement data.

Using Spreadsheets

Spreadsheet software has become a common tool used by many educators, especially to build personal databases. For example, teachers may develop one or more spreadsheets to use during the course of a school year. Spreadsheets store lists—that is, collections of information (numbers, text, or formulas) arranged in columns and rows. A spreadsheet list possesses the following characteristics:

- Each column has only one type of information.
- The first row in the list contains labels or column headings.
- The list does not contain any blank rows.
- The list is bordered on all four sides by blank rows and blank columns (Haag et al., 2005, p. 218).

A user can carry out calculations of the numerical content rapidly, and therefore they are often used for data processing. They also can be deployed to store nonnumerical data (e.g., a list of names or addresses).

Teachers often use spreadsheets to develop frequency distributions for student performance scores. Figure 8.4 provides an example developed by a mathematics teacher for a test given in one of his algebra classes. The teacher also records scores on both tests given during the course semester in another spreadsheet that identifies the variance of each student's test scores—individually and combined for two exams. The test score spreadsheet is shown in Figure 8.5. Note that the teacher used the spreadsheet to calculate means and then to calculate variance from the means. If even more statistical data were desired, he also could have cal-

FIGURE 8.4 Frequency Distribution of Examination Scores in an Algebra Class

Score	Frequency	Student ID	Relative frequency %	Cumulative frequency	Cumulative frequency %
62	2	12,18	8%	2	8%
65	1	3	4%	3	12%
71	1	9	4%	4	16%
75	2	2,24	8%	6	24%
79	1	1	4%	7	28%
82	3	5,8,11	12%	10	40%
85	4	4,6,7,20	16%	14	56%
86	1	14	4%	15	60%
88	2	8,19	8%	17	68%
90	2	16,22	8%	19	76%
92	2	13,21	8%	21	84%
93	1	25	4%	22	88%
95	2	10,15	8%	24	96%
98	1	17	4%	25	100%

culated standard deviations. Once stored in the computer, these spreadsheets provide a resource for making instructional and grading decisions.

Working with a small spreadsheet is rarely a problem; large lists, however, present a challenge because a user must sift through them to find specific data. The AutoFilter function in a Microsoft Excel spreadsheet is specifically designed to assist with this problem. It allows the user to disaggregate data in a large list by hiding all the rows except those that are of immediate interest. Using data effectively requires "disaggregating assessment results by multiple student characteristics, programs, interventions, educational reports, instructional practices, and such indicators as grades and attendance" (Lachat et al., 2006, p. 19). For example, a teacher may want to extract student information pertaining to current grade level, gender, and socioeconomic status. Though there are several options for disaggregating data from a large spreadsheet (e.g., using the Sum or Subtotal functions), Stein (2006) notes that the AutoFilter is a preferred choice because (a) the data remain intact, (b) data details are always visible and available within the original table, and (c) the data need not be sorted. Because of the utility and widespread availability of Excel spreadsheet software, educators should receive staff development designed to master the use of this tool.

FIGURE 8.5   **Exam Spreadsheet for an Algebra Class**

Student	ID	Test 1	VfM	Test 2	VfM	Combined points	VfM	Combined %
Addison, Peter	1	79	−4.60	83	−4.36	162	−8.97	81%
Brucker, Allison	2	75	−8.60	82	−5.36	157	−13.97	79%
Burns, Jason	3	65	−18.60	79	−8.36	144	−26.97	72%
Frank, Betsy	4	85	1.40	74	−13.36	159	−11.97	80%
Granger, Ann	5	82	−1.60	92	4.64	174	3.03	87%
Hall, Toby	6	85	1.40	88	0.64	173	2.03	87%
Heaton, Neil	7	85	1.40	90	2.64	175	4.03	88%
Hulbert, Andrew	8	88	4.40	93	5.64	181	10.03	91%
Ibovich, Stanley	9	71	−12.60	83	−4.36	154	−16.97	77%
James, Jeffrey	10	95	11.40	88	0.64	183	12.03	92%
Kelm, Susan	11	82	−1.60	89	1.64	171	0.03	86%
Lagris, Elizabeth	12	62	−21.60	71	−16.36	133	−37.97	67%
Manza, Mary	13	92	8.40	99	11.64	191	20.03	96%
Nelson, Gerard	14	86	2.40	90	2.64	176	5.03	88%
Osgood, Peter	15	95	11.40	91	3.64	186	15.03	93%
Raburn, David	16	90	6.40	98	10.64	188	17.03	94%
Rath, Janice	17	98	14.40	96	8.64	194	23.03	97%
Sagniss, Roy	18	62	−21.60	74	−13.36	136	−34.97	68%
Sewell, Thomas	19	88	4.40	82	−5.36	170	−0.97	85%
Sordibern, Nancy	20	85	1.40	83	−4.36	168	−2.97	84%
Talbot, Constance	21	92	8.40	95	7.64	187	16.03	94%
Torget, Rudolph	22	90	6.40	84	−3.36	174	3.03	87%
Unger, Bart	23	90	6.40	92	4.64	182	11.03	91%
Walker, April	24	75	−8.60	90	2.64	165	−5.97	83%
Zelaski, Carl	25	93	9.40	98	10.64	191	20.03	96%
Mean		83.60		87.36		170.96		85%

Data Security and Integrity

Security is a major concern for database management. Protection should be provided for content misuse, alterations, or deletions, regardless of whether such actions are accidental or purposeful. In addition to protecting data accuracy, school officials have legal and professional responsibilities to protect employee and student information. Security devices for school networks (e.g., firewalls) are not designed to control access to databases, and therefore separate measures are necessary.

In general, an effective security system has two primary features:

1. *Transparency.* The security system should be invisible to the extent that employees do not alter applications as a result of data being added.
2. *Accessibility.* The system ensures that authorized personnel are not prevented or hindered from using a database as intended (Haag et al., 2005).

Specific features of a security system usually include user names, passwords, encryption, and audit trails, providing a history of transactions (Hoffer, Prescott, & McFadden, 2005).

The superintendent and school board have a responsibility to establish technology policies, and this duty extends to developing and enforcing a database policy (Kowalski, 2006). At a minimum, such a policy should address these three issues:

1. *Purpose.* As examples, the policy should identify which types of databases are required or permitted and should provide a rationale for maintaining them.
2. *Disclosure.* As an example, the policy should inform employees and others that data are being maintained.
3. *Access and availability.* As an example, the policy should identify employees who by virtue of their positions are authorized to input or access data.

Whereas security focuses on access and control, the issue of data integrity is concerned with consistency and accuracy. Typically, security and integrity are intertwined and addressed generically under database management; that is, a good MIS provides controls for access, for use after access, and for protecting data integrity (Hoffer, Prescott, & McFadden, 2005).

Data Warehousing and Mining

Simply defined, a *data warehouse* is a computer storage area that accumulates, integrates, and stores data with the aim of producing accurate and timely information to support decisions (Mieles & Foley, 2005). Commonly, such a warehouse should have these attributes:

- Accumulating and storing information from various databases
- Cleansing content to eliminate incompatibilities
- Producing a uniform data format
- Providing a single information source for multiple databases
- Providing a comprehensive, complex foundation for data analysis and reporting

These features allow authorized users to retrieve pertinent, accurate information rapidly (Depka, 2006). Typically, a data warehouse is housed on an enterprise mainframe server. *Data warehousing* is a term used to describe activities pertaining to defining, populating, and using a data warehouse.

Data mining involves database analysis to identify relationships that previously have not been discovered (e.g., hidden patterns in a group of data that can be used to facilitate decisions). The analytical applications search for patterns (e.g., trends or associations) or content (e.g., entity or entity set) relationships inside a database. The deployment of data mining has increased substantially over the past ten years, largely because of technological advances. Available data mining tools vary in affordability and functionality—factors that have limited their application in schools (Schumnan, 2005). Database software, however, often have features allowing users to generate reports and data subsets; most commonly, a query language is provided to allow users to access data in different ways (Picciano, 2006).

Research on the use of data warehouses in districts and schools reveals that preparing staff to use this tool is the most frequently cited problem. This was true primarily for three reasons:

1. A small portion of educators still are not technology literate (Wenglinsky, 2005) and therefore are unable to use computers to access the warehouse.
2. Many teachers and administrators routinely make decisions without relying on data (Picciano, 2006).
3. District employees have not been prepared to use specific hardware and software used to manage data (Rice, 2005).

Establishing a data warehouse and selecting appropriate mining tools are complex tasks that typically require school administrators to retain the services of technical consultants. Managing education databases is especially challenging because of the quantity and quality of information that is stored. As an example, there are demographic data, management data, instructional data, personnel data, and so forth. Often this information is stored on various computers in different data formats. Therefore, school personnel must "cleanse" and standardize the data before placing it in a warehouse (McIntire, 2003). Data cleansing involves finding and then correcting or eliminating inaccurate or an invalid entity from an entity set. Often the process is undertaken to ensure that entity sets are consistent, a characteristic essential to complex data analysis. When building a data warehouse, school officials should remain focused on the quintessential question: *What mining tools will ensure that the data warehouse will facilitate data-driven decisions made by administrators and teachers?*

S U M M A R Y

Implementing data-driven decision making, as intended by NCLB, should be visualized as a three-dimensional task. First, *educators require accurate and comprehensive data*. In most districts, much of this information already exists but the quantity will expand, largely because of achievement testing mandates included in NCLB.

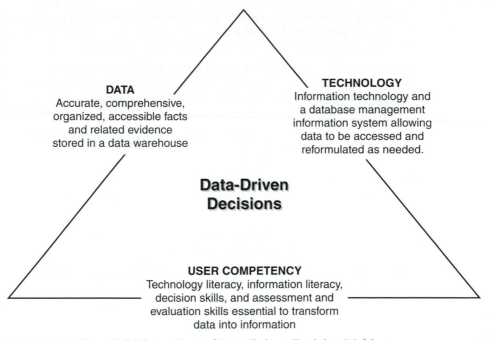

FIGURE 8.6   Essential Dimensions of Data-Driven Decision Making

Second, *educators require a technology infrastructure configured as a DMIS, allowing them to translate data into pertinent information rapidly and conveniently.* As discussed in this chapter, meeting this need typically involves creating new resources and integrating them with existing resources. Third, *educators require the knowledge and skills essential for using the information they access to make diagnostic and prescriptive decisions.* Arguably, this is the most difficult challenge because it requires a considerable investment in organized learning opportunities for administrators and teachers. The relationship among these three dimensions is depicted in Figure 8.6.

After reading this chapter, you should be able to define and describe (a) technology and information literacy, (b) the deployment of IT in schools, (c) the development and use of databases, (d) a data warehouse and data mining, and (e) the integration of technology and data via a DMIS. Equally important, you should understand why the goal of implementing data-driven decision making is likely to be attenuated if technology is not deployed appropriately.

QUESTIONS AND SUGGESTED ACTIVITIES

Case Study Questions

1. If you were Principal Martinez, what would you communicate to the superintendent about the obstacles to data-driven decision making that you discovered?

2. Given the unwillingness of district-level administrators to integrate student databases, should Principal Martinez assume the responsibility of developing a data warehouse and a DMIS for her school? Why or why not?

3. Discuss the superintendent's expectation that Principal Martinez provide leadership to implement data-driven decision making in Roosevelt Middle School. Generally, is this a realistic expectation for a principal? Is it a realistic expectation in this case?

4. What role, if any, should Principal Martinez play in structuring and providing staff development to ensure that the staff is prepared to engage in data-driven decision making?

Chapter Questions

5. What factors have prevented educators from engaging in data-driven decision making?

6. What is the difference between technology literacy and information literacy? Which is essential for data-driven decision making?

7. What is a data warehouse? What purpose does it serve in relation to data-driven decision making?

8. What is data mining? What purpose does it serve in relation to data-driven decision making?

9. What is a DMIS? What are the characteristics of an effective DMIS?

10. What are the characteristics of an effective database?

11. What is the relationship between a computer-generated spreadsheet and a database?

REFERENCES

Anderson, R. E., & Dexter, S. (2005). School technology leadership: An empirical investigation of prevalence and effect. *Educational Administration Quarterly, 41*(1), 49–82.

Brooks-Young, S. (2006). *Critical technology issues for school leaders.* Thousand Oaks, CA: Corwin Press.

Carroll, S. R., & Carroll, D. J. (2002). *Statistics made simple for school leaders: Data-driven decision making.* Lanham, MD: Scarecrow Press.

Chen, E., Heritage, M., & Lee, J. (2005). Identifying and monitoring students' learning needs with technology. *Journal of Education for Students Place at Risk, 10*(3), 309–332.

Depka, E. (2006). *The data guidebook for teachers and leaders.* Thousand Oaks, CA: Corwin Press.

Doyle, C. S. (1992). *Outcome measures for information literacy within the National Education Goals of 1990. Final report to National Forum on Information Literacy. Summary of findings.* (ERIC Document Reproduction Service No. ED 531 033)

Duffy, J. (2000). Knowledge management: To be or not to be? *Information Management Journal, 34*(1), 64–67.

The Education Trust. (2004). The real value of teachers: If good teachers matter, why don't we act like it? *Thinking K–12, 8*(1). Retrieved July 15, 2006, from www2.edtrust.org/EdTrust/ Product+Catalog/test+browse.htm

Gray, P., & Watson, H. J. (1998). *Decision support in the data warehouse.* Upper Saddle River, NJ: Prentice Hall.

Haag, S., Cummings, M., & McCubbrey, D. J. (2005). *Management information systems for the information age* (5th ed.). Boston: McGraw-Hill, Irwin.

Hoffer, J. A., Prescott, M. B., & McFadden, F. R. (2005). *Modern database management* (7th ed.). Upper Saddle River, NJ: Prentice Hall.

Jametz, K. (2001). Beyond data mania. *Leadership, 31*(2), 8–12.

Jarke, M., Jeusfeld, M. A., Quix, C., & Vassiliadis, P. (1999). Architecture and quality in data warehouses: An extended repository approach. *Information Systems, 24*(3), 229–253.

Kimmelman, P. L. (2006). *Implementing NCLB: Creating a knowledge framework to support school improvement.* Thousand Oaks, CA: Corwin Press.

Kowalski, T. J. (2002). *Planning and managing school facilities* (2nd ed.). Westport, CT: Bergin & Garvey.

Kowalski, T. J. (2006). *The school superintendent: Theory, practice, and cases* (2nd ed.). Thousand Oaks, CA: Sage.

Lachat, M. A., & Smith, S. C. (2005). Practices that support data use in urban high schools. *Journal of Education for Students Placed at Risk, 10*(3), 333–349.

Lachat, M. A., Williams, M., & Smith, S. C. (2006). Making sense of all your data. *Principal Leadership* (High School edition), *7*(2), 16–21.

Lenox, M. F., & Walker, M. L. (1993). Information literacy in the educational process. *Educational Forum, 57*(3), 312–324.

Loveless, A., & Longman, D. (1998). Information literacy: Innuendo or insight? *Education and Information Technologies, 3*(1), 27–40.

McIntire, T. (2003). Digging for data. *Technology & Learning, 23*(8), 42, 44, 46.

McMillan, S. (1996). Literacy and computer literacy: Definitions and comparisons. *Computers and Education, 27*(3–4), 161–170.

Mieles, T., & Foley, E. (2005). School staff and the data warehouse. *Technology & Learning, 26*(11). Retrieved July 12, 2006, from www.techlearning.com/story/showArticle.jhtml?articleID=-163703320

Nance, J. P. (2003). Public school administrators and technology policy making. *Educational Administration Quarterly, 39*(4), 434–467.

Owston, R. D., & Wideman, H. H. (2001). Computer access and student achievement in the early school years. *Journal of Computer Assisted Learning, 17*(4), 433–444.

Petrides, L. A., & Guiney, S. Z. (2002). Knowledge management for school leaders: An ecological framework for thinking schools. *Teachers College Record, 104*(8), 1702–1717.

Petrina, S. (2000). The politics of technological literacy. *International Journal of Technology and Design Education, 10*(2), 181–206.

Picciano, A. G. (2006). *Data-driven decision making for effective school leadership.* Upper Saddle River, NJ: Merrill, Prentice Hall.

Rice, N. S. (2005). Conquering NCLB with technology. *T.H.E. Journal, 33*(2), 42.

Rob, P., & Semaan, E. (2004). *Databases: Design, development, and deployment using Microsoft Access* (2nd ed.). Boston: McGraw-Hill, Irwin.

Salpeter, J. (2004). Data: Mining with a mission. *Technology & Learning, 24*(8). Retrieved July 12, 2006, from www.techlearning.com/story/showArticle.jhtml?articleID=18311595

Sarason, S. B. (1996). *Revisiting the culture of the school and the problem of change.* New York: Teachers College Press.

Sarmiento, J. W. (2006). *Technology tools of the analysis of achievement data: An introductory guide for educational leaders.* Retrieved July 13, 2006, from www.nwrel.org/scpd/sslc/federal_grantees/cohort2/data_institutes/binder/resources/C2DataTechToolsforAnalysis.pdf#search='Sarmiento%20and%20Technology%20Tools

Schacter, J. (1999). *The impact of education technology on student achievement: What the most current research has to say.* (ERIC Document Reproduction Service No. ED430537)

Schumnan, J. (2005). *Data mining methodologies in educational organizations.* Unpublished doctoral dissertation, University of Connecticut, Storrs.

Stein, J. D. (2006). *Spreadsheet smarts: Three laborsaving Excel functions.* Retrieved July 14, 2006, from www.aicpa.org/pubs/jofa/jan2000/stein.htm

Telem, M. (1996). MIS implementation in schools: A systems socio-technical framework. *Computers and Education, 27*(2), 85–93.

Wayman, J. C. (2005). Involving teachers in data-driven decision making: Using computer data systems to support teacher inquiry and reflection. *Journal of Education for Students Placed At Risk, 10*(3), 295–308.

Wayman, J. C., Stringfield, S., & Yakimowski, M. (2004). *Software enabling school improvement through the analysis of student data.* Baltimore, MD: Johns Hopkins University Center for Research on the Education of Students Placed At Risk.

Wenglinsky, H. (2005). *Using technology wisely: The keys to success in schools.* New York: Teachers College Press.

PART THREE

Applying Data-Based Decisions

Chapter Focus

Knowing how to structure classroom instruction to maximize student learning is critical for enhancing student achievement. No one approach to fostering student learning is adequate for addressing the inherent complexity of the teaching–learning process. In this chapter, the authors describe how to approach that complexity in ways that should foster enhanced student achievement. Specifically, they proffer selected principles of instruction and assessment that help practitioners critically reflect on their own instructional practices.

The following questions will be addressed in this chapter:

1. How do states establish an academic foundation for what occurs in schools, and what role does high-stakes testing play in assuring that academic goals are achieved?
2. Should there be national standards, or are state standards sufficient for assuring the competitiveness of students in the United States?
3. How can instruction be organized to maximize academic results?
4. What assessment regimens need to be in place to ensure that teachers and students are receiving adequate feedback about academic performance?

CASE STUDY I

Susan Brightstein moved to Wyoming because she loved the out-of-doors and wanted to experience the Equality State. She now teaches third grade in a small rural town and wants the students to achieve competency in using the reading process to better understand literary and informational texts. The specific benchmark for the standard that she is focusing on is: "(1e) Students use the reading process to apply a variety of comprehension strategies before, during, and after reading. Students make connections among texts and themselves."

Susan has read through the performance-level descriptors for the standard (see Figure 9.1), and although she finds the material understandable on one level (that is, she knows what all the words mean), she is perplexed as to what it actually requires in terms of how to teach and assess the content. What does it really

FIGURE 9.1   Grade 3

CONTENT STANDARD

1. READING

Students use the reading process to demonstrate understanding of literary and informational texts.

Benchmark Grade 3	Performance Standards Level Descriptors Grade 3

I. Students use the reading process to apply a variety of comprehension strategies before, during, and after reading.

   A. Students use knowledge of less common vowel patterns, syllabication, complex word families, and homophones and homographs to decode unknown words and understand text.

   B. Students comprehend main idea and supporting details.

   C. Students use a variety of strategies to make, confirm, and revise predictions about text, such as use of illustrations, titles, and topic sentences.

   D. Students use reading strategies of setting a purpose for reading, visualizing, and reading between the lines.

   E. Students make connections among texts and themselves.

II. Students read and interpret literature.

   A. Students understand basic elements of plot such as conflict and resolution.

ADVANCED PERFORMANCE

Third-grade readers performing at the advanced level demonstrate the ability to extend applications and connections beyond the obvious. These students understand complex ideas, making connections among a variety of texts . . . These students cite specific, appropriate evidence for their inferences. They independently use dictionaries and glossaries to unlock meaning of unfamiliar words.

PROFICENT PERFORMANCE

Third-grade readers performing at the proficient level demonstrate understanding of a variety of grade-appropriate texts. Their comprehension extends beyond the literal level, making predictions, identifying story elements, and comparing ideas and characters presented in texts. They make relevant connections among texts, and between texts and themselves. They support opinions with text evidence. Students use a table of contents or glossary to locate information. Students apply context clues, prior knowledge, and knowledge of base words to understand unfamiliar words. They read fluently, with accuracy, expression, and appropriate rate. Students monitor and self-correct for meaning.

Source: Wyoming Language Arts Content and Performance Standards. Adopted July 7, 2003. See www.k12wyus/ega/nca/pubs/standards/lang.pdf

mean for students to "make connections among texts and themselves"? Does it refer to a student's ability to relate to different characters in stories? Or does it focus on a student's capacity to interpret and comprehend fictional material?

Susan wants the students to learn what is required, but she is unable to align the standard with an instructional method and a form of assessment because she is unclear about what the actual standard requires.

CASE STUDY II

The debate about standards and student achievement has driven states across the country to strive for higher academic performance. Critics argue for enhanced excellence and claim that without better educational opportunities, America's students will not be able to compete in the "flat world" so powerfully described in Friedman's best-seller, *The World Is Flat*.

The cries for excellence through standards and testing have also been met with expressions of concern. Nowhere has this debate been more visible than in the state of Massachusetts. There, a group of concerned citizens focuses on how tests potentially undermine the educational process. These concerned citizens (or Mass CARE, Inc.) argue that the MCAS (the exit graduation examination for secondary students) has the potential for compromising the overall educational experience of high school students.

Mass CARE, Inc., wants enhanced science education but members argue that more tests are not the answer to enhanced science achievement. They assert that a "one size fits all" standardized examination represents an inadequate mechanism for assessing what academic content secondary students actually know. In essence, they oppose the use of high-stakes testing as a means of enhancing the academic performance of middle and high school students.

In an open letter to Massachusetts legislators they write:

> We cannot narrow the achievement gap by replacing teaching with test preparation. Rather, narrowing the gap requires a system that enriches the educational experiences of low-income and disadvantaged students and does not penalize them for gaps in their background . . . there is little possibility that a standardized test could provide a fair, accurate or equitable form of student assessment. (Mass CARE, Inc., 2005, para. 4)

Creating an Academic Foundation

Both of these cases illustrate the complexity of efforts to enhance student performance. The first suggests the challenges for teachers in different states to make sense of widely divergent standards. Indeed, some critics of the state standards, in this instance the Thomas B. Fordham Foundation's 2006 review of English/Language Arts standards, argue that the wide variations in the quality of state standards (with Wyoming's receiving an "F" grade from Fordham and Massachusetts an "A") limit efforts to achieve equity across school contexts and impact the quality and type of coursework taken by preservice and even inservice teachers (Stotsky, 2005). The Fordham Foundation periodically assesses state standards and identifies four reasons why some states' standards fall short. First, the standards represent too much (through committee compromise) consensus and too little academic vision. Second, the standards are not developed by persons educated in a particular discipline (e.g., as mathematicians) and as a result are often filled with factual errors. Third, the standards are too oriented to fads and insufficiently grounded on content rigor. Fourth, the standards are too parochial and insufficiently comprehensive of the best work that other states are doing.

The second case illustrates what happens even if and when good academic content standards are in place. Strong standards, to be effective, need to be aligned with instruction and assessment. That means teachers must be able to design effective instructional models for presenting content, while school districts and states must identify ways to assess student learning without limiting student educational experiences.

The Mass CARE, Inc., group asserts that the tests will limit student performance because the standardized tests being prescribed by Massachusetts are simply inadequate for measuring what students know. The parents in Massachusetts are not the only ones expressing concerns about standards and state testing. The standards movement across the United States has given rise to a new focus on school and student performance. And that new focus has created a plethora of problems around how data are used (and misused) and how standards represent an essential foundation for educators striving to improve student overall achievement.

High-Stakes Testing: Seeing beyond the Tests

The use of high-stakes tests is now evident in many states. Whether high-stakes tests are really an educational silver bullet remains to be seen. Some suggest that the use of high-stakes tests does provide evidence about student performance that adequately represents their general level of performance (Greene, Winters, & Forster, 2003). This is particularly true if the local curriculum is aligned appropriately with the defined state standards. Indeed, with adequate alignment, students will have an opportunity to learn what they need to know and, as a consequence, their performance should improve. Others claim that the tests are insufficiently comprehensive (that is, they ask too few questions to really assess a large field of knowledge) and may literally cause students (especially poor, urban students) to drop out of the educational system. Further, they argue that use of the high-stakes tests negatively influences student performance on the SAT and ACT and that no good evidence exists to suggest that the tests positively influence transfer of learning (Amrein & Berliner, 2002). Indeed, Nichols and Berliner (2007) assert that high-stakes testing is educationally counterproductive and will engender more evidence regarding the efficacy of Campbell's Law:

> The more any quantitative social indicator is used for social decision making, the more subject it will be to corruption pressures and the more apt it will be to distort and corrupt the social processes it was intended to monitor. (pp. 26–27)

Others have documented the cheating associated with the drive for enhanced student performance (the result of an overemphasis on one indicator), particularly when the tests are used almost exclusively for teacher and school accountability purposes. Levitt and Dubner (2005) powerfully describe in *Freakonomics* the prevalence of cheating on high-stakes tests and, more importantly for the purposes of this book, how administrators used data to catch teacher cheaters. Chicago administrators provided to Levitt a massive student test database for third- through seventh-grade students from 1993 to 2000, which represented 700,000 sets of tests. The tests provided a wide range of data, including all the students' answers and support information (e.g., demographics) about the teachers and students. Levitt then examined the answers for all the students and looked for "suspicious" patterns. Sure enough, they emerged. But the presence of such patterns did *not* constitute singular evidence of cheating. Using a mathematical "cheating algorithm" the authors were able to identify classrooms in which cheating likely occurred. But likelihood and certainty are two different things. Hence, Arne Duncan, the new CEO of the Chicago Public Schools, contacted Levitt and asked for assistance in making sure who the teacher cheaters really were. As a consequence, they retested students in about 120 classrooms, which represented the number of classrooms that the district could afford to retest. Levitt describes what he proposed:

> How could those 120 retests be used most effectively? It might have seemed sensible to retest only the classrooms that likely had a cheating teacher. But even if their retest scores were lower, the teachers could argue that the students did worse merely because they were told that the scores wouldn't count in their official record—which, in fact, all retested students would be told. To make the retest results convincing, some non-cheaters were needed as a control group. The best control group? The classrooms shown by the algorithm to have the best teachers, in which big gains were thought to have been legitimately attained. If those classrooms held their gains while the classrooms with a suspected cheater lost ground, the cheating teachers could hardly argue that their students did worse only because the scores wouldn't count. (Levitt & Dubner, 2005, p. 36)

We share this example from *Freakonomics* because it so aptly describes the complexity of the data-driven school world you are entering or already function in as a teacher or administrator. Until recently, a good administrator was one who knew how to interpret test scores and who could then urge teachers to use those scores to drive instruction. The connection between what the administrator urged and what the teacher did was loose at best and nonexistent at worst.

The data-driven administrator of the future is one who does much more than read and distribute test data to teachers. The "new" administrator must be one who looks at patterns (or what is hidden within the data) suggestive of either what teachers are doing or what students should be accomplishing.

The Standards Debate: The Movement to National Standards

The debate about standards is evolving toward considerable advocacy for national standards. For years advocates have asserted that true educational excellence can only be found through the standards (and the school choice) door. Hirsch (1996) described a decade ago how the learning gap between and among diverse student populations could only be mitigated by creating a national core curriculum. Such a curriculum was essential, he asserted, especially in countries with high student mobility. And the United States is a mobile country.

Hirsch's "call" was one of many that followed the 1983 *A Nation at Risk* report, which brought to the nation's attention the need for enhanced standards. Meier (2000) describes pointedly the critics' claims and concomitant demands for excellence: "American education needed to be re-imagined, made more rigorous, and, above all, brought under the control of experts who . . . understood the new demands of our economy and culture" (p. 10). And what the critics "understood" was a need for defined academic standards. Meier is an advocate for using local testing instruments (not a national test), along with more independent reviews of student work (Mathews, 2006).

The U.S. standards movement was born out of a grassroots effort to more clearly establish defined academic content expectations for students. Educators, policymakers, learned society experts, and business leaders began to create a state-by-state consensus for clear standards. And Achieve (see www.achieve.org) was formed to assist states as they develop benchmarked academic expectations.

Initially, the focus was on state standards, but President Clinton (in his second State of the Union Address) foreshadowed the need for national standards (Tucker & Codding, 1998). So in fewer than ten years (1989–1997), the nation moved from few defined standards in some states to a call for national standards for all fifty states.

Those calls went unanswered for several years, but in the interim Achieve and others have been working frantically to create standards within all fifty states that are rigorous and well defined. And policy think tanks, especially those on the conservative side of the spectrum such as the Thomas B. Fordham Foundation, have been carefully critiquing what the individual states produce and "lobbying" for national standards (Mathews, 2006). The critics argue that the states are simply not responding with the types of standards and tests U.S. students need in order to be competitive. Petrilli and Finn (2006) write:

Consider the states' reaction to NCLB. Evidence is mounting that they are responding by lowering their standards, making their tests easier, and shielding their schools from accountability. Some of this is happening in plain view; Missouri, for example, recently backed away from its high standards specifically because NCLB was fingering so many of its schools as subpar. Many other states are gaming the system behind closed doors. One sign of this quiet rebellion is the growing disparity between student performance on state exams and on the National Assessment of Educational Progress (NAEP). According to an analysis by the Thomas B. Fordham Foundation, from 2003–2005 at least 20 states posted gains on their own 8th-grade reading exams, yet none of these showed progress at the "proficient" level on NAEP. While there could be explanations for this discrepancy, one must suspect that states are finding subtle ways to make their own tests easier. (p. 49)

State standards are currently in place, but whether national standards (or a process for moving toward them that parallels what Mathews describes) are embraced is yet to be determined. That is, all states now have standards (at least in some form), and Achieve and other policy groups are reviewing those standards to ensure that state educators and legislators know how each state's standards compare to those in other states. That comparison process, in and of itself, will eventually move the nation toward some type of implicit nationalized curriculum, but the question is whether the academic bar that results will be set high enough. The critics have an answer: establish solid, rigorous national standards and then test to those standards with appropriate assessments. Sounds logical, but will national standards solve the problem or will they create new ones? Peyser (2006) suggests that the latter is a more likely scenario.

Establishing a single set of national standards and assessments would effectively make the federal government the owner and operator of America's public education system. This would in turn inevitably draw the Department of Education deeper and deeper into the business of operating schools, most likely by issuing an ever-expanding set of ineffectual yet burdensome edicts. Such an outcome is not consistent with my view of a wise and limited federal government. (p. 53)

In essence, the critics assert that national standards represent an essential road to academic excellence across all 50 states. Those cautioning against national standards argue that some positive steps are already occurring (particularly in states such as Massachusetts) and that a move toward nationalizing the curriculum would be enervating to educators.

The State of State Standards

As we already noted, all states currently have some type or form of established content standards and some type of concomitant testing program. Clearly, the No Child Left Behind legislation has forced states to move more quickly, especially on testing programs, than they might otherwise have done, but almost all the states, as we indicated earlier, were moving to create or revise standards by the time the NCLB legislation was effected.

The standards for any particular state are now easily and readily accessed. Teachers and administrators can use myriad access points, most notably each respective state's department of education website.

As those standards are accessed and reviewed, educational leaders should be aware of several considerations:

1. *The standards vary between and within states in terms of quality.* As we indicated through the case studies at the beginning of this chapter, there is unevenness in terms of quality relative to the overall strength of each state's content standards (which is why some call for national standards). Some policy entities regularly critique (or grade) those individual states' standards (see Figure 9.2 for a sample of some A, B, C, D, and F states); other groups, such as Achieve, allow educators to view and assess state educational outcomes by simply going to a website (www.achieve.org) and reaching their own interpretations.

On the date the authors wrote this section of the textbook, they reviewed Achieve's assessment of standards in three states: Ohio, Texas, and California. For each of those states, Achieve provided reports on whether the graduation diploma requirements really "measure up" and how the students performed on the National Assessment of Educational Progress (NAEP) exam.

One of the efforts of Achieve is to show how the work world of the future necessarily will require advanced academic skills. By 2010 Carnevale and

FIGURE 9.2   Thomas B. Fordham Foundation Assessment of Academic Content Standards (2006) (Selected States)

State	Overall	English	Math	Science	U.S. History	World History
Arizona	B	B	C	B	A	B
California	A	A	A	A	A	A
Colorado	C	C	D	B	D	D
Indiana	A	A	A	A	A	A
Georgia	B	B	B	B	B	A
Massachusetts	A	A	A	A	A	A
Mississippi	D	B	D	F	F	C
Nebraska	D	C	D	F	C	D
Ohio	D	C	D	B	D	F
Texas	C	B	C	F	C	C
South Carolina	B	B	D	A	C	A
Wyoming	F	F	F	F	F	F

Source: C. E. Finn, Jr., M. Petrilli, & J. Liam. (2006). *The state of the state standards: 2006*. Washington, DC: Thomas B. Fordham Foundation.

Desrochers (2003) estimate that at least two-thirds of the available jobs will require some postsecondary education. And, so the argument goes, to be really prepared for that postsecondary education, young people will need to be educated in schools that have clearly defined standards. Achieve documents how the students in states such as Texas stack up in terms of their readiness to handle college work. For example, based on 2004 data, Achieve estimates that 35 percent of the Texas students (and 40 percent nationally) will start college but only 13 percent will earn a college degree (18 percent nationally).

The concern with standards has been heightened because of the recent efforts of business leaders and others to show how the poor academic performance and weak graduation rates of students compromise America's economic competitiveness. According to the Organization for Economic Cooperation and Development (OECD), the United States ranks sixteenth internationally, with 73 percent graduating from high schools. Denmark ranks first, with virtually a 100 percent graduation rate. In essence, far too many students are academically unprepared for postsecondary education experiences in a world that will, without doubt, require postsecondary preparation.

2. *The standards are but one of the ingredients essential for quality education.* The standards establish a foundation for effective educational practice within the classroom, but without the right complements, they are insufficient for fostering student academic achievement. What are those other complements? They include good instruction and effective assessments—essentially, good teaching provided by good teachers.

Much of what effective administrators do is to make certain that they have the right teachers in the classrooms teaching content in the best way they can to the students they are assigned. Collins (2001), though writing about the business world, probably has it right for any human enterprise: "The good-to-great leaders began the transformation [process] by first getting the right people on the bus (and the wrong people off the bus) and then [they] figured out where to drive it" (p. 63). The education enterprise is similar: Good-to-great schools are those with the right teachers in the classroom.

This second condition suggests that even if the standards in your state are exemplary (that is, they are clearly defined and comprehensive and perhaps even receive the "Fordham A"), there remains much for you to do if you are to use data in ways that drive your school forward toward excellence. As we will outline later in this chapter, it is essential that standards-instruction-assessments be aligned, and it is the administrator who ensures that such alignment is in place. Further, for the alignment to create maximum value-added opportunities, it is up to the teacher to create them. In essence, you as the administrator are the one charged almost singularly with ensuring that the right staff members are in place.

3. *The standards require that professional development of new and veteran staff members becomes integral to program operations.* For far too many schools, professional development is an incidental "add on" and not a vital value-added opportunity.

Good staff development is critical to ensuring that teachers know the academic standards and understand the curriculum alignment process.

Stotsky (2005) describes that "few states are successfully aligning their [exit or high-stakes] tests, teacher training and professional development with their K–12 academic standards" (p. 7). Indeed, Stotsky found that in twenty-two different states, insufficient articulation occurs between and among the different elements. Most certainly, Stotsky's assessment and conclusions are debatable, but equally certain, a problem of alignment in some states and many school districts *does* exist. That has real implications for administrators who want to use data to enhance program excellence and student achievement.

Although the NCLB legislation is flawed in some ways and especially limiting in others (see Starnes, 2006), it has forced everyone involved in educating young people to understand that the learning process is much more than keeping young people safe and busy. Effective education requires that students make adequate progress each year toward defined academic goals, and it necessitates that administrators monitor and drive that process. Hence, a good administrator not only needs to know how to use data to make decisions, but he or she also needs to know enough about the overall instructional process in order to direct and maximize the performance of those for whom he or she is responsible.

Thus far we have discussed the essential first link in the instructional process—standards. We now outline how instruction and assessment must necessarily be tightly coupled with defined standards.

Design of Instruction for Maximizing Results

During the past several years pedagogical wars have been occurring between progressivist educators and neoconservative critics about how best to teach content. Progressivists have argued for constructivist and inquiry-oriented, student-centered approaches. Neoconservatives have postured for direct, explicit, and teacher-centered models. The debates have been evident in a variety of disciplinary fields, but most noticeably reading, mathematics, and science.

One of the unfortunate aspects of the debate has been the polarization of how people think about instruction—it is either progressivist, student-centered, or direct, teacher-centered. If only the world were ordered so simply!

We contend that good teachers must be educated to be both teacher- and student-centered and that the emphasis in their professional development, especially once they have a classroom appointment, will be dictated by the following: the types of students they are working with and the nature of content they are teaching. Chall (2000) wrote a research synthesis about the two approaches (see also Chapter 6), and although her conclusions were biased toward the teacher-centered model, her analysis favors the complexity and balanced view that we describe. Specifically, she notes: "As research becomes available, we may well find that each approach has some advantage for academic achievement at different levels of education and proficiency. We may find that the traditional approach is more effective for beginners who first acquire knowledge and skills. Then, as they move beyond the basics, a progressive approach may prove more effective" (p. 183).

Some emerging research from large urban school districts supports the balanced view. Results from the 2005 National Assessment of Educational Progress (NAEP) suggest that in urban areas such as New York City the reading instruction that includes a focus on both higher-order (comprehension) and lower-order decoding skills fosters enhanced student achievement (Manzo, 2006). Similarly, in Boston evidence seems to be surfacing to support a more balanced approach to mathematics instruction. Writes Cavanagh (2006):

> Researchers and school officials have debated for years the most effective way to teach math. The so-called "math wars," which gained intensity in the late 1990s, featured supporters of a more conceptual approach to teaching math arguing from one perspective. Backers of conceptual math see evidence of its effectiveness in foreign nations, particularly in Asia, whose students routinely outperform their U.S. peers on tests of math skill.
>
> Critics of that approach, however, said American students' shortcomings were most likely the result of a lack of fundamental math skills.
>
> In recent years, both camps have emphasized that a balance between conceptual math and basic skills is needed. (p. 14)

Research by Sternberg, Torff, and Grigorenko (1998) is also suggestive of what Chall indicates that we need to know in order to inform the instructional process and that emerging research argues for dualistic and not polaristic modeling. Specifically, they and others argue that to maximize student achievement teachers must teach for memory, analysis, and creativity: Students remember the content better and longer when this occurs. They write:

> when material is taught in a variety of pedagogically sound ways—in this case, for memory as well as analytically, creatively, and practically, students have more opportunities to learn and understand the material being taught. If they do not understand the material when it is taught in one way, they might comprehend it when it is taught in another. (p. 668)

Further evidence supporting the use of mixed instructional approaches may be found in the way so many high-stakes tests currently are being structured. Increasingly, the high-stakes graduation and achievement examinations require students to recall content, use defined skills, *and* construct responses that synthesize the content material they have learned. Even the college board examinations now favor both recall and constructed response, and students who have too much skill-driven instruction and too little opportunity for synthesis, analysis, and evaluation will be disadvantaged in their ability to perform well on the ACT or SAT.

So, what to do? We propose several principles to guide how you think about instruction. These principles are, as we note, guides to examining the way in which teachers teach the content linked to the standards. There will be exceptions to the principles, but those exceptions will require that an administrator understand all the principles well enough to determine when and how an exception is warranted. We also urge the reader to carefully review Figure 9.3 where we have graphically illustrated the connection between the models and the goals associated with the models. We have intentionally kept the model somewhat simple. If this were a book about instruction, then the figure would necessarily be more comprehensive and look much more complicated. Instead, this is a book about using data to make decisions vis-à-vis classroom practices. Hence, our point of emphasis is for you to see that instruction is an element that must be considered and to provide you with some basic ideas about how to think about the different pedagogical models. As you look at teaching strategies (e.g., direct instruction, concept attainment) consider the following:

1. Is the model teacher-centered or student-centered?
2. Does the teacher focus on specific concepts that are covered in your state's academic standards, or is the teacher trying to encourage students to develop their own concepts?
3. Is the teacher emphasizing a skill or process that the students need to repeat (or memorize) when requested to do so, or is the teacher focusing on helping students to construct their own responses to problems?

In essence, as an administrator it is imperative that you understand the goals of instruction sufficiently well to know whether and how what the teacher is doing helps students progress in their learning. Part of using data to make program decisions entails being able to look critically at a classroom and determine if the purpose of instruction is clear. Obviously, there are times when administrators will

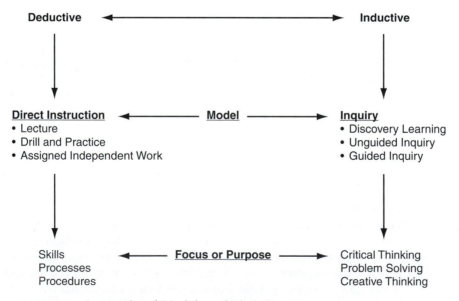

FIGURE 9.3   Instructional Models and Their Purposes

need to talk to teachers to understand the purpose (i.e., not all purposes for instruction are sufficiently transparent to be deduced through observation), but once the opportunity for reflective dialogue occurs, it should be clear to an administrator what the teacher was seeking to accomplish and how it fits within the curriculum.

And, if teachers or any others argue for a polarized view (constructivist or direct instruction), ask them to support their view empirically. We offer, as partial justification for our "mixed instructional model" view, the following observation from the National Research Council's book *How People Learn* (2000). Recall that Chall (2000) earlier evidenced a bias (based on her reading of the research) toward teacher-centered models, but then qualified it with the observation that for some students and purposes, student-centered strategies might make more sense. In *How People Learn* (National Research Council, 2000), the bias (again supported by research) is toward student-centered strategies, but then the authors offer the following qualifying observation:

> A common misconception regarding "constructivist" theories of knowing (that existing knowledge is used to build new knowledge) is that teachers should never tell students anything directly but, instead, should always allow them to construct knowledge for themselves. This perspective confuses a theory of pedagogy (teaching) with a theory of knowing. Constructivists assume that all knowledge is constructed from previous knowledge, irrespective of how one is taught . . . even listening to a lecture involves active attempts to construct new knowledge. . . . Nevertheless, there are times, usually after people have first grappled with issues on their own, that "teaching by telling" can work extremely well. . . . However, teachers still need to pay attention to students' interpretations and provide guidance when necessary. (p. 11)

All of this suggests the complexity of the instructional process. To help you better cope with that complexity, we proffer the following principles. These principles of instruction are for you to consider as you interact with teachers (or think about your own teaching) about how they design and structure instruction in their classrooms. We assume that they (that is, the teachers) are determining the strategy after they have identified the instructional goal or academic content standard they want the students to achieve.

One other note before we introduce the instructional principles relates to "noncognitive" points of emphasis in a school or classroom. As we write this book, the Knowledge Is Power Program (KIPP) academies have received a great deal of national publicity for the high performance of their students. A close examination of KIPP educational practices suggests that although teachers in KIPP schools do place heavy emphasis on *clear instructional goals,* it is equally evident that they focus heavily on shaping students' attitudes—that is, how they look at their own behavior (self-discipline) and think about their own academic potential. Research supports this emphasis as a means to improving student performance. Tough (2006), for example, writes that researchers have found that "the self-discipline scores [of students] were a more accurate predictor of GPA than the IQ scores by a factor of two" (p. 69).

The instructional principles that we articulate below address how the teachers organize instruction. The research associated with the KIPP-type experiments suggests that equally important is how the administrators and teachers help shape the attitudes of students to ensure that they understand and work toward achieving their own individual potential. In essence, a school might be doing everything "right" but still be failing if the students are not acquiring the mental habits to appreciate and act on their own academic abilities.

Principles of Instruction

Principle 1: The more skill oriented the goal of a lesson, the more the teacher should use a teacher-centered (deductive) strategy.

Beginning golfers are often told to take lessons to ensure that their practice does not reinforce bad habits (or the incorrect use of a particular golfing skill). Similarly, it makes little sense to allow students to "discover" the long division process. True, many students could discover it, but equally true, many would do so over an extremely long period of time, or they would learn the skill in a way that encouraged errors. In a perfect educational world, where time was not a factor, one might make a compelling case for the discovery of a skill or process. But in our world (your world), it is simply not logical to expect students to inductively learn all they need to acquire for academic success.

Administrators who want results need teachers who know how to efficiently and effectively achieve defined educational goals. If one of those educational goals is enhanced achievement vis-à-vis defined academic content standards, then teachers need to know that in most instances the best, most effective way to teach a skill or process is to use direct or explicit instruction.

In sum, when teachers are covering new skills, new factual material, or when time is of the essence, a teacher-centered strategy is preferred.

Principle 2: The less well academically prepared the students are, the more the teacher should use a teacher-centered strategy.

Students who come to school ill prepared (that is, typically children from less well-educated families, or families of poverty, or those with special learning needs or early learning deficiencies) need teachers who are more direct in their teaching approaches (Chall, 2000). As Chall notes, one of the reasons why the teacher-centered approach is efficacious is that it "makes clear to the student what the objectives are and specifies the learning tasks to be mastered in an increasing order of difficulty. Because of the explicitness, it is of particular benefit to those who are less well prepared" (p. 177).

Because the teacher is directive and controlling does not mean a lesson is necessarily boring. Teacher-centered lessons can be engaging, but they require that a teacher understand how to connect the skills and content being taught to the lives of the young people they are teaching.

A teacher-centered, direct instruction lesson has a defined structure (see Rosenshine, 1983).

1. Provide daily review.
2. Present new skill or content in step-by-step fashion.
3. Provide time for student practice.
4. Offer feedback to students on their performance.
5. Provide time for independent practice.
6. Perform ongoing periodic reviews.

The lesson described in Figure 9.4 offers an example of a direct instruction lesson. The teacher in this instance is teaching an explicit skill that is linked directly to a defined state academic standard. As you read this case (or watch any teacher teach a skill or concept using direct methods), consider the following types of questions (see also Lasley, Matczynski, & Rowley, 2002):

1. Does the teacher state the objective for a lesson?
2. Does the teacher connect the lesson objective with a defined state academic content standard?
3. Does the teacher teach the skill in a step-by-step fashion?
4. Are students given an opportunity to practice the skill?
5. Are students provided with feedback about their performance?
6. Are students given ample opportunity for independent practice? And do they appear to know the skill before they begin independent practice?

Teacher-centered instruction should match content to be learned with the learning needs of those who need to acquire the content; it does *not* place students in a passive or inactive role. Students should be asked lots of questions and be highly interactive with the teacher as they are both taught the content in a step-by-step fashion and practice skills with feedback on their performance by the teacher.

Beck and McKeown (2007) also illustrate how varied teacher-centeredness can be in classrooms. Far too many educators see teacher-centeredness as high teacher control and low student engagement (lecture or drill and practice). Teacher-centered instruction takes many forms. It can entail direct or explicit instruction (described above), or it can involve having a teacher systematically teach, for example, vocabulary through "rich" texts to enhance student comprehension, with the teacher selecting specific and conceptually challenging texts that contain terms or vocabulary that students would find unfamiliar. The teacher then carefully defines the terms, provides contextually different representations of the terms (through the texts), helps students examine examples and nonexamples of each term's use (in and outside selected texts), and then has students generate their own conceptually appropriate uses (examples) of the terms. In essence, the students "explore" each term's meaning under very controlled, teacher-centered conditions.

Principle 3: The teacher maximizes the use of time on content directly related to the importance of the defined academic content standards being taught.

FIGURE 9.4   Case Study: Direct Instruction

Mr. Dale Carthridge begins his mathematics unit with the following statements:

"During the past several weeks we have been studying how to add and subtract fractions. Last week we investigated how to multiply fractions. Let's take a couple of minutes to review the process that we followed in multiplying $\frac{3}{4} \times \frac{1}{2}$." At this point Mr. Carthridge reviews the steps the students should follow in multiplying fractions. Once the class completes the review, Mr. Carthridge begins a new segment of the unit.

"Today, class, we are going to learn how to divide fractions. There will be two purposes for our lesson. First, you will list the specific steps that must be followed in dividing fractions; and second, you will describe why you follow the steps used in the division process."

"Let's begin. First, I want you all to get your slates out and put them on your desks." (Mr. Carthridge has slates and chalk that the students use during math drill and practice exercises.)

"I am going to work three problems on the board. You will see each step labeled clearly, but I want you to perform the work on your slates as I perform the work on the board. The problem we will start with is $\frac{1}{2} \div \frac{3}{8} = ?$"

The teacher then puts the acronym PIRMS on the board: Problem Invert Reduce Multiply Solve. "Let's look at what each of these letters in the acronym means for $\frac{1}{2} \div \frac{3}{8}$. I call this the PIRMS process."

Mr. Carthridge works the first problem slowly, and next to each of the words he identifies the step the students must follow. When he is finished, the problem on the board looks similar to the one in Table 9.1.

The students have the same problem worked out on their slates. As Mr. Carthridge presents each step, he carefully talks them through the process: "First, class, you state the problem, which in this case is $\frac{3}{4} \div \frac{1}{3}$. Next, class, Step 2: You invert the fraction on the right side. To remember this, just think that it's right to invert on the right. Sharonda, what does invert mean?" (Sharonda correctly describes how to invert.)

Mr. Carthridge meticulously describes the first problem and then erases, at the end, all the numbers on the right side of Table 9.1 and puts a new problem on the board: $\frac{3}{4} \div \frac{1}{3} = ?$ Once again he very carefully describes the mathematical processes step-by-step. The students follow each step by performing the steps on their personal slates. At the end, Mr. Carthridge erases the problem and all the steps.

TABLE 9.1   Sequential Organizer for Solving Division Problem

STEP 1:	Problem	$\frac{1}{2} \div \frac{3}{8} =$
STEP 2:	Invert	$\frac{1}{2} \div \frac{8}{3} =$
STEP 3:	Reduce	$\frac{1}{2} \times \frac{8}{3} = \frac{1}{1} \times \frac{4}{3}$
STEP 4:	Multiply	$\frac{1}{1} \times \frac{4}{3} = \frac{4}{3}$
STEP 5:	Solve	$\frac{4}{3} = 1\frac{1}{3}$

"Now, class, I'm going to give you a third problem. But in this case, you will be helping me. Let's begin. I'll start by giving you a problem: $\frac{3}{5} \div \frac{1}{2} = ?$ Joshua, what's the second step that we use?"

"You invert the numbers and multiply."

"Which numbers?"

"The $\frac{1}{2}$."

"Why?" responds Mr. Carthridge.

"Because it's on the right side," says Joshua.

"Yes, and a little later you'll also know the more technical reason for inverting the $\frac{1}{2}$. What's the next step after we have $\frac{3}{5} \times \frac{2}{1}$? Jasmine?"

"You simplify."

"And what do you mean by simplify, Jasmine?"

"You see if any of the numbers are factors of the other numbers."

"Excellent. I like how you explained that. Well, are any of the numbers factors and can you simplify? Lanita?"

"No."

"Good. So what's the next step?"

"You multiply."

"Yes. First you multiply the numerators, and then you multiply the denominators. What would you get if you do that? Troy?"

"6/5."

"Correct. So $\frac{3}{5} \times \frac{2}{1} = \frac{6}{5}$. Now the last step is to solve the problem. Remember last week I indicated that this means putting the improper fraction $\frac{6}{5}$ into its lowest terms. And what would that be? Nathan?"

"$1\frac{1}{5}$."

"Yes.

"Now I want you to do one on your slate. When you finish, please show all your work, and hold your slate up so I can see your work. Now, try $\frac{3}{7} \times \frac{2}{3} = ?$"

The students work the problem and hold up their slates. Mr. Carthridge moves around the room and checks the students' progress. He then gives them three more problems: $\frac{1}{5} \div \frac{1}{3} = ?$; $\frac{2}{9} \div \frac{4}{5} = ?$; and $\frac{1}{4} \div \frac{1}{2} = ?$ After students complete each problem, Mr. Carthridge reviews each step with the students to make certain everyone understands.

Source: T. J. Lasley, T. J. Matczynski, & J. B. Rowley. (2002). *Instructional Models: Strategies for Teaching in a Diverse Society*. Belmont, CA: Wadsworth, pp. 268–269.

Few classroom variables have been researched with as much depth as has the concept of time-on-task (or academic learning time). Since the early process-product studies of the 1970s, researchers have noted that the amount of time devoted to instruction influences the amount of student learning (see Berliner, 1979). Even those with incredible natural talents spend lots of time developing and refining their skills. Tiger Woods is an accomplished golfer, but he practices long hours to maintain his excellence.

Deductive strategies such as lectures are more time efficient, but even with such approaches it is imperative that teachers make certain that they allocate the time necessary to ensure that students have an opportunity to learn the material being taught. Administrators who want results need to be very cognizant of how teachers use time. Are they providing students with enough time to really process (or think through) ideas? Are they limiting the number of topics focused on during a lesson? Teachers who cover too many topics, too quickly, will significantly mitigate student learning (see National Research Council, 2000). Interestingly, the now famous Singapore curriculum (in mathematics) limits the number of topics covered by teachers, and consequently ensures that students spend more time on those topics that are covered. Further, the Singapore curriculum evidences both an emphasis on content mastery and a focus on problem solving relative to that content.

Teachers and administrators need to be aware that time-on-task entails more than just spending lots of time on a topic in practice or problem solving. Researchers agree that unless feedback is occurring (to the students) the overall impact of the time spent will be reduced. As the authors of *How People Learn* note:

> Concepts such as "deliberate practice" emphasize the importance of helping students monitor their learning so that they seek feedback and actively evaluate their strategies and current levels of understanding. Such activities are very different from simply reading and rereading a text. (National Research Council, 2000, p. 236)

The effective use of time is actually quite complex. Given that this is a book about using data to make decisions and not a book about instruction per se, we necessarily abbreviate our presentation of the research on this topic. Readers, however, are encouraged to review texts such as *How People Learn* or to examine the extensive research and instrumentation available for academic learning time, especially if they are going to be thoughtful observers of the teaching–learning process.

> Principle 4: The teacher organizes instruction so that students have opportunities to memorize, analyze, and creatively encounter the content that the teacher is presenting.

Sternberg and colleagues (1998) refer to this emphasis on memory, analysis, and creativity as triarchic intelligence. Their research is a cautionary note for all who want to polarize the teaching–learning process into either a deductive or inductive process. Acquisition of information is often accomplished through very teacher-centered modeling. But analysis and creativity is inherently more inductive and complex. It takes more time, but it also results in enhanced retention. Research support for this assertion is provided by Pogrow (2006). Citing studies by James Catteral and others, Pogrow notes that "a national database showed that participation in dramatic productions increased the reading scores of low income students . . . [because of] the more sophisticated uses of language from students than are called for in the typical classroom" (p. 227).

Sternberg and colleagues (1998) provide additional support when they note:

> an educational intervention based on the theory of successful intelligence improved school achievement on performance assessments measuring analytical, creative, and practical achievements and on conventional multiple choice memory assessments. . . . Triarchic thinking does not impede—and actually facilitates—factual recall, presumably because students learn the material the way they are taught in multiple ways and can better capitalize on their strengths and weaknesses. (p. 669)

The Sternberg research, which is reinforced in the literature by other researchers (see National Research Council, 2000; Pogrow, 2006), suggests that any one-size-fits-all approach to teaching *all students* will fail to achieve the learning outcomes that most educators desire. Good teachers know how to use different teaching strategies to accomplish different purposes. The children they work with may influence the type of instruction they use at times, but it will not (and should not) affect the need to help students explore content in different ways.

Our point is that teachers do not use a variety of instructional strategies in order to be pedagogically cute; they use them in order to be pedagogically effective—that is, to help students learn material better and retain it longer. The effectiveness occurs because teachers, through stimulus variation, are better able to maintain the interests and attention of students, and the students, through varied modes of learning, are able to experience content in ways that enhance achievement (Borich, 1999).

> Principle 5: The teacher should identify some content (or power standards) that need to be taught in more depth and then provide lots of examples to ensure that students acquire the content (See National Research Council, 2000).

One of the real problems confronting teachers is the sheer volume of content that needs to be taught. As an example, in the authors' home state, the number of standards and indicators makes it difficult for teachers to really cover all the academic content, especially in an area such as social studies.

One way to deal with this "coverage" problem is to identify "power standards" that have more academic "reach." This requires that you as an administrator be reasonably knowledgeable of the content standards for your state *and* that your teachers must be able to make decisions about where they will devote the most time in order to maximize student content exposure.

The authors of *How People Learn* capture the notion: "The goal of coverage need not be abandoned entirely. . . . But there must be a sufficient number of cases of in-depth study to allow students to grasp the defining concepts". . . (National Research Council, 2000, p. 20). Students who have depth in the right domains (and on certain power standards) can then more readily transfer that knowledge to other domains of learning. Teachers want students to do well on achievement tests, but even more importantly they want them to be able to transfer their understandings (what they have learned) into multiple contexts. That transfer will only be accomplished if teachers make wise choices about what content to emphasize, how to teach that content, and then work with students to deal effectively with the understandings and misunderstandings of students.

We articulated five instructional principles for you to consider in the previous section. Quite candidly, there are a plethora of principles that could or should be considered, but these five, to us, represent instructional keys. They suggest that knowing *which* standards to teach in depth and *how* teachers should teach to the content standards are both vitally important. Teachers have to make choices and an administrator is, of necessity, in a position to influence those choices. As teachers and administrators interact, it is important to remember that there is no one pedagogically right way, but there are multiple possible instructional options. The administrator's role is one of looking at student performance data and asking reflective questions such as:

1. Are the students having difficulty with constructed response items?
2. Are the students unable to recall key facts or use important academic skills?
3. Are the students unable to critically think through different types of learning problems?

The yes or no answers to these types of questions will influence how administrators need to work with the teaching staff, with the guiding principles that we have proffered as a guide for the professional development decisions that are made; that is, in what areas does the professional staff need more work if the students'achievement is to be enhanced?

Design of Assessment to Direct Student Learning

In Friedman's book *The World Is Flat* (2005), he describes the process of globalization and the electronic flattening of the world. Friedman powerfully describes how UPS and Wal-Mart have changed the way products are made, transported, sold, and monitored for performance. In the "round" world in which most of us grew up, the connection between the point of creation and the point of sale was often not tightly coupled. In the "flat" world, as soon as a barcode registers a widget "sold," a message is delivered to the manufacturer to make another widget.

In the education world, a similar flattening is occurring. UPS need not feel threatened! But educators who continue to ineffectively align standards-instruction-assessment should. This book is about how to flatten the educational process. In the old pedagogical world, a teacher decided what to teach, often with some assistance from a district curricular guide. The classroom was the teacher's domain, and he or she was relatively disconnected from the rest of the educational world. The teacher might administer a standardized test, but the results would take weeks if not months to secure, and as a result they never significantly impacted what teachers did to design instruction based on student learning needs.

In the flat education world, instruction is linked to standards, and assessments are a result of a systemic process to gather evidence about the achievement of the students (Chappuis & Chappuis, 2002). Further, when standardized tests are administered, the results are delivered quickly and are then used to shape and direct student learning. Indeed, some tests (such as those from Northwest Evaluation Association or NWEA) are administered electronically, with results delivered to students and teachers within hours or days (not weeks or months). The Measures of Academic Progress (MAP) are used to track students' academic progress. Those results compare students to other students who are at a similar age or grade, and they also describe the students' current achievement level on a defined curriculum scale (see www.NWEA.org) that is anchored to the academic standards of each state. Especially important is the fact that teachers receive almost immediate feedback on student performance.

In the previous section we described some basic instructional principles that a data-driven administrator might consider as he or she observed a classroom. In this section we offer three basic assessment principles to consider. Before proffering those principles, we offer a caution. The assessment and accountability process is just beginning to mature in the United States. Psychometricians are still much better at assessing for factual knowledge than they are at measuring depth of understanding (National Research Council, 2000). That fact necessarily limits the degree to which assessment results can be used to judge overall teacher performance but it does not preclude teachers from designing and developing lots of alternatives (or teacher-made assessments) to assess what students know. Indeed, it almost demands that they do so.

Principles Assessment

Principle 1: Standards, instruction, and assessment procedures must be aligned to maximize student learning.

Student learning expectations are outlined in standards. Those expectations should be oriented to ensure that students know certain facts or content to deal with a practical problem, use certain skills to solve those problems, and as a result create a product that exhibits what they know (Chappuis & Chappuis, 2002).

For all four of these to occur teachers need to design meaningful and appropriate instruction (see previous section) and determine whether (and to what degree) students know, can use, and can produce the results that are reflective of the expectation. Good assessment is focused on more than just knowing something. It connects what is known to a defined achievement target (a standard) and then varies depending on what the teacher wants the student to demonstrate. In science, for example, a teacher might want students to know certain science facts, be able to reason (through hypothesis testing) the relationship between those facts, use a skill in the lab to test the hypothesis, and then produce a product or written report that exhibits the understanding that the students possess (Stiggins, 2001).

To assess meaningfully all four levels (knowing, reasoning, demonstrating a skill, and producing a report) requires that a teacher know the content standards and understand instructionally all the different ways to teach and assess what students have learned.

Principle 2: Assessment is *for* learning and not *of* learning.

In the "round" world of the past, teacher assessments were mostly of learning. That meant that teachers focused on material to be covered (we have to get through the book) as opposed to what material needed to be learned: that is, toward an emphasis on content facts as opposed to content facts *and* an understanding in depth of what those facts mean (Chappuis & Chappuis, 2002).

Teachers who assess for learning are carefully matching what they are expecting students to learn with an assessment technique. Figure 9.5 demonstrates what this might look like using the four "targets" (knowledge, reasoning, skills, products). Notice that the assessment approach is matched with the target not for

FIGURE 9.5   Best Matches between Learning Targets and Assessment Methods

Target to Be Assessed	Selected Response	Essay	Performance Assessment	Personal Communication
KNOWLEDGE MASTERY	Multiple-choice, true-false, matching, and fill-in items can sample mastery of elements of knowledge	Essay exercises can tap understanding of relationships among elements of knowledge	Not a good choice for this target—three other options preferred	Can ask questions, evaluate answers, and infer mastery, but a time-consuming option
REASONING PROFICIENCY	Can assess application of some patterns of reasoning	Written descriptions of complex problem solutions can provide a window into reasoning proficiency	Can watch students solve some problems or examine some products and infer about reasoning proficiency	Can ask student to "think aloud" or can ask follow-up questions to probe reasoning
SKILLS	Can assess mastery of the knowledge prerequisite to skillful performance, but cannot rely on these to tap the skill itself	Can assess mastery of the knowledge prerequisite to skillful performance, but cannot rely on these	Can observe and evaluate skills as they are being performed	Strong match when skill is oral communication proficiency; also can assess mastery of knowledge prerequisite to skillful performance
ABILITY TO CREATE PRODUCTS	Can assess mastery of the knowledge prerequisite to the ability to create quality products, but cannot use these to assess the quality of products themselves	Can assess mastery of the knowledge prerequisite to create quality products, but cannot use these to assess the quality of products	Can assess both proficiency in carrying out steps in product development, and attributes of the product itself	Can probe procedural knowledge and knowledge of attributes of quality products, but not quality of product

Source: Adapted from Richard J. Stiggins (2001), *Student-Involved Classroom Assessment*, 3rd ed. (p. 93) Upper Saddle River, NJ: Merrill Prentice Hall. Copyright © 2001 by Prentice Hall, Inc. Adapted with permission.

convenience (i.e., multiple-choice tests are easier to grade) but because the teacher is attempting to assess in particular what students know at a particular level of understanding. In addition, teachers need to be aware that just because selected response approaches are used does not preclude the use of constructed response methods. Marshall (2007), in describing some of the work by the Center for Performance Assessment, notes that it is possible and appropriate to incorporate writing and enhanced critical thinking into multiple-choice-type tests, with the teacher requiring that students explain in writing why an incorrect answer or "distractor" is wrong.

In other methods texts, readers can find in-depth discussions about how best to develop selected response tests such as fill-in-the-blanks or multiple choice (see, for example, Ornstein & Lasley, 2004) or how to create essay tests that measure student knowledge. Our goal in this section is to suggest that data-driven administrators are critical observers of how teacher assessments are used in the classroom. That is: Does the teacher establish varied achievement targets for students? Does the teacher use varied "matched" methods for determining whether those targets are achieved? Is the teacher providing students with ample opportunities to express what they know through both selected response and constructed response approaches?

> Principle 3: Norm- and criterion-referenced tests are used to assess an understanding of broad achievement levels and not of specific instructional approaches for particular students.

The use and misuse of standardized tests has been a topic of heated debate for the past decade, especially with the implementation of NCLB and high-stakes testing in so many states.

Good teachers use both formative (ongoing) and summative (end of learning activity) assessments to determine what students have learned and what they still need to learn or relearn. They also understand that the performance of any one student on any one day has limitations. For one student to do poorly on a standardized test is "suggestive" of where he or she might stand as a learner; for a whole class to do poorly is compelling evidence of an instructional problem. It means that either the students did not learn what was required (which suggests something about how the teacher taught the material) or that the test did not assess (or match) what they learned. The opposite is also true; it is important not to assume that high student performance on certain types of standardized tests means high student achievement. The authors of *How People Learn* (National Research Council, 2000) write:

> in addition, many standardized tests that are used for accountability still overemphasize memory for isolated facts and procedures, yet teachers are often judged by how well their students do on such tests. One mathematics teacher consistently produced students who scored high on statewide examinations by helping students memorize a number of mathematical procedures (e.g., proofs) that typically appeared on the examinations, but the students did not really understand what they

were doing, and often could not answer questions that required an understanding of mathematics. (p. 141)

Standardized tests are most appropriately used by data-driven decision makers when taken as one form of information about students and teacher performance, not the source of information. As Chappuis and Chappuis (2002) note, standardized tests are best used by teachers to rank-order students for the purpose of deciding who (which students) may need special or enhanced assistance. And they are best used by data-driven decision makers to determine where the strengths or weaknesses are within an instructional system and where future resources and professional development might be directed.

SUMMARY

Administrators who understand how to use data to make effective decisions must be aware of the complex dynamics associated with good teaching. Those dynamics include, but are not limited to, the use of academic content standards to ground instruction, the use of instructional strategies that help students acquire defined learning targets, and the use of assessment techniques that help teachers know what learning has occurred and also needs to occur in the future.

Data-driven administrators are not simply individuals who look at numbers and reach conclusions. They are persons who understand how to shape results by helping teachers better interface standards, instruction, and assessment. In order to do that effectively necessarily means that an administrator understand, at some reasonable level, what the content standards are for his or her state, what instructional alternatives exist to teach the requisite content, and what assessment approaches are available for teachers. Not all data-driven administrators can be or will be gifted teachers. But all must be sufficiently knowledgeable about the standards–instruction–assessment nexus to be critical observers of classroom practices.

QUESTIONS AND SUGGESTED ACTIVITIES

Case Study Questions

1. Susan Brightstein (Case Study I) found the reading standards for her state to be unclear. What steps can or should be taken by a teacher or administrator when particular academic content standards are not clear?

2. The testing debate continues in most states. In what ways have high-stakes tests helped to improve education in America? In what ways do high-stakes tests represent a threat to the educational achievement of young people?

3. Visit the Thomas B. Fordham website (www.edexcellence.net) and review the content standards for your state. In what ways do you agree with the Fordham assessment for your state? Disagree?

4. Do you tend to favor high-stakes tests as a means of ensuring educational quality, or do you agree with groups such as Mass CARE (see Case Study II) that they compromise education? See the Greene, Winters, and Forster (2003) and Amrein and Berliner (2002) studies and compare and contrast their arguments. Nichols and Berliner (2007) have a book highly critical of high-stakes testing. Examine their arguments carefully and identify ways in which you believe they have it "right" and "wrong."

Chapter Questions

5. Why is the data-driven administrator's role so much more complex than what was expected previously of school administrators? Are principals being adequately prepared to deal with that complexity?

6. The "call" for a national curriculum has been in evidence for a decade, but increasingly policy leaders are arguing for a move toward nationalizing learning targets. What factors are contributing to the move toward a national curriculum?

7. The *Coleman Report* (in the 1960s) and *A Nation at Risk* (in the 1980s) represent two different approaches to understanding academic achievement expectations. In what ways are the conclusions similar? Different?

8. Why is it so difficult for states to align academic standards with appropriate assessments?

9. Why would it be inappropriate to rely exclusively on either direct instruction or inquiry as an instructional approach to the delivery of academic content?

10. What is triarchic intelligence? How can teachers teach to ensure that students maximize their overall achievement?

11. When is it imperative that teachers consider identifying certain "power" academic standards to emphasize in their instruction?

12. Why is it important for different learning targets to be established by teachers in the course of an extended unit of study?

13. Why is it inappropriate to use a student's performance on one standardized test (such as the Iowa Test of Basic Skills) to assess his or her overall academic abilities?

REFERENCES

Amrein, A. L., & Berliner, D. C. (2002). High-stakes testing, uncertainty, and student learning. *Education Policy Analysis Archives, 10*(18). Retrieved February 9, 2006, from http://epaa.asu.edu/epaa/v10n18/

Beck, I., & McKeown, M. (2007). Increasing young low-income children's oral vocabulary repertoires through rich and focused instruction. *Elementary School Journal, 107*(3), 251–271.

Berliner, D. C. (1979). Tempus educare. In P. L. Peterson & H. J. Walberg (Eds.), *Research on teaching: Concepts, findings, and implications* (pp. 120–135). Berkeley, CA: McCutchan.

Borich, G. (1999). *Observation skills for effective teaching.* Upper Saddle River, NJ: Merrill, Prentice Hall.

Carnevale, A. P., & Desrochers, D. M. (2003). *Standards for what? The economic roots of K–16 reform.* Washington, DC: Educational Testing Service.

Cavanagh, S. (2006, January 11). Big cities credit conceptual math for higher scores. *Education Week, 25*(18), 1, 14–15.

Chall, J. (2000). *The academic achievement challenge.* New York: Guilford.

Chappuis, J., & Chappius, S. (2002). *Understanding student assessment.* Portland, OR: Assessment Training Institute.

Collins, J. (2001). *Good to great.* New York: Harper Business.

Friedman, T. (2005). *The world is flat.* Cambridge, MA: MIT World.

Greene, J. P., Winters, M. A., & Forster, G. (2003). Testing high stakes tests: Can we believe the results of accountability tests? *Civic Report, 33.* Retrieved February 9, 2006, from www.manhattan-institute.org/html/cr_33.htm

Hirsch, E. D., Jr., (1996). *The schools we need.* New York: Doubleday.

Lasley, T. J., Matczynski, T. J., & Rowley, J. B. (2002). *Instructional models: Strategies for teaching in a diverse society.* Belmont, CA: Wadsworth.

Levitt, S. D., & Dubner, S. J. (2005). *Freakonomics: A rogue economist explores the hidden side of everything.* New York: Morrow.

Manzo, K. K. (2006, January 11). NAEP results offer scant insight into best reading strategies. *Education Week, 25*(18), 14.

Marshall, K. (2007). Marshall Memo 167. Marshall cites the following: Reeves, D. (2007). Top five tips to use student writing to improve math achievement. Center for Performance Assessment. Retrieved from www.makingstandardswork.com.

Mass Care, Inc. (2005). *Massachusetts students need deeper science education, not another MCAS test.* Retrieved December 30, 2005, from www.parentscare.org/scienceedstatement.pdf

Mathews, J. (2006, September 3). National school testing urged. *Washington Post,* p. A01.

Meier, D. (2000). *Will standards save public education?* Boston: Beacon Press.

National Research Council. (2000). *How people learn.* Washington, DC: National Academy Press.

Nichols, S. L., & Berliner, D. C. (2007). *How high-stakes testing corrupts America's schools.* Cambridge, MA: Harvard Education Press.

Ornstein, A. C., & Lasley, T. J. (2004). *Strategies for effective teaching* (4th ed.). New York: McGraw-Hill.

Petrilli, M. J., & Finn, C. E., Jr. (2006). A new federalism. *Education Week, 6*(4), 48–51.

Peyser, J. A. (2006). Hoop hassles. *Education Week, 6*(4), 52–55.

Pogrow, S. (2006). Restructuring high poverty elementary schools for success: A description of the hi-perform school design. *Phi Delta Kappan, 88*(3), 223–229.

Rosenshine, B. (1983). Teaching functions in instructional programs. *Elementary School Journal, 83*(4), 335–352.

Starnes, B. A. (2006). What we don't know can hurt them: White teachers, Indian children. *Phi Delta Kappan, 87*(5), 384–392.

Sternberg, R., Torff, B., & Grigorenko, E. (1998). Teaching for successful intelligence raises student achievement. *Phi Delta Kappan, 79*(9), 667–669.

Stiggins, R. (2001). *Student-involved classroom assessment.* Upper Saddle River, NJ: Merrill-Prentice Hall.

Stotsky, S. (2005). *The state of state English standards.* Washington, DC: Thomas B. Fordham Foundation.

Tough, P. (2006, November 26). What it takes to make a student. *New York Times Magazine,* 44–51, 69–72, 77.

Tucker, M. S., & Codding, J. B. (1998). *Standards for our schools.* San Francisco: Jossey-Bass.

10 Effective School Improvement

Chapter Focus

Since the early 1980s, research on highly effective schools has produced a list of characteristics that distinguish these institutions from other schools. Often, mandated or proposed school reforms were tied to one or more of them. Even so, a number of authors (e.g., Murgatroyd & Morgan, 1993; Schenkat, 1993) have concluded that all these characteristics had not been infused into a single model. Not all models, however, are equally incomplete or ineffective, and over time several of them have been shown to be more useful than others. Although the most effective paradigms are not identical, they are highly similar. Most notably, they:

- Rely on data to diagnose problems and prescribe solutions.
- Set challenging, realistic, and measurable goals.
- Require periodic assessments.
- Prescribe continuous evaluation that is both formative and summative.

The content of this chapter identifies basic characteristics of effective models and describes two paradigms possessing them. Then attention is given to seven components considered fundamental to effective school improvement; these components have helped educators to improve schools of all different sizes, income levels, and minority populations. Last, leadership is examined in relation to school improvement.

CASE STUDY

Spring Elementary School is a K–5 city school with a very diverse student population (27 percent African American; 50 percent Caucasian; 15 percent Asian; and 4 percent Hispanic). Nearly 40 percent of the students are part of economically disadvantaged families, and approximately one-third of them have been scoring below the proficiency level on the state achievement tests.

Two years ago, after Joan Kimble became principal, she set four goals intended to improve student learning. The first focused on inputs, the next two involved process, and the fourth addressed outcomes:

1. Increase the amount of resources available for instruction by 2 percent.
2. Involve parents more directly in the school.
3. Increase teacher collaboration in instructional planning.
4. Reduce the percentage of students scoring below the proficiency level on the state achievement tests.

She revealed these goals to teachers at the second faculty meeting over which she presided.

Principal Kimble anticipated that the objectives would spawn questions and comments, but her expectation proved to be incorrect. There was only one query and it was voiced by a novice teacher: "Will there be negative repercussions if the goals are not met?"

Principal Kimble responded that the goals were not intended to evaluate teacher performance directly. She then asked the faculty to vote on adopting the goals; the vote was unanimous. She then appointed four teachers to serve with her on an ad hoc committee to evaluate goal attainment.

Within days after the faculty meeting, Principal Kimble met with the district's assistant superintendent for business to address the input goal. Adjustments were made to the school's budget to ensure that the resources for instructional-related activities were increased by 2.5 percent. Principal Kimble then retained a consultant, Professor Brian Wilcox, to facilitate the implementation of the remaining goals.

The consultant met with the faculty on three occasions, once each month during October, November, and December. Each session was held in the school's media center, lasted one hour, and occurred at the end of a regular school day. During these meetings, Professor Wilcox primarily identified resources and recommended practices that he said would aid teachers in their efforts to meet the process and outcome goals.

The evaluation committee waited until early April to hold its first meeting because it wanted to have results from the state proficiency test before convening. Principal Kimble provided evidence pertaining to the first and last goals. Financial statements provided by the assistant superintendent for business indicated that the school's budget had been adjusted to ensure that resources for instructionally related activities were increased by 2.5 percent. Results from the state proficiency exam revealed that the percentage of students scoring below the proficiency level had dropped from 32 percent to 29 percent. Neither the principal nor the other committee members, however, had physical evidence related to the two process goals. The committee decided that the best way to evaluate these goals (increased parental involvement and teacher collaboration) was to collect data from teachers.

A four-question, open-ended survey was developed and then distributed via email to all professional staff to collect data pertaining to the process goals. The same two questions were asked for each process goal: "To what extent has this goal been met?" "What evidence do you have to support your response to the previous question?" Overwhelmingly, faculty members indicated that parental involvement and teacher collaboration had increased; however, they provided only anecdotal evidence to support their contentions. The following were typical responses to the evidence queries: "I spent more time meeting with parents this school year." "I worked closer and longer with other teachers this year."

Over the next month, the evaluation committee members held two additional meetings, during which they discussed other possible evidence that might be pertinent to the process goals. Unable to reach agreement on this topic, they decided to make final decisions and issue their report. In mid-May, about two weeks before the school term would end, the committee voted unanimously that all four goals had been met.

After reading the committee's report, the district superintendent, Dr. Elizabeth Parsons, phoned Principal Kimble. She expressed appreciation for having received the report and praised the principal for having developed the goals. However, she challenged the committee's summative evaluations. With respect to the input goal, she pointed out that the report failed to identify how the 2.5 percent increase in funds appropriated for instruction was actually expended. With respect to the process goals, she asked why no evidence, other than teacher opinions, had been assessed and evaluated by the committee. And most notably, she had reservations that declaring that a slight improvement in state test scores for a single year justified the committee's declaration regarding the outcome goal. Dr. Parsons concluded the discussion with Ms. Kimble by giving her three recommendations:

1. The language in the committee's report should be edited to indicate that *it appears* progress had been made toward achieving the goals.
2. The goals should be retained for the following school year.
3. The district's assistant superintendent for instruction should meet with the ad hoc evaluation committee to assist it in developing more and better sources of evidence that could be used to determine the extent to which the goals are met.

Effective Paradigms

Unfortunately, the school-improvement strategy described in the preceding case study has not been unusual. In many districts and schools, reform has been conceptualized primarily as increasing inputs (e.g., adding resources), adjusting process (e.g., doing something differently), and stating outputs in a manner that make them difficult to evaluate. In truth, the effects of the change initiatives on actual student learning have often been ignored, misinterpreted, or exaggerated—largely because improvement goals were established without consideration as to how they could be evaluated objectively or because those evaluating the goals did not know how to collect and analyze evidence.

Basic Characteristics

Though school improvement plans should not be simplistic, they *should* be simple. A study in Kentucky of high-performing, high-poverty schools (Kannapel & Clements, 2005) suggested that elaborate and complex forms of improvement planning have a negative relationship to achievement. This fact should not surprise experienced teachers or administrators. Ask a principal if he or she could predict effective instruction based on the elaborateness or complexity of teachers' individual lesson planning and the answer will usually be "no." Doubt about the relationship between elaborate planning and positive outcomes, however, does not mean that planning is unimportant; rather, it means that administrators often believe that elaborateness and complexity do not guarantee instructional improvement.

After critiquing school improvement efforts, Karns (2001) concluded that success depends on three types of teacher activity, and correspondingly the extent to which administrators are aware of the essential nature of these activities. First, teachers accurately assess student skills and academic needs to ensure that they understand students completely and administrators recognize that teachers cannot teach students whom they do not know. Second, teachers understand course frameworks, state standards, and the nature of state testing programs, and administrators recognize that teachers cannot teach what they do not know. Third, teachers collaborate and engage in discourse about student learning, and administrators recognize that teachers cannot teach effectively if they do not know how students learn and what they have learned.

School improvement models should be rooted in the conviction that both technical and adaptive solutions are essential. Technical solutions entail the application of established knowledge (e.g., in the case of schools, in areas such as pedagogy and educational psychology). Adaptive solutions lie outside the realm of existing expertise (Heifetz & Linsky, 2002) and are more difficult to pursue because they require administrators and teachers to challenge current practices and then to pursue experimental approaches. As Fullan (2005) explains, "addressing an adaptive challenge requires complex learning in politically contentious situations where there are many internal forces pulling us back to the status quo" (p. 46). Consequently, effective school-improvement models must recognize the essential nature of organizational learning.

Though there are now many school-improvement paradigms, the purpose here is to demonstrate that in order to be effective they need not be complex, esoteric, or lengthy. Two models, one developed initially for business and then adapted to schools, and the other developed specifically for schools, are summarized.

The PDCA Cycle

One simple but effective school improvement model is the *PDCA Cycle* (also known as the *Shewart Cycle* and *Deming Wheel*). According to Capezio and Morehouse (1995), the model was first created by Walter Shewart and then revised by Edward Deming (1986). The acronym (PDCA) represents four essential stages that span diagnostics, innovative experimentation, evaluation, and eventually institutionalization. These stages are described below in relation to school improvement.

- *Plan.* This stage begins with diagnosing problems. For example, administrators seek to determine reasons for low student test scores. Then experimental activities intended to eradicate the problems are planned. In the case of districts and schools, such planning should center on viewing disaggregated data and other pertinent evidence that provides information for improving instruction.
- *Do.* Once selected activities are planned, they are implemented on an experimental basis. Initially, the changes are small, ensuring that they can be implemented properly. In education, these changes have a direct instructional focus.
- *Check.* Assess, evaluate, and monitor the changes to determine if they are producing their intended results. All primary instructional activities, including those that have not been changed, should be studied to determine effectiveness and check if unanticipated problems have emerged.
- *Act:* If the changes are successful, implement them on a larger scale. This means institutionalizing the changes. Doing so requires preparing teachers and administrators across a school district, first by demonstrating that the changes have been successful and then by providing them with the knowledge and skills to implement the changes across all schools.

Let us take a practical example. A building principal met with three fifth-grade teachers to discuss instructional effectiveness. Although students in their classes had similar achievement test scores, one teacher's students had progressed more rapidly. After discussing why progress had been greater in one of the classes, the principal concluded that setting quarterly student goals for the district's benchmark exam was a possible reason. The other two teachers were persuaded to adopt the same practice. The annual achievement test scores then confirmed that the intervention accelerated student progress in their classes. The following school year, the principal required all teachers to adopt this intervention. This example reveals how the principal deployed the PDCA cycle. She engaged several teachers in a process in which they collectively questioned the possible causes for student outputs, experimented and tested a hypothesis, and then made an effective intervention a normative standard for the school.

According to the Florida Bureau of School Improvement and Assistance, principals in "F" schools (i.e., poor-performing schools) during the 2003–04 school year unanimously identified the PDCA cycle as having had the greatest positive effect on school improvement. The average school grade point increase for "F" schools that year was 51. Such outcomes demonstrate that coherent and understandable school improvement models often have a positive effect on school performance.

Five School-Level Factors Model

Another simple but effective model evolved from school-improvement research conducted by Marzano (2003). He identified five school-level factors that can dramatically influence student achievement. In chronological order, they are:

1. *A guaranteed and viable curriculum.* This factor is a combination of opportunities for students to learn and the time it takes for them to learn. The curriculum actually taught must be aligned with the state or adopted (espoused) district curriculum. All too often there is a disjunction between the intended and actual curricula.
2. *Challenging goals and effective feedback.* Challenging goals require school personnel to set high expectations for all students. Then progress toward those goals and expectations is monitored, ensuring that students, teachers, and principals receive effective feedback about teaching and learning. To be effective, the feedback must be timely, substantive, and formative in nature (i.e., intended to provide information that leads to further improvements).
3. *Parent and community involvement.* Multiple studies (e.g., Desimone, 1999; Epstein, 1991; Jeynes, 2005; Sheldon & Epstein, 2005) have found that parent and community involvement have a positive effect on student achievement. Marzano (2003) states that such involvement centers around communication allowing and encouraging participation in the day-to-day instructional activities and school governance.
4. *Safe and orderly environment.* In a safe and orderly environment, students' basic needs are more likely to be met, thus allowing them to focus more directly on learning. In such schools, rules, expectations, and consequences are consistent, and expectations and support for student responsibility are incorporated in the daily life of the school.
5. *Collegiality and professionalism.* Collegiality and professionalism involve both process and accountability. From a process perspective, teachers and administrators examine student work and teaching practices collaboratively and objectively; from an accountability perspective, teachers and administrators accept responsibility for structuring and facilitating student learning.

Marzano (2003) believes that by addressing these components in the prescribed order, schools can significantly improve student achievement without having to drastically add resources. He also notes that his explicit omission of leadership as one of the five factors does not diminish its importance. He views leadership as "an overarching variable that impacts the effective implementation of the school-level factors" (p. 20). And, as discussed in the next chapter, the school-level factors commingle with teacher and student-level factors to engender student achievement. Though Marzano's model is not exactly the same as several other popular models, it does broadly capture the fundamentals of both Scheerens and Bosker's (1997) and Levine and Lezotte's (1990) school-improvement models.

Fundamental Components of School Improvement Models

Though there are many improvement models, the most effective share seven components. Each of these elements is briefly described to ensure that you have information that allows you to assess and evaluate reform programs.

Results-Driven Goals

Success most often occurs through unrelenting attention to purpose. Marzano (2003) says schools must have a guaranteed and viable curriculum. Schmoker (2006) adds that goals need specificity as demonstrated by the following statement: Within one year, 80 percent of the students in East Side High School will score at the proficient level in mathematics. *Goals bring focus and clarity to school improvement efforts, and therefore, they must be clear, concise, measurable, and understandable.*

Schmoker (2006) described the effects of goals in District Two located in Manhattan, part of the New York City school system. In 1987, District Two was serving more than 20,000 students, half living in poverty and 10 percent being immigrants. Officials in that troubled district began by eliminating long-winded, ambiguously worded goals and replacing them with new statements that were measurable and linked to assessment. This focused transition helped District Two become one of the highest performing units in the New York City system.

Frequently, educators set goals without considering if they can be measured, at least objectively. To understand the importance of results-driven goals, consider the following goal statements from two schools:

School A: "Students will be the focus of our instruction and make improvements in learning."
School B: "Ninety percent of students will score 3.0 on a 4.0 rubric scale in writing."

In which school are the principal and faculty more likely to know if the goal was accomplished? In School A, the word "focus" is undefined and no level of improvement is specified. In School B, the objective is quite clear—and measurable. As the Cheshire Cat argues in *Alice in Wonderland,* "If you don't know where you're going, then any road will take you there." Having clear direction to achieve your final destination and, just as importantly, how you are going to effectively measure it if you get there, are critical components of any school improvement effort.

Goals must be formulated from a need supported by data. Otherwise, considerable time and effort may be spent on something that merely puts a Band-aid on a serious problem. In his book on using data in problem solving, Preuss (2003) posits that an approach must be taken that helps dissolve problems, not just identify the symptoms, because remedies that do not consider root causes are unlikely to eliminate symptoms.

Data

Ask teachers if they use data to make decisions about students or to differentiate instruction and chances are they will roll their eyes. Why? Because for a long time they were given unusable data, and though administrators talked about differentiation, that critical word was not defined. Equally important, most teachers were not taught *how* to differentiate among data in relation to improving student learning. The significance of this condition is framed by another fact: *Schools that exhibit significant improvement almost always have educators who know how to access and use data to make critical interventions.* In effective schools, both quantitative and qualitative data and summative and formative measures inform critical decisions. Moreover, data used to make these decisions, especially those directly pertaining to student achievement, are constantly updated and monitored.

Monitoring students includes more than just noting summative results; the process also requires evaluating each student's individual achievement and assisting teachers to prescribe and apply different strategies. Too often, educators wait until students have failed before attempting meaningful assistance, and then their effort is often too little, too late. Monitoring should be designed to determine necessary interventions, not merely to prescribe remediation.

An example of successful monitoring is found in Johnson City, New York. The mathematics department head at one high school there met with teachers quarterly to review assessment reports. In a single year, the passage rate on the New York Regents Exam went from 47 percent to 93 percent (Schmoker, 1999). Such outcomes demonstrate that school improvement efforts are highly dependent on the ability of educators to access and use data to make important decisions.

Battelle for Kids, a nonprofit organization in Columbus, Ohio, has one of the largest longitudinal databases of value-added data in the United States. This organization has been working with 115 Ohio school districts as part of a statewide school improvement collaborative called Project SOAR. The project utilizes annual achievement data to apply Sanders's[1] value-added methodology to determine growth.

In one Project Soar study, researchers reviewed specific grade levels in which students had shown significant growth over a one-year period. The grade levels reviewed were those in which growth moved from low to very high progress in one year. At Bond Hill Academy in Cincinnati, a school with evidence of high growth, three teachers, including an intervention specialist, did the following:

- They collaborated regularly by sharing data showing where students were academically.
- They held on to high expectations.
- They determined if students had exhibited improvement by examining their work and assessment data.

---

[1]William Sanders is manager of value-added assessment and research for SAS Institute in Cary, North Carolina.

Grouping and regrouping were regular intervention strategies, and according to the principal, the focus on instruction and the teaching of the academic standards were relentless. When necessary, the teachers retaught lessons, modified assignments, and provided the additional time needed for students to master a particular standard. What these teachers did is not highly complicated but their methods are scientific.

The Learning First Alliance studied five high-poverty districts making great strides in improving student achievement: Providence, Rhode Island; Minneapolis, Minnesota; Aldine Independent School District, Texas; Kent County Public Schools, Maryland; and Chula Vista Elementary School District, California. The Learning First Alliance is a partnership of sixteen education associations with more than 10 million members. Its goal is to improve public education based on solid research. What these districts have in common is that they all made decisions based on reliable, useful, and robust data. The districts also used multiple measures of individual and school performance to monitor growth and inform instruction (Togneri, 2003).

A Providence administrator noted:

> Our decisions are made based on data, qualitative and quantitative. We look at student achievement data on an ongoing basis. We address it at principals' meetings. On Thursday of last week we had a half-day data analysis session with all the [teacher leaders]. We had voluntary professional development sessions on data analysis and interpretation. We use data all the time. The schools have to develop a school improvement plan and allocate their budgets based on data. (Togneri, 2003, p. 20)

In these districts, leaders made data *safe* and *usable;* data were used to initiate change—not to assign blame.

Data Systems

In addition to ensuring usable data, a system must be in place to regularly capture, display, and share data so they can be easily used. (This topic was previously discussed in Chapter 8.) In the aftermath of enacting NCLB, robust data systems have been created both at state and local levels. They contain a considerable amount of information about individual students, ranging from their daily attendance to annual performance on statewide tests. An emergent art is how one takes the voluminous data, digs through them systemically, and pulls out the salient pieces to drive appropriate practice.

Many districts currently use a data information system available on a commercial basis to do this. These systems enable users to connect dots that create a story before action. For example, Battelle for Kids generates customized, high-level reports on specific grade-level and subject-area progress in school districts. Furthermore, these reports provide quick access to information detailing how previously high- and low-achieving pupils are progressing. In a simple picture one can quickly view progress that was compiled from hundreds of data points. Consider the example in Figure 10.1, which reveals that adequate progress is being made by all students.

Again, the attributes of good data systems, including their construction and maintenance features, were detailed earlier in Chapter 8. The point here is to emphasize that these systems are integral to school improvement.

Instruction Connected to Learning

Results provide a picture of goals and data. But instruction really generates both and drives results. Sanders's important research (Sanders & Rivers, 1996) clearly suggests the impact of highly effective or ineffective teachers over time with student performance. Highly effective teachers raised student scores by more than 50 percentile points when compared to previously similarly achieving students who had a string of ineffective teachers. Sanders's findings are not research isolates. A Haycock and Huang study (2001) demonstrated that the best teachers have six times the impact as the least effective teachers in the same school. The conclusion is clear: Teaching matters and it matters a great deal.

The Learning First Alliance's research accentuates two simple lessons learned about school improvement: "Students learn what they are taught; students will learn more if they are taught well" (Togneri, 2003, p. 49). This study also found that specified outcomes (goals), district curriculum (helping teachers know what to teach), data (informing their work), and strategies to support improvement (professional development) were influential factors in school improvement.

Humorist Will Rogers advised, "Why not climb out on the limb of the tree? That's where the fruit is." If we know instruction is the key, why don't we do more to improve it?

FIGURE 10.1   Sample of a Sixth-Grade Mathematics Report

School Effect Rating						
Grade	Subject	Year	Test	Effect Rating	Student N	Testing Pool
6	Math	2005	OPT	High+	190	TerraNova

Diagnostic Group Ratings									
Low Achievers	N	Low Average	N	Average Achievers	N	High Average	N	High Achievers	N
High+	14	High+	25	High+	40	High+	50	High+	61

Elmore (2005) concluded that schools remain somewhat protected by a buffer regarding what constitutes good teaching. This buffer, real or imagined, prevents, discourages, or keeps others away from reviewing instruction. As a result, teacher success in many schools is determined by effective student management, good parental relations, peer acceptance, and "reasonable" student performance. And the principal generally stays away from teachers so judged to be effective.

Building on this description, Eaker suggested, "The traditional school often functions as a collection of independent contractors united by a common parking lot" (as cited in Schmoker, 2006, p. 23). Elmore refers to this independence as a "logic of confidence" (as cited in Schmoker, 2006, p. 31) and not a logic of quality.

The sad truth is that teaching remains a fairly isolated act. To improve instruction, administrators must empower teachers and provide them time to interact in ways that are helpful, constructive, honest, and collaborative. The intersection of these attributes is where improvements in teaching and learning occur. Instruction is what teachers do, and doing it effectively so that students learn is very difficult. Some of the demands of effective instruction include actively engaging students, employing grouping and regrouping strategies, knowing students as learners, paying attention to quality student work, and closely monitoring individual student progress. Newmann and Wehlage (1995) note that high-performing schools exhibit three important characteristics:

1. A professional learning community
2. A focus on student work through assessment
3. Altered instructional practices that produce better results

A study conducted by researchers at Mid-continent Research for Education and Learning identified nine categories of instructional strategies that affect student achievement. The research technique used for the study was a meta-analysis combining the results from several studies. One goal was to identify strategies that would have a high probability of enhancing student achievement for all students in all subject areas at all grade levels.

The outcomes of the meta-analysis were analyzed by Marzano, Pickering, and Pollock (2001). The nine strategies, in descending order of effect size, were:

1. Identifying similarities and differences (e.g., helping students use something familiar to deal with a complex problem)
2. Summarizing and note taking
3. Reinforcing effort and providing recognition (e.g., focusing on the attitudes of students and helping them understand the importance of effort)
4. Homework and practice
5. Nonlinguistic representations (e.g., using graphic organizers)
6. Cooperative learning
7. Setting objectives and providing feedback
8. Generating and testing hypotheses
9. Questions, cues, and advance organizers

Perhaps the most important issue is not whether teachers are teaching the curriculum, but rather whether students are mastering the content of the curriculum. The difference between teaching and learning was illustrated in a cartoon in which a young boy was bragging to a friend that he taught his dog, Spot, to whistle. When the friend asked for a demonstration and the dog was not able to produce, the dog's owner replied, "I said I taught Spot to whistle, I didn't say he learned to do it!"

In the Battelle for Kids study mentioned earlier (involving schools that moved from "low progressing" to "high progressing" in certain grade levels), the emergent findings for principals were that in many cases the turnaround occurred through the implementation of *intentional*, *planned*, and *coherent* strategies to raise academic growth for students (Lynch, Nicholson, Peters, & March, 2006). The most common turnaround strategies included specific changes to curriculum, pedagogy, personnel, or infrastructure. These findings corroborate what Bratton, Horn, and Wright (1996) conjectured in their review of statewide value-added data in Tennessee. The question is no longer *whether* to improve instruction, but rather *how* to do it. Part of the solution lies in the next element—effective professional development, a key school structure for improving student achievement.

Professional Development

One way to understand effective professional development is to know what it is not. The process:

- Does not involve telling
- Should not always mean training
- Should not be isolated
- Should not be the first thing in the budget that gets eliminated
- Should not be something that is "done to" people

Most certainly, effective staff development is not what is commonly known as "pay and spray." In this process, speakers give interesting, one-shot, often motivational talks that might serve as a springboard for more intensive professional development. More often than not, however, interest in the topic and its development end with the speech (Guskey, 2003).

According to the National Staff Development Council, effective staff development is results-driven, standards-based, and job-embedded. The recent revision of this organization's standards for this process was guided by these three questions:

1. What are all students expected to know and be able to do?
2. What must teachers know and do in order to ensure student success?
3. Where must staff development focus to meet both goals?

Professional development involves a set of activities designed to help educators learn new skills, acquire new knowledge, and develop new attitudes. Professional development's ultimate goal should always be to improve student performance. Improving performance does not just take the form of improved student test scores—it could also include improved behavior or attendance. Educators' work with students and professional development must be aimed at ways to improve that relationship to ultimately contribute more to students' education.

When teachers or administrators are asked where their best ideas came from that resulted in changed behavior, many respond, "from each other." When people can truly and honestly share ideas regarding practices that are or are not working, positive change happens. Collaborating is more than just being friendly with a colleague across the hall. Professional collaboration involves real sharing, listening, questioning, and learning from others. All five districts featured in the Learning First Alliance study focused on sharing in ways to foster professional growth (Togneri, 2003).

Staff development is reflective of a normative re-educative approach to change (Kowalski, 2003). That is, a new performance standard is deemed preferable and employees are taught the underlying merits and necessary implementation approaches. Although staff development in school districts can be and occasionally has been successful, a caveat is in order. When the proposed new standard is incongruent with fundamental assumptions embedded in a school's culture, teachers usually regress to their old behavior shortly after staff development is completed (Hoy & Miskel, 2005; Kowalski, 2006). Consequently, staff development should be planned in relation to known problems involving school climate, and especially school culture.

Organizational Learning

Today's most widely discussed approach to sharing ideas is probably DuFour and Eaker's approach to building a professional learning community. DuFour worries that the term "professional learning community" has been "used so ubiquitously that it is in danger of losing all meaning" (DuFour, 2004, p. 6). He describes a professional learning community as a place where the focus is on (a) learning rather than teaching, (b) working collaboratively, and (c) being held accountable for results.

He also identifies three fundamental characteristics:

1. Relentless attention to whether children are learning
2. A culture of collaboration
3. A focus on results

One example of an effective professional learning community in action is Adlai Stevenson High School in Lincolnshire, Illinois, where Richard DuFour was formerly the principal and later district superintendent. Every three weeks, each of the school's 4,000 students receives a progress report. Interventions are planned immediately when necessary, and students are required—not simply invited—to participate in tutoring, take extra classes, and identify other ways to extend themselves.

The idea behind "intervention rather than remediation" is taking action before students fail. Forcing students to attend summer school to retake a failed class is remediation. Using short-cycle assessment data to give the student what he or she needs is intervention.

Finally, DuFour (2004) suggests that members of a professional learning community judge their effectiveness based on outputs (results) rather than on inputs (specific initiatives). In schools where the inverse is true, administrators tend to become complacent once an improvement model or specific initiative is adopted.

Simply adopting a new model, initiating a new program, or pursuing a new strategy, however, does not ensure school improvement. The key question is, "Is it working for you?" The purpose of staff development should be to improve student learning. Though administrators may assess how these learning experiences change teacher behavior, they generally fail to assess if they ultimately have a positive influence on students.

Schmoker (2006) reinforces many tenets of Marzano's accumulated research and DuFour's professional learning communities. He recommends that school leaders should rely on the following conditions:

- A coherent curriculum with the responsibility to teach fewer standards while teaching them better and in a more in-depth way
- A renewed commitment to teaching critical thinking and literacy
- Evidence that most lessons contain elements essential to success
- Periodic classroom tours predominantly intended to identify and report back to the faculty on schoolwide patterns of strength and weakness (p. 136)

Schmoker suggests that far too often, teachers engage students in too much busywork with little or no attention to standards. He has also taken the controversial position that the reason many children do not learn has little to do with socioeconomic factors or school funding. Instead, he argues, the negative outcome is driven by inadequate or inappropriate instruction.

Collaborative Teams

When asked to identify the best team on which they have ever participated, most individuals respond that it was an athletic team, a committee, grade-level partners, or some other short-term activity involving a small group of people. When asked to explain their response, they often say that the team had clear goals (knew what they needed to accomplish), evidenced collaborative efforts (worked together successfully), and achieved significant results (accomplished something important).

Collaboration involves much more than just meeting together. According to DuFour (2004), the process is defined by the following characteristics:

- Participants act as a team day after day, week after week to meet defined student needs.
- Participants are honest and confront difficult issues when necessary.

■ The process is inclusive rather than exclusive; every member of the school's professional community is involved.

Collaboration teams drive the school improvement process. In an elementary school, for example, grade-level teams interact and engage in discourse about present and future student expectations, student progress, and needed instructional improvements. Moreover, teachers develop and deploy a common formative assessment program intended to monitor student achievement. Among the most important routine questions they ask are, "Are students learning what they need to learn? Who needs additional time and support to learn?" (DuFour, 2004, p. 9).

Little (1990) suggests that school improvement is most surely and thoroughly achieved when teachers engage in frequent, continuous, and increasingly concrete and precise talk about their practice. This means that teachers must be provided time to collaborate, they must know how to cooperate and consult with peer professionals, and they must use the time they are provided judiciously to reflect on practice.

Knowing versus Doing

In *The Knowing-Doing Gap*, authors Pfeffer and Sutton (2000) demonstrate, quite convincingly, that there is no shortage of knowledge about how to improve performance. The application of this knowledge is another matter. Pfeffer and Sutton estimate that organizations spend billions of dollars training employees, retaining consultants, and purchasing new supplies and equipment, yet they have little evidence to prove that these investments were made in a manner that boosts organizational effectiveness.

Errors in applying Edward Deming's paradigm of Total Quality Management (TQM) demonstrate the gap between knowing and doing. Numerous authors (e.g., Bonstingl, 1996; Leonard, 1996) have promoted the paradigm as an effective school-improvement strategy. Immensely popular, TQM actually has been attempted across all types of organizations, including schools, with varying degrees of success. Inconsistent outcomes, however, appear to result from improper application procedures and not the model itself. As an example, research on TQM has revealed a proclivity among high-level executives to ignore or devalue the need to provide staff development so that their employees can apply the model as intended. In stressing this fact, Pfeffer and Sutton (2000) cited a study examining TQM training across five organizations in which top-level executives understood and promoted the adoption of TQM. Despite their knowledge and encouragement, essential employee training did not occur in four of these organizations and in the fifth, it occurred on only a limited basis.

Standing alone, understanding school-improvement models is insufficient to ensure authentic reform. A school must also have the capacity to change. This capacity spans both human and material resources (Kowalski, 2006); that is, school employees must have the knowledge and skills to apply a change model as intended, and they must have supplies, equipment, and time to ensure proper application.

School Improvement and Leadership

School-improvement planning and models also require effective leadership because leaders continuously focus on what needs to be done to make schools more effective (Kowalski, 2003). Heifetz and Linsky (2002) describe leadership as an improvisational art. They suggest that vision, core values, and strategic plans provide a general framework but not a daily and continuous script. Said differently, school improvement is a journey and not a roadmap. Consequently, educators, including classroom teachers, must continuously make decisions about the improvement voyage—a responsibility that is far more complex and risky than following a map. In this vein, accessing, analyzing, and applying data are characteristics of effective school leadership.

Jim Collins (2001) posits that effective leadership also entails "confronting the brutal facts" (p. 70). In the case of schools, this means that administrators and teachers are expected to (a) diagnose their schools' weaknesses, (b) acknowledge that they exist, and (c) commit to eliminating or at least diminishing them.

Leaders also play a symbolic role in school improvement. They model desired behaviors, such as collegiality and risk taking, and emphasize the cultural importance of acknowledgment, success, and celebration. They engage others in relational communication essential to uncovering negative assumptions and replacing them with positive beliefs that allow visions to be achieved (Kowalski, 2005)

In the eyes of many, leadership appears to be an impossible and unduly idealistic role. Long ago, however, Peter Drucker (1966) predicted that institutions requiring geniuses or supermen to manage them would not survive. In truth, organizations must learn to be effective under the stewardship of average human beings who are committed to achieving extraordinary results. Recognizing the fact, Hamel's (2000) advice to aspiring leaders is to "win small, win early and win often" (p. 68). The power of appreciative inquiry is to look for starting points of strength and success and build on them.

There is an old adage that the road without obstacles usually does not lead anywhere. The road to improved student achievement is filled with challenges. To address them effectively, educators must be prepared to overcome both technical and adaptive challenges. As noted earlier in this chapter, the former entail the application of known knowledge. For example, a principal may face the technical challenge of having teachers who do not know how to access, interpret, and use data in their practice. The latter involves the development of new knowledge. For example, a principal may face the adaptive challenge of working with teachers to determine why students are not progressing in mathematics and then experimenting with alternative approaches in an effort to resolve the problem. Failing to meet either challenge deters the school-improvement journey (Heifetz & Linsky, 2002).

Random and isolated efforts are almost always ineffective because they typically cannot be replicated, and they fail to consider the social systems dimension of schools (Hoy & Miskel, 2005). This reality is a primary reason why organizational learning and effective leadership are critical to school reform. Summarizing research conducted with businesses, Mai and Akerson (2003) identified two broad leadership roles that have proven to be effective: critic/provocateur and learning advocate/coach. Mai (2004) subsequently applied these roles to schools and identified actions and techniques associated with each of them. The following were identified as being integral for a critic/provocateur:

- *Creating a climate conducive to learning and change:* demonstrating that it is safe to be a critic and encouraging constructive criticism of current practices
- *Posing potent questions:* critically examining possible improvements through dialogue that encourages creative thinking
- *Provoking critical review:* aggressively challenging underlying assumptions of the school's culture, especially those that encourage and sustain ineffective practices
- *Setting expectations for disagreement and debate:* reminding teachers why criticism and creative thinking are encouraged
- *Managing the debate process:* managing the conflict, ensuring that it does not become malevolent, reducing power differences among participants, and reinforcing a spirit of collegiality

The following were identified as critical to being a learning advocate/coach:

- *Facilitating discourse on practice:* drawing out valuable, tacit knowledge that causes teachers to think about improvement and to see themselves as innovators and problem solvers
- *Sponsoring innovation:* encouraging collaboration, invoking a sense of urgency, and encouraging risk taking
- *Using data to coach:* using data to challenge the status quo, and encouraging others to develop and apply data to their practice and to make important decisions

In summary, leadership is essential to school improvement, and though the role is undeniably complex, risky, and demanding, it is not impossible. Unfortunately, educators historically have neither been prepared academically nor socialized in their workplaces to assume this responsibility. In the context of a rapidly changing world, however, new expectations have emerged. Both administrators and teachers are encountering demands that focus more directly on what should be done to improve schools. Although these demands clearly produce anxiety for educators, they also constitute an opportunity for them to make education a mature, legitimate, and highly respected profession.

SUMMARY

This chapter summarized several proven improvement models that can be replicated across schools. The purposes were twofold. First, you should understand that successful improvement paradigms need not be complex. Second, you should understand that schools seeking reform without being guided by the characteristics in these models are doomed to fail.

Former President Lyndon Johnson once lamented, "Doing the right thing is easy. It's knowing what to do that is hard." In the case of schools, Glickman (2002) concluded that the key components of effective schools are "not a mystery" (p. 46). Moreover, we have many time-proven, research-based solutions for poor-performing schools. Even so, a large gap exists between the "most well-known, incontestably essential practices and the reality of most classrooms" (Schmoker, 2006, p. 2). In part, the gap is perpetuated by a lack of knowledge, skills, and appropriate dispositions.

As noted several times in this chapter, school improvement should be perceived as a continuous journey. Accordingly, visions, strategies, and activities are not commodities that should be replicated mindlessly. Both administrators and teachers must become leaders, practitioners willing to and capable of making critical decisions about what should be done to improve schools. More than any other single expectation, the call for leadership defines the essential nature of data in making critical decisions.

QUESTIONS AND SUGGESTED ACTIVITIES

Case Study Questions

1. Evaluate the manner in which Principal Kimble set the improvement goals and then presented them to the faculty. As a teacher, would you be satisfied with the process?

2. After reading this chapter, do you consider the topics addressed in the goals (parental involvement, teacher collaboration, and student achievement test scores) to be appropriate in relation to school improvement? Why or why not?

3. Were Principal Kimble's goals effectively developed? Why or why not?

4. Do you agree with the superintendent's apprehensions and recommendations regarding the evaluation committee's report? Why or why not?

5. What is anecdotal evidence? Under what circumstances can such evidence be useful?

Chapter Questions and Activities

6. Conduct your own knowing–doing gap. Describe how you use data to accelerate school improvement. Is your procedure consistent with what is known about effective practice?

7. Develop two clearly written, easily understood, measurable, results-driven goals for a school, subject area, or classroom.

8. Why is leadership important in relation to school improvement?

9. To what extent do school improvement models depend on accurate data?

10. What is the difference between an intervention and remediation? What needs to occur to ensure that teachers intervene rather than remediate?

11. Discuss the extent to which teachers know (a) their students as complete individuals, (b) what they are supposed to teach, (c) how students learn, and (d) what their students actually learn over the course of an instructional unit.

12. What are the differences between quantitative and qualitative data? Give examples of each that pertain to student performance.

REFERENCES

Bonstingl, J. J. (1996). *Schools of quality: An introduction to total quality management in education* (2nd ed.). Alexandria, VA: Association for Supervision and Curriculum Development.

Bratton, S., Horn, S., & Wright, P. (1996). *Using and interpreting Tennessee's value-added assessment system.* Knoxville: Value-Added Research and Assessment Center, University of Tennessee.

Capezio, P., & Morehouse, D. (1995). *Taking the mystery out of TQM: A practical guide to total quality management* (2nd ed.). Franklin Lakes, NJ: Career Press.

Collins, J. (2001). *Good to great: Why some companies make the leap—and others don't.* New York: HarperBusiness.

Deming, W. E. (1986). *Out of the crisis.* Cambridge, MA: Massachusetts Institute of Technology, Center for Advanced Engineering Study.

Desimone, L. (1999). Linking parent involvement with student achievement: Do race and income matter? *Journal of Educational Research, 93,* 11–30.

Drucker, P. F. (1966). *The effective executive.* New York: Harper & Row.

DuFour, R. (2004). What is a professional learning community? *Educational Leadership, 61*(8), 6–11.

Elmore, R. (2005). Building new knowledge: School improvement requires new knowledge, not just good will. *American Educator, 29*(1), 20–27.

Epstein, J. L. (1991). Effects on student achievement of teachers' practices of parent involvement. In S. B. Silvern (Ed.), *Advances in reading/language research: Literacy through family, community, and school interaction* (Vol. 5, pp. 261–276). Greenwich, CT: JAI Press.

Fullan, M. (2005). *Leadership sustainability: System thinkers in action.* Thousand Oaks, CA: Sage.

Glickman, C. (2002). *Leadership for learning: How to help teachers succeed.* Alexandria, VA: Association for Supervision and Curriculum Development.

Guskey, T. (2003). What makes professional development effective? *Phi Delta Kappan, 84*(10), 748–750.

Hamel, G. (2000). *Leading the revolution.* Boston: Harvard Business School Press.

Haycock, K., & Huang, S. (2001). Are today's high school graduates ready? *Thinking K–16, 5*(1), 3–17.

Heifetz, R., & Linsky, M. (2002). *Leadership on the line: Staying alive through the dangers of leading.* Boston: Harvard Business School Press.

Hoy, W., & Miskel, C. (2005). *Educational administration: Theory, research and practice* (7th ed.). New York: McGraw-Hill.

Jeynes, W. H. (2005). The effects of parental involvement on the academic achievement of African American youth. *Journal of Negro Education, 74*(3), 260–274.

Kannapel, P., & Clements, S. (2005, February). *Inside the black box of high-performing high-poverty schools: A report from the Prichard Committee for Academic Excellence.* Lexington, KY: Prichard Committee for Academic Excellence.

Karns, M. (2001). New models for reform. *Leadership, 31*(1), 28–32.

Kowalski, T. J. (2003). *Contemporary school administration* (2nd ed.). Boston: Allyn and Bacon.

Kowalski, T. J. (2005). Evolution of the school superintendent as communicator. *Communication Education, 54*(2), 101–117.

Kowalski, T. J. (2006). *The school superintendent: Theory, practice, and cases* (2nd ed.). Thousand Oaks, CA: Sage.

Leonard, J. F. (1996). *The new philosophy for K–12 education: A Deming framework for transforming America's schools.* Milwaukee, WI: ASQC Quality Press.

Levine, D., & Lezotte, L. (1990). *Unusually effective schools: A review and analysis of research and practice.* Madison, WI: National Center for Effective Schools Research and Development.

Little, J. (1990). The persistence of privacy: Autonomy and initiative in teachers' professional relations. *Teachers College Record, 91,* 509–536.

Lynch, J., Nicholson, M., Peters, K., & March, J. (2006). *Intentionality, coherency, and leadership: Principal explanations of factors contributing to rapid changes in student academic growth.* Columbus, OH: Battelle for Kids.

Mai, R. (2004). Leadership for school improvement: Cues from organizational learning and renewal efforts. *Educational Forum, 68*(3), 211–221.

Mai, R. P., & Akerson, A. (2003). *The leader as communicator: Strategies and tactics to build loyalty, focus effort, and spark creativity.* New York: AMACOM.

Marzano, R. (2003). *What works in schools: Translating research into action.* Alexandria, VA: Association for Supervision and Curriculum Development.

Marzano, R., Pickering, D., & Pollock, J. (2001). *Classroom instruction that works: Research-based strategies for increasing student achievement.* Alexandria, VA: Association for Supervision and Curriculum Development.

Murgatroyd, S., & Morgan, C. (1993). *Total quality management and the school.* Philadelphia, PA: Open University Press.

Newmann, F., & Wehlage, G. (1995). *Successful school restructuring.* Madison, WI: Center on Organization and Restructuring of Schools, University of Wisconsin.

Pfeffer, P., & Sutton, R. (2000). *The knowing–doing gap.* Boston: Harvard Business School Press.

Preuss, P. (2003). *School leader's guide to root cause analysis using data to dissolve problems.* Larchmont, NY: Eye on Education.

Sanders, W., & Rivers, J. (1996). *Cumulative and residual effects of teachers on future student academic achievement.* Knoxville: University of Tennessee, Value-Added Research Center.

Scheerens, J., & Boskers, R. J. (1997). *The foundations of educational effectiveness.* New York: Pergamon.

Schenkat, R. (1993). *Quality connections: Transforming schools through total quality management.* Alexandria, VA: Association of Supervision and Curriculum Development.

Schmoker, M. (1999). *Results: The key to continuous school improvement.* Alexandria, VA: Association for Supervision and Curriculum Development.

Schmoker, M. (2006). *Results now.* Alexandria, VA: Association for Supervision and Curriculum Development.

Sheldon, S. B., & Epstein, J. L. (2005). Involvement counts: Family and community partnerships and mathematics achievement. *Journal of Educational Research, 98*(4), 196–206.

Togneri, W. (2003). *Beyond islands of excellence: What districts can do to improve instruction and achievement in all schools: A leadership brief.* Washington, DC: Learning First Alliance/Office of Educational Research and Improvement, U.S. Department of Education.

11 Implementing and Monitoring Decisions

Chapter Focus

Once administrators have good data, they are still in the precarious position of knowing how to proceed with what they know. In this chapter the authors describe both the complexity of making decisions and why program implementation sometimes fails (even with adequate data) and can succeed (even with limited data). Administrators seldom know all that is required for making decisions, but they still have to make them. How can that be done to better assure success? Further, even if extensive data exist, that data might be interpreted to mean different things to different people.

The particular questions to be addressed in this chapter are:

1. What is the difference between a single-loop and double-loop learning approach?
2. What is the difference between first-order change and second-order change?
3. Why do even well-thought-out change processes so often result in failure?
4. How can administrators enhance the chances for success of change efforts?
5. What are the different types of school accountability models, and what is the essential characteristic of each model?

CASE STUDY

John Spinoza is the quintessential administrator. He always goes the extra mile, is more of a leader than a manager, and almost never fails to file necessary paperwork required by the district office. In essence, Shadylawn Elementary is, on the surface, fortunate to have a strong, focused principal. And, since he is so purposeful, most certainly Shadylawn is operationally effective. The student population is relatively affluent and the state's accountability system (which uses a status model of accountability—see description in this chapter) suggests that the school is a strong performer, with almost all students demonstrating proficiency.

He wants his school, however, to be even more effective. Indeed, the school he leads is within a large suburban district and is consistently cited as a "school of excellence," but he wants to document and reward that excellence. As a result, he decides to more fully embrace value-added modeling (VAM) to assess the degree of influence (amount of learning) each teacher creates for each child. With VAM he believes that he has a method (perhaps *the* method) for more fully rewarding (and perhaps even dismissing) those teachers who create (or cannot engender) the student academic growth that he and the central administration want for Shadylawn Elementary.

John was convinced that value-added modeling was "the answer" after reading an article in the American Association of School Administrators' monthly magazine. In that article (see Hershberg, Simon, & Lea-Kruger, 2004), the authors describe how "value-added assessment [could] . . . serve as the foundation for an accountability system at the level of individual administrators" (p. 14). Finally, a sure method to hold his teachers and himself accountable!

John's teachers are less enthused. They contend that the standardized tests being used by the school and school district are not sufficient to assess the critical thinking and advanced reasoning skills of students. In essence, they argue that the mandated testing procedures are simply not of sufficient quality to make reliable judgments about the efficacy of their teaching. Indeed, one of the teachers, while doing some personal research for the union on VAM, identified studies (Kane & Staiger, 2001) that highlighted statistical sampling problems. The teacher noted that Kane and Staiger even question whether VAM should be used at all for high-stakes decisions by school administrators.

The tension between Shadylawn teachers and John is increasing. Interestingly, all have the same goal: academic excellence. John sees VAM as the path to this goal. The teachers question the model and doubt whether it should be implemented for *any* high-stakes purposes.

Implementing Data-Driven Decisions

On the surface, it appears quite simple to look at data and then make a decision. In fact, the process of making decisions using data is quite complex. First, administrators need to ask clear, relevant questions. Second, they need to know whether they have the appropriate data. Third, they need to determine if the problem they are trying to deal with is one that can be solved using the data that are available.

Trusting the available data is complicated by both the quality of the existing research and the politics of interpreting data. As we discussed in earlier chapters, there are a wide variety of ways to explore a problem (see Chapters 5–7), but the methods one uses influence the results achieved. Administrators need to take real care in reviewing research because the rhetoric often does not match the data (see Bracey, 2006a). Bracey asserts:

> Despite the limitations of individual statistics and public cynicism about being able to prove anything, people remain remarkably trusting when it comes to statistics. . . . This acceptance would be dangerous at any time, but given today's polarized politicization of education . . . it is particularly hazardous now. (p. 79)

First, then, administrators need to take care in both collecting and assessing data. But even if they have access to good data, the next step is using (and disaggregating) the data to make appropriate decisions relative to clearly defined problems and taking time to really think through what the data mean, especially in terms of change (see Earl & Katz, 2006). Although there are many reasons to use data, we will briefly explore two of the most common: to foster innovations and to assess ongoing programs. That is, administrators are often seeking data to either foster or justify change or to evaluate, assess, and monitor a program that is being implemented within the school district.

One of the certainties of life is change. And one of the absolute certainties of educational life is the *need* to change if young people in the United States are to be nationally and internationally competitive. Heifetz (1994) distinguishes between the different types of change and the concomitant problems that accompany those change models. Type I problems are those for which traditional solutions are sufficient and appropriate. Type II problems are those that are reasonably well defined but for which a clear solution is not readily apparent (see Marzano, Waters, & McNulty, 2005). Type III problems are sufficiently complex that current approaches (and thinking) are simply not efficacious. Obviously the problem "type" influences the solution or innovation proposed.

Some innovations and changes are incremental in nature. An administrator is not dramatically changing a practice but rather subtly implementing a "treatment" that he or she believes will improve a practice that is already occurring. These changes are described by Marzano, Waters, and McNulty (2005) as first-order changes, and typify what occurs in most school districts. Programs in reading or math or science are not eliminated and then new ones initiated each year; rather, established programs are tweaked or modified (with, hopefully, appropriate teacher professional development) to enhance their effectiveness. Indeed, many school districts have clear procedures for accomplishing ongoing incremental improvement.

Hillsborough County Public Schools comprise a very large school district in Tampa, Florida (i.e., 14,517 teachers, 202,247 students, and almost 5,000 new students each year). Using a process developed by Davenport and Anderson (2002), they utilize a clearly defined step-by-step process for collecting, analyzing, and using data: data collection and disaggregation, timeline development (teachers discuss practices and develop timelines for implementing ideas), instructional focus, assessment, tutorials, enrichment, maintenance, and monitoring. This process is not structured to create change; rather, it is organized to ensure that teachers know where students are in their learning and to identify what and how instruction should be modified to enhance student achievement. (See Figure 11.1 for a more detailed description of the steps in the data collection and analysis process.)

Other innovations are more dramatic in nature. That is, a conscious effort is made to fundamentally change the way people think and act regarding a particular educational practice. In Chapter 6 we highlighted the efforts of one of the coauthors of this text to help create a new high school. That school (the Dayton Early College Academy) represents a second-order change because all those involved

FIGURE 11.1   Steps to Continuous Improvement

Step 1   *Disaggregate Data*

Disaggregate test scores to identify weak and strong objective areas.

Key need: State assessment results for incoming and outgoing students.

Step 2   *Instructional Timeline Development*

Develop an instructional timeline that encompasses all objective areas and time allocations based on the needs of student groups and the weight of objectives on state tests.

Key need: State performance standards.

Step 3   *Instructional Focus*

Using the instructional timeline, an instructional focus sheet is disseminated that states the objectives, target areas, instructional dates, and assessment data.

Key need: Completed instructional calendar.

Step 4   *Frequent Assessments*

After the instructional focus is taught, administer an assessment to check for understanding.

Key need: Teacher-made or commercial assessments.

Steps 5 and 6   *Tutorials and Enrichment*

After the assessments have been administered and evaluated, teachers should target the needs of their students with ongoing tutorials and enrichment.

Key need: Alternative resource materials.

Step 7   *Maintenance*

Maintenance is a continuous process to ensure that students retain and strengthen the skills and concepts learned earlier.

Key need: Bank of maintenance questions.

Step 8   *Monitor*

Monitoring is a multifaceted step that involves everyone, from the principal to the students.

Key need: Ongoing assessment sheet.

Source: Adapted from K. Fielder (2006, July). *Systemic change.* Paper presented at the National Staff Development Council Conference, Washington, DC. See also P. Davenport & G. Anderson (2002). *Closing the achievement gap.* Houston, TX: American Productivity and Quality Center.

began to rethink everything from whether to use Carnegie units as a means of documenting student learning to the restructuring of the school day around educational projects (and academic gateways) rather than class periods and a standardized curriculum.

Part of the rationale for second-order change in high schools, especially urban high schools, is the acute shortage of effective instructional delivery mechanisms (i.e., far too many students are dropping out and far too few are opting for more rigorous coursework). That is, with large numbers of urban students either physically or psychologically dropping out, educators are forced to rethink the structure of the school day and the defined curriculum. And, regrettably, for far too long policymakers and practitioners have eased requirements in the hope that it would mitigate student dropouts. That approach has neither reduced the dropout problem nor more effectively engaged those students who remain in the system. Instead, it has resulted in large numbers of students simply being unprepared for entrance into college or the workforce.

In essence, for years educators have tried to use single-loop learning approaches to solve a double-loop learning issue. Marzano and colleagues (2005) describe the difference:

> Single-loop learning occurs when an organization approaches a problem from the perspective of strategies that have succeeded in the past. When a particular strategy is successful, it reinforces its utility. If a strategy is not successful, another is tried until success is achieved. In a sense, then, single-loop learning teaches us which of our current set of strategies works best in different situations. Double-loop learning occurs when no existing strategy suffices to solve a given problem. In these situations, the problem must be conceptualized differently or new strategies must be conceived. Double-loop learning, then, expands an organization's view of the world while adding new strategies to an organization's repertoire. (pp. 66–67)

Secondary educators have been trying single-loop learning for years to enhance what occurs in secondary schools. Attend almost any professional association meeting and you will see efforts directed at how to modify the organizational structure or academic curriculum of secondary schools and to do so in ways that might enhance the educational opportunities provided to students. The circumstance is understandable. Why drastically change an institution or practice if a subtle change can achieve the desired results? Unfortunately, the urban secondary education problem may not be solvable with first-order changes. It likely requires second-order change, which may explain why so many efforts at innovation have met with so much failure. To paraphrase Marzano and colleagues (2005): The failure to recognize when to use second-order change approaches coupled with a natural desire to use first-order approaches results in the wrong outcomes.

The explanation is in part due to an unwillingness for people and organizations to change and in the leaders to use the types of behaviors that make change possible. It is also attributable to the fact that people tend to solve problems using the "mental maps" that they carry with them and that have been constructed based on prior personal and professional experiences (see Marzano, Waters, & McNulty, 2005).

As a result of these mental maps, we tend to assume that schools must have a certain type of structure or that students must learn in particular ways. These assumptions tend to encourage the use of first-order change strategies. They also implicitly foster formulas about how to address problems. Consider, for example, a noneducation problem that has education implications: poverty. How has poverty been addressed over the past fifty years in the United States? In the 1960s, policymakers looked at the data and, using their assumption that "the system" was responsible for poverty, argued for creating massive antipoverty government programs (e.g., President Johnson's Great Society initiative). More recently, those Great Society efforts have been perceived as enabling helplessness on the part of the poor. The "popular" approach now espoused is to create a growing economy and to use tax cuts as a way of fostering that economic growth (see Wessel, 2006).

Notice that to deal with the poverty problem you could either push for first-order change (i.e., refine President Clinton's 1996 efforts to limit the time a person is eligible for welfare) or push for a second-order change: Dismantle welfare and require the poor to economically assimilate. In fact, some argue for a bit of both (i.e., encouraging people to complete high school and delay child bearing and then linking new benefits to those who act responsibly), but others are either-or oriented. Everyone is looking at the same data, but the conclusions they reach and the approaches they advocate vary greatly.

Interestingly, when second-order change is undertaken, it places a unique burden on both those leading and those following. Leaders have to exhibit the fortitude to push through the problems and conflicts; followers have to evidence sufficient faith to believe that the proposed changes will work. The Great Society programs of the 1960s did not work, but were they truly wrong ideas or did U.S. citizens simply lose faith before the approach had time to work? Wessel (2006), regarding the government antipoverty programs, writes:

> There is today, however, a different sense about the potency of any government response to poverty than when the War on Poverty was born. "There was a sense in those early . . . days that the possibilities were endless," Lisbeth Schorr, who worked in the Johnson White House, recalled at a recent retrospective sponsored by the Brookings Institution and Georgetown University. "Of course," she said, "nobody knows what would have happened if we had been able to continue and expand what we started." (p. A10)

Similar second-order change jitters most certainly occur in education. During the past half century many second-order innovations have been tried and many have failed. The question is whether they failed because they were truly bad ideas or because educators lacked the political will and educational imagination to refine (and stick with) the innovation to enhance the likelihood of its success. But why would they lack that will? Is it because they do not have the "right stuff" or is it some other systemic reason? In the next section, we proffer three explanations for why second-order educational changes often fall short and why implementation and monitoring are imperative.

Why the Implementation Process Fails

Much of the change that administrators initiate is not second-order in nature, nor should it necessarily be. Ongoing second-order change is physically and emotionally exhausting for all involved, both leaders and followers. As Heifetz and Linsky (2002) assert, "When you lead people through difficult change, you take them on an emotional roller coaster because you are asking them to relinquish something— a belief, a value, a behavior—that they hold dear" (pp. 116–117).

The critical question is why change fails so often, even when leaders *do* endeavor to collect substantial data about the need or direction for change. We suggest three reasons, any one of which is sufficient to derail even the most efficacious change process.

First, even when data are collected, the data may not be sufficient in scope to fully address a problem. That is, what, if any, biases are evidenced in the data collection process, and do those biases intentionally or unintentionally exclude critical information? As we have noted repeatedly in this book, education, like politics, is ideological. The result is that those proposing change may search for data but search only in those places that reinforce their dispositions regarding the direction for change. This can be seen especially in areas such as reading and mathematics, where dramatic differences of opinion exist regarding best practices (e.g., in mathematics debate has raged about whether the emphasis should be on rote memorization or inquiry approaches, and in reading the "phonics–whole language" wars have divided educators and researchers about "what works").

As you explore any change possibilities, ensure that studies embodying a range of methodologies and perspectives are represented. Also ensure that you are drawing on more than just conceptual or ideational contributions. A range of views requires that you access concept articles from ideologically diverse periodicals such as *Phi Delta Kappan* and *Education Next* and research manuscripts from journals such as the *American Educational Research Journal*.

It is also imperative to determine whether the rhetoric of some studies extends far beyond the data. One illustration of this is presented by Bracey (2006b) as he describes advocacy arguments for private schools. Specifically, education critics such as Doyle argue that partial evidence of poor-quality public education is the fact that teachers in public schools send their own children to private schools. Yet a close examination of the data, asserts Bracey, would suggest that between 1990 and 2000 the percentage of public school teachers with children in private schools actually dropped (12.1 percent in 1990 to 10.6 percent in 2000). If you read only Doyle–type articles, you reach one conclusion. If you read only Bracey contributions, you reach another. Our recommendation: Read both and do so with a critical eye; discuss the articles with knowledgeable professionals and then decide what makes personal sense for you and those you serve.

A second reason change often fails relates to "implementation fatigue." The change process is exhausting and many who undertake change simply do not have the will to work through all the phases. This is especially true for those who do not ground change on sufficient data or research. The more confident you are of what you are doing (and the concomitant support, research and philosophical, for what you propose), the better your chances for success as you move through the change process (i.e., from awareness for the need to change to creating and implementing changes in practice).

Love (2002) articulates some key principles of change which should be considered as any innovation is undertaken, especially within any standards-based environment:

1. Change is both an individual and an organizational phenomenon.
2. Change is a process that takes personal time and professional persistence.
3. Change is purposeful and requires clear goals and defined procedures for assessing results. Organizations that are continuously improving have ongoing mechanisms for setting goals, taking actions, and assessing the results of their being made. That is, how much time is being spent on implementing the innovation? Have teachers been adequately prepared to use the innovation? Are the teachers being given adequate support and professional development?
4. Change requires ongoing data collection. Specific data collection processes need to be in place to track student progress. This might be accomplished through classroom observations, teacher interviews, teacher self-assessments, and a review of classroom artifacts or materials used by teachers during the instructional process.

In the No Child Left Behind accountability era, so much of what administrators confront entails demands for curricular relevance and instructional effectiveness. One of the truly impressive things about how the Hillsborough County Public Schools (Florida) is endeavoring to use data relates to the way administrators are systematically preparing teachers to understand the instructional approaches being used and how to interpret the data being collected vis-à-vis the performance of students. Without such a systematic effort both to collect and analyze data and to develop the persons/teachers responsible for using the data, even the best-intentioned efforts will fail. (Later in this chapter we will discuss how similar systematic data analysis professional development is occurring in Michigan and Connecticut.)

Far too often, when confronted with the inevitable program conflicts and change resistors, those involved in change accommodate resistance by retreating to past practices; they return to what they know. That is, they view the antidote to implementation fatigue to be a retreat to the known. Actually, the best antidote to implementation fatigue is good data collection. Hence, if you are implementing a new curriculum (such as a standards-based curriculum), the change process might entail, at minimum, the following (see Love, 2002):

1. *Identify and define specifically what is being implemented.* Does everyone agree about what the curriculum looks like and how it should be aligned and structured?
2. *Identify the indicators that would suggest where positive progress constitutes change.* As you consider changes, be certain that you not only thoroughly research what changes you want to make, but also assiduously examine the implementation process by considering what specifically is being implemented.

What are the key implementation indicators, and how will data be collected on those indicators?

Finally, implementation processes are compromised when personnel changes occur prematurely, among leaders or followers. Some leaders, quite simply, are not willing to see the change process through to its completion. They like the thrill of instituting change (and creating awareness) but are fatigued by the labor-intensive nature of the actual change process. The early stages of change are fun and exciting; the latter stages are difficult and frustrating. Many who lead simply do not have the "right stuff" for confronting the problems associated with change. Heifetz and Linsky (2002) assert, "The deeper the change and the greater the amount of new learning required, the more resistance there will be and, thus, the greater the danger to those who lead" (p. 14). Many leaders simply change jobs or "abandon ship" when danger emerges. Urban school districts have been especially afflicted by this circumstance. Rapid leadership changes at all levels in urban districts make even good innovations difficult to implement because continuity in the senior leadership is not present.

Leaders who want change need to be aware of their obligation to see the process through. Change is not easy. It is, remember, individual and organizational (see Love, 2002). Leaders are not without some resources, however, and those resources (e.g., good data and the "right people") need to be accessed as changes are implemented.

How to Improve the Chances of Success

Heifetz and Linsky (2002) identify some of the resources needed for success in a change environment. If you are going to use evidence to make decisions, it helps ground what occurs but it does not mitigate the emotional reaction of those impacted by proposed changes. Heifetz and Linsky offer some simple but powerful perspectives to keep in mind:

1. *Distinguish the role you are in from who you are as a person.* Far too many leaders see their "role and self" as synonymous. The key is to limit the degree to which the proposed evidence-based change is you. In the words of Heifetz and Linsky, "When you take 'personal' attacks personally, you unwillingly conspire in one of the common ways you can be taken out of action—you make yourself the issue" (p. 191). The leader who can listen to criticism without being devastated by it and who can consider a critique without using "attack-defense" responses is a person who has a chance to make changes and make a difference.

2. *Have confidants, but remember that they are not the same as allies.* You will need someone with whom you can have thoughtful, in-depth discussions. Such "confidants" are persons you can trust with your deepest thoughts and

concerns. Even with good data, changes will still be difficult because they may impact the way people think of themselves and their roles. Allies are persons who share your values and often your approaches but, as Heifetz and Linsky assert, "because they [often] cross a boundary, they cannot always be loyal to you; they [may] have other ties to honor" (p. 199). You need allies and confidants—that is, leaders who make changes and implement tough decisions need both persons they can trust with their deepest thoughts and concerns (confidants) and individuals who share their views and approaches but who may disagree with specific proposed practices (allies).

Heifetz and Linsky (2002) articulate other ways of anchoring yourself as a leader when making tough decisions, but we selected these two because they so epitomize why so much good change is compromised once the "going gets tough." That is, leaders often become too absorbed in the change (they view it as a referendum on themselves), and they fail to understand that they need *both* persons they can trust (noncritical advocates) with all their thoughts and concerns and persons who share their views/approaches but who may, of necessity, argue against some aspects of the change that they propose (critical friends).

Aligning Tests with Assessing Performance

"Anchored" administrators know how to use data in ways to create meaningful and appropriate action. Change should never occur for the sake of change. Change is necessarily grounded on a problem that needs to be solved in order either to enhance the culture of the school or to engender better learning on the part of the students. This sounds simple but clearly defining a "problem" can often be quite complex. A problem can entail systemic issues over which an administrator has little control or specific school-based factors that can be strongly influenced by administrative action.

As an example, consider the problem of one urban midwestern school district, which for several years was in academic emergency (it moved out of academic emergency in 2006–07) as defined by its state education agency (see Figure 11.2). That is, it met fewer than eight of the state's twenty-five report card accountability indicators (e.g., one indicator is 93 percent student attendance rate). Looking at the figure, you will notice that as an academic emergency district it met a low number of indicators, had a low performance index score (i.e., a weighted value assigned to each performance level on any state achievement test), and missed AYP. So what might this mean for an administrator in terms of trying to use data to determine a district's needs and foster school improvement? And does it matter what types of tests are being used to assess the growth of students? Further, does it matter what type of accountability system is in place within a state or at the national level to measure student achievement growth? We first discuss the accountability question and then address the issue of aligned tests.

FIGURE 11.2   How Academic Status Is Determined (2005–06)*

	Methodology for Determining District Rating				
	State Report Card Indicators met		**Performance Index Score**		**AYP Requirements**
Excellent	24–25	OR	100–120	AND	Met or Missed AYP
Effective	19–23	OR	90–99	AND	Met or Missed AYP
Continuous Improvement	0–18	AND	0–89	AND	Met AYP
	13–18	OR	80–89	AND	Missed AYP
Academic Watch	9–12	OR	70–79	AND	Missed AYP
Academic Emergency	0–8	AND	0–69	AND	Missed AYP

Source: S. Lowery (2006). Dayton Public Schools: Dayton, Ohio.

*Note: The categories may be redefined annually. The descriptors presented in this figure are for 2005–06.

There are four different types of school accountability models currently in use in the United States: status models, improvement models, growth models, and value-added models (see Council of Chief State School Officers, 2005). *Status models* essentially take a performance snapshot of student proficiency at a particular point in time and answer this question: "On average how are students performing this year?" (p. 3). *Improvement models* are a type of status model and essentially measure changes between defined groups of students (e.g., this year's third graders compared to last year's third graders) and address this question: "On average, are students doing better this year as compared to students in the same grade last year?" (p. 4). Critics assert that such approaches have very limited utility because they are nothing more than measuring this year's apples to last year's oranges (Stewart, 2006). *Growth models* track the achievement progress of students from year to year and focus on "How much, on average, did students' performance change?" (p. 4). With growth models, educators need at least two scores for each student so that they can measure where the student was last year as compared to where the student is this year. *Value-added models* (VAM) represent a type of growth model where efforts are made "to isolate the specific effects of a particular school, program, or teacher on student academic progress" (p. 5). In essence,

VAM focuses on attempting to appropriately attribute student growth by separating "non-school factors (such as family, peer, or individual influence) from a school's performance" (p. 5). The VAM model examines two possible questions: "On average, did the students' change in performance meet the growth expectation? . . . By how much did the average change in student performance miss or exceed the growth expectation?" (p. 5). William Sanders's work, which we refer to at several points in this book, is an example of VAM. The proponents of VAM view it as an inherently fairer method of measuring effectiveness because it takes into account some of the complexity associated with deriving a specific score. Rather than a single score on a standardized exam (status model), VAM "can identify effective teachers and effective schools that are helping low-achieving children progress even when . . . the students' standardized scores are below average and their scores are not meeting AYP requirements" (Stewart, 2006, p. 2).

The critics of VAM are vocal. They have concerns with how value-added data might be used to "judge" or evaluate certain teachers because of "statistical errors" and the existence of "simply too many variables" (Stewart, 2006).

All of this accountability focus seems quite complex, and it is, but is it something you should be knowledgeable about as an administrator or teacher? The answer is yes, in order to better understand or represent what is actually occurring at the school or in the classroom within which you work. If a status model is the only "growth" measure used, educators would know how each class had performed but they would not know whether that performance represented real academic growth or whether this year's third graders are simply smarter than last year's. The different models have emerged to help educators and others better understand how students are actually performing.

To return to our academic emergency district, suppose all the students matriculating there came from high-poverty families; that is, they are from families that are challenged to provide young people with the requisite social and intellectual capital they need for success. If the status model were the only one used, the "snapshot" of performance taken annually would likely almost always make the students appear as weak performers (even though they may be evidencing academic growth). Meanwhile, the affluent district contiguous with the poverty school district might appear to be highly successful. The annual snapshot for the wealthy district (where parents are able to invest much more time and significantly greater resources in their children's education) would make their schools appear highly successful or effective.

At the present time, the different educational providers are using varied accountability structures, sometimes by choice, sometimes by the unintended consequence of legislated action. The differences have emerged largely because of all the time and financial costs associated with measuring student performance. Quite simply, measuring student proficiency is complex, and mitigating that complexity is expensive. The No Child Left Behind legislation relies on status models (e.g., Adequate Yearly Progress), but that approach tends to favor the wealthy districts described above compared to the neighboring, more impoverished, and typically urban Academic Emergency districts. In essence, NCLB tends to reward high-performing schools and does not adequately take into account why they might be high performing. In 2005–06, 8,446 schools were identified as "in need of improvement," which means they failed to make AYP (Archer, 2006).

Murray (2006) argues that pass percentages represent an inappropriate and potentially pernicious way to monitor educational progress. After analyzing the misleading nature of percentage-passed measures, he writes, "Doesn't this mean that the same set of scores could be made to show a rising or falling group difference just by changing the definition of a passing score? Answer, yes." (p. A12). In essence, the use of pass percentages represents a misleading accountability measure—and it is that approach that characterizes NCLB.

Growth models are now emerging to better document the ways in which a school or school district is performing. Recall that growth models address this question: How much did students' performance change? Consider a couple of different ways to assess that growth (and there are several ways). Fixed growth would measure students against some fixed standard: Students should gain X amount of learning each year, with the same growth standard being applied to all schools. Seems logical. The problem is that for some urban students, that fixed standard may never allow them to catch up and reach desired performance levels. Also, what fixed level/standard should be set? If that standard is fixed at one level (say, too low), no school might fail and all schools would be expected to foster the "defined" level of growth.

Another approach is *position maintenance*, which describes the amount of growth a student needs to evidence each year in order to maintain a certain academic "position." That is, if a child scores at the 50th Normal Curve Equivalent (NCE) on the third-grade reading test and scores at the 50th NCE on the fourth-grade reading test, then he or she grew a year to maintain that position. Obviously, for low-achieving students this may not be sufficient to "encourage" growth, and some would contend that other measures would need to be in place to accelerate growth for low achievers so that they could catch up. In essence, one of the critical questions being asked is whether the growth models being used adequately reflect academic performance needs across all student demographic groups.

Many administrators examine data but fail to see beyond or behind the data. Suppose that your school district uses a position-maintenance model but your state uses a fixed-growth approach. You could have students who evidence growth but still may not meet the criterion or target levels fixed by state agencies.

Our point is that it is imperative to have district growth measures (and testing procedures) aligned with state requirements and to ensure that what is being measured (and how it is measured) are consistent with expectations at both the local and state levels. Complicating the issue even more is the fact that proficiency levels in some states may not be sufficient to really measure whether the students possess the requisite skills. Peterson and Hess (2006) and others have documented that differences sometimes (unfortunately) exist between proficiency (or fixed-growth standard) at the state level and proficiency as defined by the National Assessment of Education and Progress (NAEP). That is, some states have lower defined proficiency standards (e.g., Oklahoma and Tennessee) and others have higher levels established for proficiency (e.g., Massachusetts, Maine, and South Carolina), with the result that their students appear either *more* or *less* proficient than they really are.

Not only must school districts consider the types of accountability models and tests used, but even if they have aligned systems, it is imperative that they determine whether the local growth expectations are sufficient for adequately and effectively measuring student growth and addressing state and national (NCLB) mandates. That is, do state expectations compare favorably to National Assessment of Educational Progress (NAEP) requirements for proficiency? (The latter focuses on the Peterson and Hess issue regarding how states define proficiency, which is often lower than that defined by NAEP.)

Clearly, then, the growth modeling question is one that administrators need to have some awareness of, but they often cannot control what states or local governing authorities do to document growth. They can, however, more directly influence the different testing regimens that they use in their schools. In that regard, it is imperative to ensure that the structure of required tests matches or aligns with the needs of the district. For example, the district cited earlier (which was in Academic Emergency) was able to move in 2006 to Continuous Improvement (see Figure 11.2). That movement, in part, was because district assessment personnel ensured that the tests they used locally matched structurally with state-mandated tests; that is, they used both selected and constructed response items. With selected response, students are choosing among options (such as multiple choice), and with constructed response, students are creating an answer. Because the state-mandated tests contained both types of items, the local tests were selected to match. (It is also important to note that the district leadership during this time was relatively stable, at the central office, at middle management, and at school board levels.)

Engaging in Inquiry to Ensure Good Decisions

Making decisions using appropriate evidence is not an easy process. Earl and Katz (2006) describe the "cycle of inquiry" as essential for any effective data-based decision-making process. That process includes, at minimum, two features:

1. A system in which access to data is ongoing and comprehensive
2. A system that ensures appropriate, timely feedback on the data received

Data collection is not something that occurs and then is discontinued. For real school improvement to occur, it must be systemic (see Figure 11.1 for one example). Indeed, some states are now attempting to be more systematic in the technical assistance they provide to help schools that are in need of improvement. Michigan, for example, created a team of skilled educators who could work more directly and intensely with low-performing schools. That team developed a how-to book for helping turnaround schools, which included almost step-by-step methods for effecting positive change. Archer (2006) writes:

Teams of educators from schools in the state listed as needing improvement under the federal No Child Left Behind Act now get two days of training. . . . Education departments in other states also have bought the guide to incorporate its lessons into their own work. (Information can be found at www.michigan.gov/mde) (p. 55)

Connecticut is engaged in similar efforts. The state's education department hosts a "data fair," where schools and school districts can gather to examine how others are tracking student progress and measuring the effectiveness of school improvement strategies (Archer, 2006). In essence, more and more states are realizing that schools in need of improvement must have technical support if they are going to have any chance of meeting the NCLB mandates.

The use of data is part of the school's routine way of approaching problems and answering critical questions. Recall in Chapter 5 our description of the four Cs: collecting, connecting, creating, and confirming. That process has many variations, but all play to the same theme of collecting and systematically analyzing data. For example, Davenport and Anderson (2002) structure our four Cs as eight steps (see, again, Figure 11.1), and when that occurs student learning is enhanced because of alignment between and among all elements of the system. Teachers who use and disaggregate data to actively understand what is occurring in a classroom, rather than to passively rank how students perform, are simply going to be more effective. Davenport and Anderson (2002) describe this with a poignant anecdote:

> When we looked more closely at the data from the poorer schools, one teacher, in particular, stood out. Her name was Mary Barksdale. Something different was happening in Mary's third grade classes. Despite the fact that 94% of her students were considered "at risk," virtually all of them had mastered each section of the TAAS.
>
> What was Mary doing differently in her classroom?
>
> . . .we found [that she used] . . . a dynamic process of continuous assessment and re-teaching for those students not up to mastery. When Mary's students missed questions on their tests, she didn't see it as a failure on their part. Instead, she set out to determine what part of her instruction had not come across. She then [retaught] . . . that section before moving on. (p. 45)

Some data analysis problems will be general in nature: Are African American students performing as well in mathematics as the white students? What ethnic student groups are underperforming? Data can then be used to determine whether a concern/problem is real or whether insufficient evidence exists to support the problem's existence.

Other data problems are more specific in nature. For example, completing an item analysis on an administered test can reveal a great deal about what students are or are not learning regardless of their racial group or socioeconomic status. Key item analysis questions for selected response items might include the following (see Depka, 2006):

1. On which items did students do extremely well?
2. On which items was an incorrect response chosen more often than a correct response?

3. Are there questions that students did not attempt to answer?
4. Are there questions with evenly balanced responses across items?
5. On which items did only a small number of students answer correctly? (p. 44)

For each of these questions, it is imperative to ask why a circumstance (i.e., a pattern of student responses) may be true and to then determine what decisions (instructional or curricular) might need to occur to ensure that problems are mitigated or eliminated in the future. With such information, a selected response item analysis chart (see Figure 11.3) can be constructed, the patterns can be identified, and tentative hypotheses as to why a certain pattern exists can be proffered.

Our central point is that good inquiry enhances the quality of the evidence-based decision making that occurs. If you are using aligned tests and if the standards for performance for students are appropriate and if you have in place procedures for analyzing student performance (item analysis), you will be in a position to make good decisions at both the district and the classroom level.

In essence, good evidence-based decision making requires an iterative questioning process (Depka, 2006):

1. What data sources are available and are they sufficient and adequate?
2. How can the available data be made understandable to all the appropriate stakeholders?
3. How should the data be organized to ensure its transparency?
4. What do teachers or administrators need to be part of the data analysis process? That is, once the data are available and organized, who needs to view them?
5. How should and can the results of the analysis be used to improve educational practice? What are the action steps that need to be taken from the point of analysis to prescriptions for action?

FIGURE 11.3   Item Analysis Chart: Selected Responses

| Item | Response Questions | | | | |
	A	B	C	D	E
1	10%	40%*	20%	25%	5%
2	80%*	15%	0%	0%	5%
3	14%	26%	52%*	8%	0%
4	10%	70%*	5%	2%	13%
5	25%	50%*	15%	5%	5%

*Indicates correct response

Source: Adapted from E. Depka (2006). *The data guidebook for teachers and leaders.* Thousand Oaks, CA: Corwin Press, p. 44.

SUMMARY

The evidence-based decision-making process appears linear. In fact, it is often somewhat nonlinear. True, it has the appearance of linearity but in actuality good administrators are always asking questions and continually looking for data to suggest what their next steps might be. This "continuous looking" process is part of any good maintenance and monitoring process. Indeed, Davenport and Anderson (2002) diagrammatically show monitoring and maintenance as something that occurs throughout the data analysis process.

We are arguing that as an evidence-based decision maker, you must move closer to a process described by LeGault (2006) in *Th!nk* and rely less on the types of concepts presented in Gladwell's (2005) *Blink*. In *Blink* Gladwell argues that human intuitive senses are useful for making decisions on both a personal and professional level. We agree that they are useful, but educators, as professionals, must rely on evidence, intuition, and experience; clearly intuitive instincts are important for any professional, but those instincts are improved when "informed" with evidence and experience. In *Th!nk,* LeGault argues that it is through systematic and critical thinking (statistics and analysis) that real progress toward excellence occurs. Data-based decision making requires such intellectual dispositions. Most professionals are better off *thinking* and *blinking,* especially those in education. To do this, to "think" and to "blink," we in education have to move away from a reliance on egalitarian intelligence (i.e., deriving a "popular" or easy decision) to a reliance on more empirical dispositions (i.e., using what can be observed or documented to determine appropriate next steps). Far too many administrators and school boards use egalitarian approaches for politically expedient reasons: They want to appease often diverse and often contentious groups. We suggest a move toward the empirical because so much of what is now being evidenced and tacitly encouraged is what is popular, which may explain, in part, the increasingly poor comparative performance of U.S. students on writing, mathematics, and problem-solving tasks (LeGault, 2006) and may also explain why so many "fad," unstudied practices find their way into educational settings.

So why the overreliance on egalitarian approaches? We suggest two reasons. First, really digging through data to make decisions takes time and effort. As a result, far too many schools and school districts use what is familiar or what is convenient as opposed to what is needed and well researched. That means that educators need not only to ensure that they are using "curriculum-sensitive" tests (i.e., state and standardized tests aligned with state standards) but also that they are, in Marzano's (2003) words, using "assessments that actually measure the content the teachers teach" (p. 57).

Marzano argues that to secure such direct and aligned measures, educators need to create report cards that "track student performance on specific knowledge and skills" (p. 57). One school in Dayton, Ohio (the Dayton Early College Academy), does this by tracking the performance of every student on the state academic standards and the associated content indicators. The DECA students do not receive formal report cards but instead receive periodic assessments regarding their progress vis-à-vis the academic indicators in each of the disciplinary areas. Such detailed data provide better formative assessments of student progress and more clearly document the direction for future learning; the process is also more labor intensive.

A second reason why egalitarian approaches are often relied on is that educators do not possess a comprehensive understanding of the assessment process. They go with what is politically or practically easy because it mitigates the need to look more comprehensively at the educational environment. Lots of factors have to be considered in designing a vital school: school level (viable curriculum, appropriate curricular goals), teacher level (effective instructional strategies, logical sequencing, and pacing of curriculum), and student level (supportive home and motivation to learn) (see Marzano, 2003). Unless these factors are all considered and assessed, it will be difficult to create an atmosphere conducive to learning (see Figure 11.4).

Our point is that evidence-based decision makers who know how to implement decisions are more than data nerds. They are persons who begin to look broadly at the school and classroom environments. What is working? What is not working? Why? And they are not just looking at state test scores and standardized tests. They are looking at school, teacher, and student factors that might influence those scores.

The complexity of educating young people is why it creates such challenges and opportunities. Making good decisions is difficult but clearly quite possible, especially when systems are set up that demonstrate alignment and reflect comprehensive assessment approaches.

Finally, providing appropriate leadership is critical to the success of any school administrator or teacher leader. Once a decision has been made to initiate some type of change, whether first or second order, the process of knowing what responsibilities to emphasize in order to successfully implement the change needs to be carefully considered. Marzano and colleagues (2005) note that with first-order changes it is imperative, for example, to "champion" the capacity of the staff to succeed and to acknowledge program implementation successes. With second-order changes, the administrator not only understands the curriculum and instructional practices at a school, but also clearly appreciates "how the selected initiative will affect current practices in curriculum, instruction and assessment" (p. 116). In essence, the administrator is moving from an advocate-of-practice to a reflector-on-practice.

What a powerful way to end our discussion on data-based decision making! Some years ago Schön (1984) studied the problems of practice in a number of different fields and examined the process of reflecting *in* and *on* practice. Strong leaders reflect on what they are doing and what they are accomplishing, and they do that with data. They collect data and use them in order to know what is happening and then they study them carefully (and continue to collect information) as they effect defined changes. They implement and monitor and by doing so they behave more professionally. It is also important to note that the responsibilities are not the sole domain of a single person. Change is communal in nature, and good

FIGURE 11.4   Factors Related to Student Achievement

School-Level Factors

Guaranteed and viable curriculum

Challenging goals and effective feedback

Parent and community feedback

Safe and orderly environment

Staff collegiality and professionalism

Teacher-Level Factors

Instructional strategies

Classroom management

Classroom curriculum

Student-Level Factors

Home atmosphere

Learned intelligence and background knowledge

Student motivation

Source: Adapted from Marzano (2003), pp. 58–59.

school administrators work with leadership teams in ways that maximize the success of any type of change effort.

Readers need to be aware of the fact that it takes a unique set of learnable leadership skills to deliver on the promise of change, especially when using data. We cited in Chapter 5 the work of Collins (*Good to Great*). One of Collins's observations is that in highly successful companies there are levels of leadership skill. The highest level (level 5) consists of leaders who are humble, personally convicted by the ideas they espouse, and absolutely passionate about inspiring others to achieve the organization's mission. Collins (see Bisoux, 2007) notes that the "truth is that level 5 leadership is painful—not everyone is up to it" (p. 18). We agree. Using data to make decisions will often mean that unpopular decisions have to be made. It takes a certain amount of guts and political acumen to know how and when to make those decisions and to do so in a way that keeps an organization moving forward.

Special note: Readers are encouraged to read Marzano, Waters, and McNulty (2005), *School Leadership That Works,* which provides an extensive discussion on the change process and the leadership behaviors associated with different types of change. Our book describes how to use data to inform decision making. Marzano and colleagues examine in detail the actual change process and how leaders can shape and influence it to better ensure success.

QUESTIONS AND SUGGESTED ACTIVITIES

Case Study Questions

1. This chapter begins with a case study describing one administrator's approach to assessing student learning. Review our description of the different accountability models (e.g., status, improvement, growth, and value-added) and identify potential problems with using just one of these methods to ascertain a school's effectiveness and student performance.

2. What are the key differences between Type I and Type II problems? Provide a personal example (from your educational experiences) of each type. What type of problem would you assert is being evidenced at Shadylawn Elementary by Mr. Spinoza and his teachers?

3. We argue that much of the change required in schools is *not* second-order in nature. Do you agree? Why or why not?

4. Has the change process in the schools you have worked in been more *think* or *blink* oriented? What factors contributed to the approach you have experienced? Why is it imperative that educators be more *think* oriented when they confront problems such as those at Shadylawn?

5. What school, teacher, or student level factors (see Figure 11.4) would you find most often are *not* considered when doing comprehensive data analysis in your school?

6. Which methods of monitoring student growth are used in your school? Are they sufficient? Appropriate?

Chapter Questions and Activities

7. Identify a Type I problem that is evidenced in the school environments in which you have worked. Was a traditional solution used to solve it? Was the solution used successful? Why or why not?

8. Identify a Type II problem that you have experienced as an educator. What solutions were attempted? Who determined the solutions to be used? Were the approaches successful? Why or why not?

9. We identified several reasons why change often fails. Do you agree with the reasons we identified? What others would you identify that have contributed to unsuccessful change efforts?

10. In the last part of this chapter we discuss Marzano's description of the "environmental" factors related to student achievement (see Figure 11.4). He created a survey instrument to assess all the school-, teacher-, and student-level factors. Obtain a copy of his instrument (see *What Works in Schools: Translating Research into Action*, ASCD, 2003) and using that instrument assess an educational environment within which you are working now or have worked in the past. If you cannot access the instrument, simply ask and answer a question for each factor (e.g., Does the school evidence a safe and orderly environment—yes or no?).

REFERENCES

Archer, J. (2006). Building capacity. *Education Week, 26*(3) 53–55.

Bisoux, T. (2007). Thinking big. *BizEd, 6*(1), 16–21.

Bracey, G. W. (2006a). How to avoid statistical traps. *Educational Leadership, 63*(8), 78–81.

Bracey, G. W. (2006b). *Reading educational research.* Portsmouth, NH: Heinemann.

Council of Chief State School Officers. (2005). *Policymakers' guide to growth for school accountability: How do accountability models differ?* Washington, DC: Author.

Davenport, P., & Anderson, G. (2002). *Closing the achievement gap.* Houston, TX: American Productivity and Quality Center.

Depka, E. (2006). *The data guidebook for teachers and leaders.* Thousand Oaks, CA: Corwin Press.

Earl, L. M., & Katz, S. (2006). *Leading schools in a data-rich world.* Thousand Oaks, CA: Corwin Press.

Gladwell, M. (2005). *Blink: The power of thinking without thinking.* New York: Little, Brown and Co.

Heifetz, R. A. (1994). *Leadership without easy answers.* Cambridge, MA: Belknap Press of Harvard University.

Heifetz, R. A., & Linsky, M. (2002). *Leadership on the line.* Boston: Harvard Business School Press.

Hershberg, T., Simon, V. A., & Lea-Kruger, B. (2004). The revelations of value-added: An assessment model that measures student growth in ways that NCLB fails to do. *The School Administrator, 61*(11), 10–14.

Kane, T. J., & Staiger, D. O. (2001). *Volatility in school test scores: Implications for test-based accountability systems.* Paper presented at the Brookings Institution Conference, Washington, DC.

LeGault, M. R. (2006). *Th!nk.* New York: Threshold Editions.

Love, N. (2002). *Using data/getting results: A practical guide for school improvement in mathematics and science.* Norwood, MA: Christopher-Gordon Publishers.

Marzano, R. J. (2003). Using data: Two wrongs and a right. *Educational Leadership, 60*(5), 56–60.

Marzano, R. J., Waters, T., & McNulty, B. A. (2005). *School leadership that works.* Alexandria, VA: Association for Supervision and Curriculum Development.

Murray, C. (2006, July 25). Acid tests. *The Wall Street Journal,* p. A12.

Peterson, P., & Hess, F. (2006). Keeping an eye on state standards: A race to the bottom? *Education Next, 6*(3), 28–29.

Schon, D. (1984). *The reflective practitioner.* New York: Basic Books.

Stewart, B. (2006). *Value-added modeling: The challenge of measuring educational outcomes.* New York: Carnegie Corporation of New York.

Wessel, D. (2006, June 15). In poverty tactics, an old debate: Who is at fault? *The Wall Street Journal,* A1, A10.

INDEX

equality, 29
liberty, 28
Education Statistics Quarterly (NCES), 149
The Education Trust, 143, 174
Educators
  behavior of, 26–27
  goals of, 17
  leadership and, 9
  role of, 9
Effectiveness variables, 83–85
Elitism, 90
Elmore, R.F., 7, 10, 229
End of course (EOC) exams, 104
English as a Second Language (ESL), 168
Epstein, J.L., 33, 224
Erickson, F., 155
Erlandson, D.A., 19
Espoused theories, 66
Espoused values, of culture, 34
Essay questions, 165
Estler, S., 36, 63
Ethical decision-making model, 61–63
  boundaries in, 62
  ethic of caring, 62
  ethic of critique, 62
  ethic of justice, 62
Ethnographic records, 159
Evidence-based decision making, 116
Ewing, E.A., 80
Expected utility decision-making model, 60
Experiential learning, process, 20
Experimental research. *See* Quantitative research
Expertise, 85
External data sources, 148–53
  direct, 149–50
  nondirect, 150–53

F
Feedback form, for teachers, 158
Field studies, 133
Filley, A., 86
Findings, confirming, 114–17
Finn Jr., C.E., 5, 9, 198
Firestone, W.A., 33
Five school-level factors model, 224
Fluid participation, 64
Foley, E., 185
Forster, G., 196, 217
Fowler, F.C., 29, 39

Fraternity, 29
Freakonomics (Levitt and Dubner), 197
Frequency, in decision making, 54
Friedman, T., 212
Frymier, J.R., 7
Fullan, M., 6, 11, 33, 80, 222
Fuller, E., 113
Furger, R., 118
Fusarelli, L.D., 11, 16, 72

G
Gambler's fallacy, 44
Garbage can decision-making models, 64–66
  counterproductiveness in, 65
  example of, 66
  fluid participation, 64
  preferred solutions, 64
  problems, 64
Gardner, H., 127
Garmston, R.J., 84
Gastil, J., 90
Getzels, J.W., 17, 39, 40
Gibb, J.R., 89
Giesecke, J., 63, 64
Gladwell, M., 255
Glasman, L., 8
Glasman, N.S., 8, 28
Glass, T., 32
Glickman, C., 236
Goldring, E.B., 77
Good to Great (Collins), 103
Grandori, A., 56
Gray, P., 182
Greatschools, 150–52
Great Society programs, 244
Greene, J.P., 196, 217
Gregory, G.H., 160
Griffiths, D.E., 57
Grigorenko, E., 203, 210
Group decision making, 72–94
  advantages and disadvantages, 78–80
  decision behavior in groups, 74–78
  dysfunctional conflict, 88–91
  ineffectiveness, factors in, 84–85
  leading groups, 80–83
  problems with, 87–88
  processes, 91–93
  quality of, 83–84
  stages in, 80